THE CAUSES AND COSTS

OF

DEPOSITORY INSTITUTION FAILURES

Innovations in Financial Markets and Institutions

Editors:

Robert Eisenbeis and Richard W. McEnally
University of North Carolina at Chapel Hill
Chapel Hill, North Carolina, U. S. A.

Other books in the series:

England, C. and Huertas, T.:
The Financial Services Revolution

Gup, B.:
Bank Mergers: Current Issues and Perspectives

Kormendi, R., Bernard, V., Pirrong, S., Snyder, E.:
Crises Resolution in the Thrift Industry

Hancock, D.:
A Theory of Production for the Financial Firm

England, C.:
Governing Banking's Future

Kaufman, G.:
Banking Structures in Major Countries

Anderson, S., and Born, J.:
Closed-End Investment Companies

THE CAUSES AND COSTS OF DEPOSITORY INSTITUTION FAILURES

edited by

ALLIN F. COTTRELL, MICHAEL S. LAWLOR
and
JOHN H. WOOD

Wake Forest University
North Carolina

SPRINGER SCIENCE+BUSINESS MEDIA, LLC

Library of Congress Cataloging-in-Publication Data
The causes and costs of depository institution failures / edited by
Allin F. Cottrell, Michael S. Lawlor and John H. Wood.
p. cm. -- (Innovations in financial markets and institutions)
Includes bibliographical references and index.
ISBN 978-94-010-4290-1 ISBN 978-94-011-0663-4 (eBook)
DOI 10.1007/978-94-011-0663-4
1. Savings and Loan Bailout, 1989- 2. Savings and loan association failures--United States. 3. Bank Failures--United States. 4. Deposit insurance--United States. I. Cottrell, Allin, 1953- . II. Lawlor, Michael S. III. Wood, John H. (John Harold) IV. Series.
HG2151.C38 1995
332.3'2'0973--dc20 95-34988
CIP

Originally published by Kluwer Academic Publishers in 1995
Softcover reprint of the hardcover 1st edition 1995

Printed on acid-free paper.

CONTENTS

CONTRIBUTING AUTHORS

James R. Barth
Department of Finance,
Auburn University

Rebel A. Cole
Board of Governors
of the Federal Reserve System

Allin F. Cottrell
Department of Economics,
Wake Forest University

Nurhan Davutyan
School of Business,
Michigan Technological University

R. Alton Gilbert
Assistant Vice President,
Federal Reserve Bank of St. Louis

Carl D. Hudson
Department of Finance,
Auburn University

John S. Jahera
Department of Finance,
Auburn University

Michael S. Lawlor
Department of Economics,
Wake Forest University

Gregory A. Lilly
Department of Economics,
Elon College

Joseph A. McKenzie
Federal Housing Finance Board

Thomas S. Mondschean
Department of Economics,
DePaul University

William P. Osterberg
Economist and
Assistant Vice President,
Federal Reserve Bank of Cleveland

Sangkyun Park
Economist,
Federal Reserve Bank of New York

Rowena A. Pecchenino
Department of Economics,
Michigan State University

James B. Thomson
Economist,
Federal Reserve Bank of Cleveland

Lawrence J. White
Arthur E. Imperatore
Professor of Economics,
Leonard J. Stern School of Business,
New York University

John H. Wood
Reynolds Professor of Economics,
Wake Forest University

ACKNOWLEDGMENTS

These papers were presented at the Graylyn Conference Center of Wake Forest University on October 9–10, 1993. We are grateful to Warren Samuels for suggesting the project, to Zachary Rolnik of Kluwer for help in seeing it through to completion, to Provost David Brown and Dean Gordon Melson of Wake Forest University for arranging financial support, and to the Graylyn staff for a smooth and pleasant meeting. In addition to those whose papers are published here, we wish to express our gratitude to the following participants for lively and useful discussions: Robert Clower of the University of South Carolina, Curt Hunter of the Federal Reserve Bank of Atlanta, Haluk Unal of the University of Maryland, and Paul Huck, Bobby Lamy, John Moorhouse, Charles Moyer and Andrew Yates of Wake Forest.

I

INTRODUCTION

Allin F. Cottrell, Michael S. Lawlor and John H. Wood

Wake Forest University

1 THE BACKGROUND

A RECURRING THEME of American financial history before 1934 was crisis characterized by the failure of a few large financial institutions followed by runs on other institutions because of contagious fears regarding the solvency and liquidity of the financial system. The banking panics of 1931 and 1933 showed that the Federal Reserve System, inspired by the panic of 1907 and intended to be a lender of last resort, was not a solution. Furthermore, bank failures were frequent even in years free of financial crisis. Nearly a quarter of commercial banks failed during the agricultural depression of the 1920s. The median annual commercial bank failure rate between the Civil War and 1920 was one of every 250 banks, about 80 banks a year at the turn of the century. After the introduction of federal deposit insurance—administered by the Federal Deposit Insurance Corporation which also added another level of bank supervision—in 1934, the incidence of commercial bank failures fell dramatically despite the fact that vulnerable unit banking structures were retained in many states. About 50 banks a year (of 15,000 banks) failed between 1934 and 1942, but there were only 156 failures during the next thirty-two years. This improvement was largely attributed to federal deposit insurance, although unprecedented economic stability and nearly unbroken farm prosperity received some of the credit.

It was too good to last. The 1970s saw a return to the interest-rate instability of the 19th century, a slowing of economic growth, and an acceleration of inflation. Bank failures began to rise, averaging 10 per year between 1975 and 1981 and then increasing from 42 in 1982 to 206 in

1989 before falling to 120 in 1992. The nearly one-percent average annual failure rate between 1982 and 1992 exceeded by one-third that prevailing between the Civil War and 1920.

Savings and loan associations suffered even more severely. They had also failed in large numbers during the 1930s, received federal deposit insurance (administered by the Federal Savings and Loan Insurance Corporation), and prospered during the stable quarter-century following World War II. However, fluctuating interest rates began to damage the solvency of these inherently risky institutions—which borrow short to lend long and whose borrowers have continuous call options at face value on their mortgage debt—as early as the 1960s. The failure rate of S&Ls was twice that of banks until 1988, when 7 percent of S&Ls failed compared with 1.5 percent of banks.

The most dramatic potential cost of the failures of the 1980s and early 1990s compared with those occurring before 1934 is the burden on the taxpayer imposed by Congress's decision to bail out the insurance funds. Before the institution of federal deposit insurance the Comptroller of the Currency assumed control of the balance sheets of failed national banks and paid depositors from the sale of assets. The process often required several years, but depositors were fully compensated in seventy-five percent of failures. Similar procedures were used by state authorities, and the annual losses suffered by depositors of failed banks between 1865 and 1919 was 0.2 percent of deposits. The FDIC and FSLIC adopted a more ambitious procedure. Although not required to do so by law, they took pride in immediate restitution to the depositors of failed institutions. In most cases they paid another bank or S&L to assume the obligations of an insolvent firm without inconvenience to depositors, most of whom were unaware of any change except the name of their depository. However, neither insurance fund was sufficient for the reimbursement of depositors of large insolvent institutions, and instead of forcing closure and following the pre-1934 payout procedure, the FDIC and FSLIC allowed those institutions to continue operations in the hope that their fortunes would turn. Unfortunately, time increased the burden of these "zombies" on the insurance funds, which by the end of the 1980s had become insolvent. In the Federal Deposit Insurance Improvement Act of 1991, congress allowed the FDIC to borrow $30 billion from the U.S. Treasury. S&L closures were more costly. A common estimate of the present value of the bailout of the

FSLIC is $150 billion; the actual figure will depend on the proceeds from the sale of S&L assets.

Not surprisingly, the events of the 1980s inspired a renewed interest in the causes and costs of financial institution failure, and several questions that had seldom been asked in the post-World War II economics literature resurfaced. Why do financial institutions fail? What are the costs of their failure? How do they differ from other firms and industries? What are the implications of the answers to these questions for financial market regulation? The papers in this volume critically survey and extend previous analyses of these questions. Taken together, they enable us to take stock of what we have learned and point to the areas about which we still have much to learn.

2 The papers

Several papers employ versions of the "structure–behavior–outcomes" approach, which is explicitly set forth by Rebel Cole, Joseph McKenzie, and Lawrence White. This approach avoids the pitfalls of earlier studies which tended to focus on portfolios immediately before failure without making connections with the environment and decisions resulting in those weak portfolios. For example, James Barth, Carl Hudson, and John Jahera address the view that the deregulations of the early 1980s were the primary cause of the S&L failures later in that decade, a view that led to Congress's rejection of the Bush Administration's proposal to increase the powers of insured depository institutions in favor of the more restrictive Federal Deposit Insurance Corporation Improvement Act (FDICIA) of 1991, which raised capital requirements and mandated prompt corrective action against weakly capitalized banks and S&Ls. They begin with the premises that risk-taking behavior is determined by the constraints (including deposit insurance and regulation) facing S&Ls and their attitudes toward risk (stock S&Ls having more to gain from risk-taking than mutuals), and find that S&Ls which moved most heavily into the direct investments (that is, for their own accounts) in land and office buildings permitted by the legislation of the early 1980s failed more frequently than conservative S&Ls which deviated less drastically from the traditional emphasis on home mortgages, and that this behavior was more characteristic of stock than of mutual S&Ls, of the less stringently regulated state-chartered S&Ls than of federal associations, and of weakly capitalized or insolvent institutions.

Cole, McKenzie, and White also find that the thrift insolvencies of the late 1980s (outcomes) were a consequence of thrifts' risk-taking in the early part of the decade (behavior) stimulated by the combination of flat-rate deposit insurance, low net worth caused by rising interest rates, and regulatory laxity (structure). The same sequence is linked to the costs of S&L bailouts. They also find support in their results for the FDICIA.

The FDICIA sought to narrow the discretion of regulators in dealing with troubled institutions by mandating prompt corrective action and limiting the use of the Federal Reserve's discount window. Responding to the question of whether the former is practicable, William Osterberg and James Thomson show that the resolution costs of failed commercial banks are explained by available balance-sheet items well in advance of closure. In contradiction to the charge in a Congressional staff study that Federal Reserve discount lending to troubled banks extended their lives and thereby raised their eventual charges against the insurance fund, Alton Gilbert finds no relation between bank borrowing from the Fed and the length of time they remained open after their identification as problems. Furthermore, borrowing banks tended to reduce their risk exposure—an indication of strict supervision—during their last year of operation.

For most observers, including the authors of the first two papers, moral hazard produced by deposit insurance and lax regulation was the chief culprit of the depository institution debacle of the 1980s. Even the greater incidence of failure in the Southwest, especially Texas, may have been caused by regulatory disruption arising from the move of the Ninth District Federal Home Loan Bank from Little Rock to Dallas in 1983. Gregory Lilly, however, finds several puzzles in this story. For example, why did the vast majority of stock S&Ls refrain from risky behavior? Furthermore, given that so many technically insolvent institutions were not closed, meaning that regulatory forbearance was negotiable so that they were not forced to take risks, why did so many mutuals fail? And why, if insured deposits are so easily obtained, as implied by the moral hazard explanation, were the expansions of risky S&Ls financed mainly by more expensive borrowed money? Lilly finds answers to these puzzles not in risk-taking but in its opposite. In view of the high and rising inflation of the 1970s, shifts from the traditional fixed-rate mortgages (and the severely constrained variable rate mortgages) into direct investments in land and buildings seemed the best inflation hedges available to S&L managers. But they were unlucky, especially in Texas, where real estate values fell the farthest.

The role of deposit insurance in the failures of the 1980s is also questioned by Allin Cottrell, Michael Lawlor, and John Wood. Using annual U.S. data from 1864 to 1989 and accounting for other factors associated with bank failures, particularly farm prices, they find that *lower* failure rates have accompanied federal deposit insurance. For example, the fall in farm real estate values during the 1980s exceeded that of the 1920s (both falls were preceded by large run-ups of land prices and farm debt), but farm bank failure rates were much smaller in the later decade. They do not challenge the theoretical existence of a moral hazard incentive in deposit insurance but interpret their results to imply that the actual empirical influence of moral hazard might not be substantial and might have been neutralized by other New Deal reforms, particularly stricter bank regulation and the acceptance of risky investments by federal agencies. This interpretation is supported by an examination of state deposit insurance in North Central unit-banking states between 1908 and 1930 that shows failure rates to be positively associated with state insurance schemes unaccompanied by supporting regulatory restraints.

Nurhan Davutyan applies Poisson and negative binomial estimation to bank failures between 1947 and 1991, and finds evidence of structural change in 1980, although he is unable to find significant relationships between bank failures and various aggregate measures of bank profits—a result which calls attention to the robustness of total bank profits during the decade.

The last two papers are concerned with the causes of economywide bank runs and credit crunches. Sangkyun Park extends earlier theoretical explanations of runs with a model of incomplete bank-specific information in which it is rational to run on solvent as well as insolvent banks when a large number of failures is observed. Thomas Mondschean and Rowena Pecchenino present a model in which the tendency of banks to expand and contract together is rational behavior and argue that it explains several recent financial episodes, including bank real estate lending in the 1980s.

3 What have we learned?

A better question might be: Of what have we been reminded? The most striking conclusion of these papers taken as a group is that regulation begets regulation. Legal restrictions on portfolios have produced a system of extremely delicate financial institutions hard-pressed to defend themselves against a harsh, rapidly changing environment. The required maturity mismatching of S&Ls exposed their capital positions to the volatile interest rates of the 1970s and early 1980s, and induced them to seek and then to exploit increased investment powers. Whether these powers were intended for risk-taking, as argued in the first two papers, or for risk aversion, as argued by Lilly, made no difference to the outcome. S&L managers were unlucky in their choices, especially in Texas, incompetent or worse in their administration of the unfamiliar activities, and weakness turned into debacle. Unwilling to lift portfolio restrictions or abandon deposit insurance with flat-rate (or nearly flat-rate) premiums and their spur to risk-taking, Congress has resorted to stricter capital regulations to limit the costs arising from other restrictions.

However, we (and Congress) have also been reminded that the quality of regulation depends on the knowledge, preferences, and incentives of the regulators, and their behavior during the 1980s has resulted in a narrowing of their discretion. Among other limits on their range of decisions, the FDICIA mandates that the regulators must in future take prompt corrective action (see Osterberg and Thomson) and the Federal Reserve is required to be more careful in its lending to troubled institutions (see Gilbert). But even perfect application of the law may not be sufficient to render it beneficial. The demonstration by Cottrell, Lawlor, and Wood that reductions in bank failures follow the institution of deposit insurance only when accompanied by substantial increases in regulation and taxpayer underwriting of risky investments raises the possibility that deposit insurance may impose net costs on society even when properly administered.

The regulatory implications and other costs of a system pervaded by the adverse incentives of deposit insurance—active incentives for risk-taking by institutions and passive incentives to forego the acquisition of knowledge by investors, which exacerbates the information problems discussed by Park—requires us to compare these costs with the benefits of deposit insurance and the growing body of regulation that it compels. Federal deposit insurance was an attempt to end the failures and sometimes crisis caused by a system of small banks dependent on local conditions and the failure of the Federal Reserve to perform its lender-of-last resort responsibilities. We hope the latter problem is behind us and the future of the second is promising. The remaining public welfare justifications of taxpayer-backed deposit insurance are the related desires to protect the small saver and further insulate the payments system from depository institution risk-taking and depositor irrationality. The first is questionable because the small part of private wealth in checking accounts (consider your average checking account balance as a proportion of your monthly income) is exceeded by bank and S&L claims on the U.S. government (cash, Federal Reserve deposits, and U.S. securities). Since it could be arranged that the owners of checking accounts be given first claim on bank assets, the only real concern for depository institutions' solvency is that arising from their non-monetary liabilities. (These points have been made by Litan, 1987.) However, since U.S. securities provide a wider range of maturities, are less risky and more liquid, and usually offer higher yields than time deposits, one could argue that investors would suffer no loss from the withdrawal of federal deposit insurance—or rather would suffer no loss if the U.S. Treasury ended its policy of discouraging demand for its debt by hindering the access of small investors. For example, instead of raising the minimum denomination of Treasury bills from $1,000 to $10,000, as it did in 1970 when depositors began to shift to the higher-yielding bills, it might, as in the United Kingdom, sell and redeem its debt over post office counters in denominations as small as £5.

Banks and S&Ls might attempt to redress the adverse competitive effects of the withdrawal of federal deposit insurance by administering one or more insurance programs of their own. (They might learn how to go about it from the record of early programs in Calomiris, 1989.) However, no private system is likely to be as popular with prospective depositors as the present system, which is underwritten by taxpayers. This guarantee, with its implied transfer of wealth from taxpayers to bankers (bank owners and the consumers of bank perquisites), is presumably the main explanation of deposit insurance and its supporting regulations.

References

Calomiris, Charles W. 1989. "Deposit Insurance: Lessons from the Record." Federal Reserve Bank of Chicago *Economic Perspectives* (May/June): 10–30.

Golembe, Carter 1961. "The Deposit Insurance Legislation of 1933: An Examination of its Antecedents and its Purposes." *Political Science Quarterly* (No. 2): 181–200.

Kane, Edward 1987. "The Risks of Capital Forbearance: The Case of the FSLIC and Zombie S&Ls." *Contemporary Policy Issues* (January): 77–83.

Kaufman, George 1985. "Implications of Large Bank Problems and Insolvencies for the Banking Industry and Economic Policy." *Issues in Bank Regulation* (Winter): 35–42.

Litan, Robert E. 1987. *What Should Banks Do?* Washington, D.C.: The Brookings Institution.

White, Lawrence J. 1991. *The S&L Debacle: Public Policy Lessons for Bank and Thrift Regulation.* New York: Oxford University Press.

2

S&L CLOSURES AND SURVIVORS: ARE THERE SYSTEMATIC DIFFERENCES IN BEHAVIOR?

James R. Barth, Carl D. Hudson and John S. Jahera, Jr.

Auburn University

DURING THE 1980s, the S&L industry experienced its worst performance since the 1930s. More than a thousand institutions failed and were resolved by regulators from January of 1980 through December of 1992 at an estimated present-value cost of nearly $130 billion. The resolution of additional troubled S&Ls will likely result in a final cost of $150 billion or more. These costs, when measured relative to the size of the industry in the 1980s, are actually greater than those incurred for S&Ls in the Great Depression.

This devastating development and a related but far less serious problem in the banking industry—see Barth, Brumbaugh, and Litan (1992)—led to sweeping proposals by the Bush Administration in the spring of 1991 to reform the federal deposit insurance system and to restructure the regulation of the banking industry (U.S. Treasury Department, 1991). One of the major controversies over these proposals is the extent to which narrowing (rather than widening, as was proposed by the Bush Administration) the range of powers available to federally insured depository institutions is an appropriate way to protect taxpayers from another S&L-like debacle. Some have argued that deregulation of the S&L industry during the early 1980s was the fundamental cause of all the problems. Certainly, there is evidence showing that those S&Ls with access to the broadest investment powers accounted for a disproportionate share of the total failure resolution costs. Such evidence contributed to the defeat of the Bush Administration's proposals for granting broader powers to depository institutions. Instead, the Federal Deposit Insurance Corporation Improvement Act (FDICIA), which is much more limited in scope, was enacted. More specifically, the FDICIA contains provisions imposing higher and stricter capital requirements on both banks and S&Ls. In addition, the legislation mandates prompt corrective action against weakly capitalized institutions.

In view of the controversy over the appropriateness of broader powers being granted to federally insured depository institutions, it is important to understand exactly what the S&L survivors did so differently from the institutions that were closed. The main purpose of this paper, therefore, is to examine the operating strategies of institutions that ultimately were closed by regulators during the 1980s, versus those that survived the decade. We attempt to determine whether the fundamental cause of the S&L debacle was indeed asset deregulation (i.e., permitting S&Ls to diversify away from mainly home mortgage loans and to move more heavily into commercial real estate loans and investments in the early 1980s). We analyze publicly available data obtained from the Federal Home Loan Bank Board (FHLBB) and its successor, the Office of Thrift Supervision (OTS), for all federally insured S&Ls in operation at some time during the period 1980 through 1989. This retrospective analysis should help identify differences in behavior that led to closure as opposed to survival for S&Ls. Only through such analyses can one discern the important lessons taught by the S&L debacle, and thus enact appropriate laws and regulations for our nation's insured depository institutions.[1]

1 Risk-taking and the S&L industry

Stockholders of S&Ls have two types of options available to them that provide an incentive toward greater risk-taking behavior. The first is related to the fact that, as with any firm, the stockholders of an S&L have a call option on the assets. The second is related to the institution's access to federally insured deposits, which means that stockholders also have a put option on those same assets. Stockholders will therefore rationally attempt to maximize the combined value of these two options, given their risk preferences and the regulatory environment in which they operate. In the 1980s, S&Ls paid deposit insurance premiums irrespective of risk. This meant that the value of the options would be increased by engaging in high-risk activities. Furthermore, the degrees of freedom available to engage in high-risk activities are enhanced when the range of assets that S&Ls can acquire is quite broad. But, more importantly, the incentive to engage in

[1] For more detailed discussions of the various problems of the entire S&L industry, see Barth (1991), Brumbaugh (1988), Kane (1989), and White (1991).

relatively risky activities is most pronounced when S&Ls are permitted to operate in an environment of lax regulation and supervision without adequate owner-contributed equity capital (see Furlong and Keeley, 1989).

With capital standards set appropriately and with prudent regulation and supervision, the value of the option to turn the keys to an S&L over to the federal insurer (i.e., exercise the put option) would be virtually nonexistent.[2] Otherwise, the value of both the call and put options can be increased, thereby enhancing the overall value of the institution for the stockholders. The basic problem is that there is no incentive on the part of insured depositors to monitor and control the risk-taking behavior of S&Ls. This important task is therefore left to the regulator. If regulation is inadequate, S&Ls will be able to engage in risk-taking behavior that is not only subsidized by the federal insurer but which excessively increases the risk-exposure of the taxpayer (see, for example, Buser, Chen, and Kane, 1981).

The risk-taking behavior of S&Ls depends not only on regulatory constraints but also on the attitudes of these institutions toward risk. In this regard, there are two basic types of ownership for S&Ls: mutual and stock. Of the two types, it is generally agreed that mutual S&Ls are more risk averse than stock S&Ls.[3] The main reason is that the managers of these institutions, by not owning stock or stock options, cannot share fully in any gains that result from high-risk activities. On the other hand, they do stand to lose their employment if any high-risk activities fail to pay off as promised. This asymmetry in returns provides an incentive for mutual S&Ls to prefer less risky portfolios. For stock S&Ls, this is not the case. With liability limited to their stockholdings, stockholders receive any upside gains from investing in riskier assets, while incurring none of the downside losses be-

[2] Based upon the seminal work of Merton (1977) and the important insights of Ronn and Verma (1986), Barth, Page, and Brumbaugh (1990) estimate the value of the put option for a sample of S&Ls during the 1980s, showing that this value is inversely related to the tangible capital-to-asset ratio. Craine and Nelson (1990) provide an interesting analysis of the appropriate level of capital and auditing interval to constrain the value of the put option.

[3] Verbrugge and Goldstein (1981), in an early study, found that mutual S&Ls are less risky and earn lower rates of return on assets than stock S&Ls. This finding was considered evidence of expense-preference behavior on the part of mutual S&Ls, which was corroborated by Verbrugge and Jahera (1981).

yond the value of their owner-contributed equity capital.[4] It is the federal insurer who covers all losses to protect insured depositors once capital has been depleted. Of course, the greater the owner-contributed equity capital, the less the incentive to engage in riskier activities. Similarly, the narrower the range of assets that can be acquired by S&Ls, the fewer the degrees of freedom to increase risk-taking behavior.[5]

The foregoing discussion may be summarized as follows. In the S&L industry, the propensity toward risk-taking behavior is greater for stock than mutual S&Ls, greater for S&Ls with broader asset powers, and greater for inadequately capitalized institutions. In an attempt to test these hypotheses, we examined publicly available data for all federally insured S&Ls during the period 1980 through 1989.

2 Comparative analysis of closures and survivors

Table 1 provides information concerning the number of mutual and stock S&Ls during the decade as well as the number of institutions closed by the regulators. As can be seen, the proportion of stock institutions increased markedly from 1980 to 1989 as many mutuals converted to the stock form of organization. Table 2 presents an overview of the S&L industry for each year in the 1980s based upon selected variables. The total assets of all institutions increased from $604 billion at the beginning of the decade to just over $1.3 trillion in 1988. The growth came largely for those institutions converting to the stock form, with the assets of stock institutions increasing from $164 billion to $992 billion over the same period. Based upon generally accepted accounting principles (GAAP), the GAAP capital-to-asset ratio declined throughout the decade, with mutuals experiencing the most dramatic decline. Similarly, the tangible (GAAP less goodwill and other intangibles) capital-to-asset ratio eroded significantly, and was even negative for mutual institutions in several years.

It is interesting to note the change in the role of the more traditional home mortgage activities of S&Ls over the 1980s. The industry began the decade with home mortgages accounting for nearly seventy-five percent of total assets, with no significant difference in behavior between stocks

[4] Teall (1993), in a study of 349 stock S&Ls, found an inverse relationship between the proportion of stock held by insiders and the equity capital-to-asset ratio, which he suggests is indicative of greater risk-taking behavior by closely held stock S&Ls.

[5] Esty (1993) finds a positive relationship between ownership concentration and risk-taking behavior for a small sample of S&Ls.

TABLE 1
DISTRIBUTION OF S&Ls AND S&L CLOSURES
BY ORGANIZATIONAL FORM: 1980–1989

	Number of Institutions			Number of Closures		
	U.S.	Stock	Mutual	U.S.	Stock	Mutual
1980	3993	782	3211	30	7	23
1981	3751	786	2965	77	15	62
1982	3287	740	2547	241	42	199
1983	3146	727	2419	67	12	55
1984	3136	934	2202	35	12	23
1985	3246	1087	2159	37	13	24
1986	3220	1189	2031	51	23	28
1987	3147	1269	1878	50	19	31
1988	2949	1285	1664	207	94	113
1989	2878	1203	1675	46	26	20

Source: Federal Home Loan Bank Board and Office of Thrift Supervision

and mutuals. However, this proportion fell below fifty percent for both ownership types by 1989. At the same time, there was a greater shift to mortgage-backed securities, with their share of total assets increasing from less than 5 percent to nearly 14 percent.

More information on the changes in the industry during the 1980s is presented in Tables 3 and 4. The total assets of both survivors and closures are presented. The data are broken down by charter type, and by organizational form for each charter type. "Survivors" are those institutions that continued in operation throughout the entire decade. "Closures" are those institutions that were closed by the regulators. In 1980, for example, there were 1,945 federally chartered mutual S&Ls. By the end of the decade, 1,587 were still in operation and 358 had been closed. Table 4 provides similar information for stock institutions. Both the number and the total assets of stock S&Ls increased over the decade. Note that state-chartered institutions were closed at a greater rate than those with federal charters, which would appear to support the argument that more lenient state regulations caused the S&L debacle.

TABLE 2
SELECTED CHARACTERISTICS OF S&Ls
BY ORGANIZATIONAL FORM: 1980–1989

	1980	1981	1982	1983	1984	1985	1986	1987	1988	1989
Total Assets ($ billions)										
U.S.	604	640	686	813	976	1,068	1,162	1,249	1,349	1,252
Stock	164	184	207	297	510	601	719	870	992	882
Mutual	440	456	479	515	465	467	442	379	357	369
GAAP Capital (percent)										
U.S.	5.4	4.2	3.0	3.1	2.7	3.1	3.3	2.7	3.3	2.0
Stock	5.3	4.3	2.7	3.9	3.4	3.9	4.0	3.5	3.5	3.3
Mutual	5.4	4.1	3.6	2.7	2.0	2.0	2.2	1.0	2.8	−1.0
Tangible Capital (percent)										
U.S.	5.3	4.0	0.5	0.4	0.3	0.8	1.2	0.7	1.6	0.8
Stock	5.2	3.7	0.1	1.3	0.8	1.4	1.7	1.2	1.6	1.9
Mutual	5.4	4.0	1.6	−0.1	−0.3	0.02	0.4	−0.4	1.6	−1.8
Ratio of Home Mortgages to Total Assets (percent)										
U.S.	74.3	72.3	64.6	59.0	54.2	52.0	48.1	46.7	46.9	49.8
Stock	75.4	72.3	64.3	58.5	52.2	50.0	46.1	44.2	44.8	48.2
Mutual	73.9	72.4	64.7	59.3	56.3	54.7	51.3	52.3	52.3	53.5
Ratio of Mortgage-Backed Securities to Total Assets (percent)										
U.S.	4.4	5.1	8.9	11.4	11.5	10.8	13.6	16.2	15.9	13.7
Stock	3.3	5.0	9.7	10.9	12.1	11.2	15.1	18.1	17.2	14.5
Mutual	4.9	5.2	8.6	11.7	10.9	10.4	11.3	11.8	12.3	11.7

Source: Federal Home Loan Bank Board and Office of Thrift Supervision

TABLE 3
S&L Assets by Charter, Ownership Type and Survivor Status: 1980–1989

Panel A: Federal Charter

	All Mutuals		Mutual Survivors		Mutual Closures	
Year	Number	Assets	Number	Assets	Number	Assets
1980	1945	327,771	1587	274,844	358	52,927
1981	1818	345,944	1502	296,535	316	49,409
1982	1588	380,629	1399	345,979	189	34,650
1983	1550	411,514	1387	373,276	163	38,239
1984	1398	353,935	1267	323,543	131	30,392
1985	1344	354,843	1220	318,920	124	35,922
1986	1264	341,082	1150	308,354	114	32,728
1987	1193	285,814	1075	353,199	118	32,616
1988	1043	269,183	1025	264,634	18	45,493
1989	1104	294,665	1104	294,665	–	–

Panel B: State Charter

	All Mutuals		Mutual Survivors		Mutual Closures	
Year	Number	Assets	Number	Assets	Number	Assets
1980	1266	111,751	1103	92,687	163	19,064
1981	1147	110,144	1003	92,381	144	17,763
1982	959	98,214	877	85,259	82	12,955
1983	869	103,753	821	93,218	48	10,535
1984	804	111,549	764	98,178	40	13,371
1985	815	112,335	781	100,725	34	11,611
1986	767	101,116	739	90,960	28	10,157
1987	685	92,904	666	85,861	19	70,433
1988	621	87,875	616	83,356	5	45,194
1989	571	74,779	571	74,779	–	–

Note: Assets in $ millions throughout.

TABLE 4
S&L ASSETS BY CHARTER, OWNERSHIP TYPE AND SURVIVOR STATUS: 1980–1989

Panel A: Federal Charter

	All Stocks		Stock Survivors		Stock Closures	
Year	Number	Assets	Number	Assets	Number	Assets
1980	39	11,799	36	11,149	3	650
1981	79	55,165	66	49,139	13	6,026
1982	104	98,482	90	95,636	14	2,846
1983	127	148,775	111	145,276	16	350
1984	291	271,469	259	257,480	32	13,989
1985	377	328,605	338	310,557	39	18,047
1986	480	404,686	445	389,889	35	14,798
1987	575	527,409	542	508,839	33	18,570
1988	677	692,047	648	672,635	29	19,411
1989	684	658,809	663	640,030	21	18,779

Panel B: State Charter

	All Stocks		Stock Survivors		Stock Closures	
Year	Number	Assets	Number	Assets	Number	Assets
1980	743	152,448	542	126,448	201	26,000
1981	707	128,554	515	95,718	192	32,836
1982	636	108,214	486	79,737	150	28,476
1983	600	148,465	461	94,735	139	53,730
1984	643	238,993	510	169,829	133	69,164
1985	710	272,479	580	198,972	130	70,507
1986	709	314,718	596	236,518	113	78,200
1987	694	342,738	598	265,877	96	76,860
1988	608	299,755	587	292,431	21	72,235
1989	519	223,443	515	222,833	4	610

Note: Assets in $ millions throughout.

To compare the behavior of survivors and closures, year-to-year differences are calculated in several variables designed to capture both portfolio shifts and changes in capital adequacy. Tables 5, 6 and 7 present the results of difference-of-means tests across the two groups. The annual percentage changes in total assets, the ratio of direct investment to total assets, the ratio of home mortgages to total assets, the ratio of real estate held to total assets, and the ratio of tangible capital to total assets are presented. Table 5 compares all surviving S&Ls with all those that were closed at some point during the decade. With respect to changes in assets, the closures, as one might expect, exhibit significantly greater declines in the latter years of the decade.

Direct investment, which basically represents the acquisition of land and commercial office buildings for an S&L's own account, is generally considered to be far riskier than traditional home mortgage loans. Indeed, the regulation of such investment generated considerable controversy in the mid-1980s (Benston and Brumbaugh, 1988). As may be seen, both the survivors and closures sharply increased the share of their assets devoted to this type of activity, but those eventually closed showed significantly greater movement into direct investment. Similarly, the tangible capital to asset ratio for both types of institutions declined throughout most of the period. At the same time, there was a marked shift towards the use of brokered deposits to fund growth, particularly for the closures.

Table 6 compares the mutual survivors to the mutual closures. While the results are generally similar to those for all institutions, there are nonetheless differences worth mentioning. Both groups experienced a decline in tangible capital relative to assets, but the survivors were able to reverse the trend and actually increase this ratio in 1985, 1986 and 1987. As for the closures, this ratio decline continuously, with the rate of decline increasing by the end of the decade. As shown in the table, the year-to-year changes in this ratio for mutual survivors and mutual closures were significantly different from one another for each year.

Table 7 provides information for stock survivors versus stock closures. A comparison of the change in the direct investment to asset ratio for stock institutions (Table 7) and mutuals (Table 6) reveals that the former engaged in this risky activity at a greater rate than the latter. Also, the stock closures moved significantly more heavily into direct investment than did their mutual counterparts. With respect to brokered deposits, there also is a significant difference between the survivors and closures. Furthermore,

TABLE 5
ANNUAL PERCENTAGE CHANGE IN SELECTED BALANCE SHEET RATIOS FOR S&Ls BY SURVIVOR STATUS: ALL SURVIVORS VERSUS ALL CLOSURES

		1980	1981	1982	1983	1984	1985	1986	1987	1988	1989
Total Asset Growth	Survivors	–	−1.30	1.65	5.60	−6.10	−12.54	−2.70	−7.73	−1.12	−10.41
	Closures	–	3.66	4.08	13.63	−74.88	−28.43	−16.45	−5.53	26.14	−86.85
	t-statistic	–	(0.69)	(0.23)	(0.77)	(1.65)	(2.10)†	(2.87)†	(0.99)	(1.71)	(2.04)†
Direct Investment/ Assets	Survivors	0.06	0.09	0.14	0.15	0.12	0.19	0.13	0.01	0.59	0.12
	Closures	0.09	0.19	0.47	0.57	0.46	1.08	0.01	−0.11	−0.22	0.74
	t-statistic	(1.48)	(2.93)*	(2.62)†	(2.13)†	(1.91)	(4.41)*	(0.49)	(0.35)	(1.40)	(0.80)
Brokered Deposits/ Assets	Survivors	0.04	0.03	0.55	0.74	−0.38	−0.42	−0.05	0.39	0.50	0.63
	Closures	0.23	0.32	3.27	4.55	−4.13	−1.86	−0.26	3.31	3.99	1.73
	t-statistic	(2.33)†	(2.08)†	(4.83)*	(5.15)*	(5.26)*	(2.85)*	(0.64)	(4.53)*	(2.21)†	(0.74)
Home Mortgages/ Assets	Survivors	−1.76	−0.84	−4.00	−4.16	−3.25	−0.75	−2.63	0.44	0.66	0.22
	Closures	−1.45	−0.21	−6.46	−4.96	−6.95	−1.47	−1.95	−1.65	1.07	0.98
	t-statistic	(1.06)	(1.78)	(4.22)*	(0.91)	(4.56)*	(1.04)	(1.03)	(3.52)*	(0.39)	(0.49)
Tangible Capital/ Assets	Survivors	−0.37	−1.22	−1.93	−0.74	−0.76	−0.003	−0.18	−0.38	−1.13	−1.65
	Closures	−0.87	−2.02	−3.41	−2.15	−2.21	−2.58	−6.77	−11.51	−9.49	0.84
	t-statistic	(4.83)*	(5.84)*	(5.68)*	(3.98)*	(6.08)*	(5.52)*	(9.05)*	(10.17)*	(3.28)*	(1.12)

Note: * and † indicate significance at the 1 percent and 5 percent levels respectively.

TABLE 6
ANNUAL PERCENTAGE CHANGE IN SELECTED BALANCE SHEET RATIOS FOR S&Ls BY SURVIVOR STATUS: MUTUAL SURVIVORS VERSUS MUTUAL CLOSURES

		1980	1981	1982	1983	1984	1985	1986	1987	1988	1989
Total Asset Growth	Survivors	–	−0.11	−1.43	2.83	−2.56	−4.04	1.21	−3.93	0.29	–
	Closures	–	−3.00	3.95	−7.12	−14.69	−12.97	−6.75	−0.85	1.73	–
	t-statistic	–	(0.62)	(1.00)	(1.25)	(2.83)*	(4.80)*	(5.51)*	(2.06)†	(0.33)	–
Direct Investment/ Assets	Survivors	0.04	0.06	0.05	0.05	0.05	0.10	0.07	−0.01	0.69	–
	Closures	0.07	0.10	0.08	0.03	0.32	0.28	−0.16	−0.02	−1.63	–
	t-statistic	(1.44)	(1.83)†	(0.38)	(0.22)	(1.35)	(1.22)	(1.06)	(0.05)	(1.40)	–
Brokered Deposits/ Assets	Survivors	0.05	−0.02	0.21	0.45	−0.14	−0.11	−0.04	0.11	0.09	–
	Closures	0.23	0.10	1.54	3.17	−3.58	−0.47	−0.61	1.65	4.18	–
	t-statistic	(1.88)†	(0.88)	(2.59)*	(3.65)*	(3.81)*	(0.56)	(1.07)	(2.47)†	(1.58)	–
Home Mortgages/ Assets	Survivors	−1.96	−1.07	−3.96	−4.55	−2.96	−1.04	−3.29	0.89	0.73	–
	Closures	−1.67	−0.67	−5.52	−6.37	−7.31	−0.09	−2.73	0.08	3.15	–
	t-statistic	(1.05)	(1.47)	(2.53)†	(1.83)†	(4.39)*	(1.41)	(0.84)	(1.13)	(1.84)	–
Tangible Capital/ Assets	Survivors	−0.23	−0.88	−1.65	−0.49	−0.45	0.33	0.57	0.20	−0.04	–
	Closures	−0.52	−1.59	−2.93	−1.16	−2.08	−2.87	−5.99	−9.76	−16.50	–
	t-statistic	(10.08)*	(10.15)*	(5.26)*	(3.33)*	(6.64)*	(4.48)*	(8.26)*	(8.16)*	(4.59)*	–

Note: * and † indicate significance at the 1 percent and 5 percent levels respectively.

TABLE 7
Annual Percentage Change in Selected Balance Sheet Ratios for S&Ls by Survivor Status: Stock Survivors versus Stock Closures

		1980	1981	1982	1983	1984	1985	1986	1987	1988	1989
Total Asset Growth	Survivors	–	−7.11	14.99	17.33	−16.61	−34.52	−10.90	−13.93	−3.12	−17.98
	Closures	–	19.62	4.32	43.81	−140.90	−43.30	−24.73	−9.29	33.46	−86.85
	t-statistic	–	(1.23)	(0.38)	(1.14)	(1.42)	(0.57)	(1.56)	(1.07)	(1.77)	(1.83)
Direct Investment/ Assets	Survivors	0.17	0.24	0.51	0.59	0.33	0.46	0.24	0.03	0.46	−0.03
	Closures	0.16	0.40	1.16	1.32	0.61	1.82	0.16	−0.19	0.44	0.74
	t-statistic	(0.21)	(1.51)	(1.97)†	(1.54)	(0.88)	(3.79)*	(0.20)	(0.37)	(0.08)	(0.92)
Brokered Deposits/ Assets	Survivors	−0.01	0.29	1.94	1.89	−1.04	−1.15	−0.07	0.83	1.05	1.22
	Closures	0.23	0.84	6.26	6.47	−4.72	−3.15	0.04	4.80	3.91	1.73
	t-statistic	(1.55)	(1.65)	(3.45)*	(2.42)†	(3.14)*	(2.53)†	(0.27)	(3.68)*	(1.41)	(0.31)
Home Mortgages/ Assets	Survivors	−0.78	0.21	−4.18	−2.59	−4.07	−0.04	−1.36	−0.24	0.56	0.18
	Closures	−0.86	0.83	−8.08	−3.01	−6.56	−2.75	−1.28	−3.21	0.11	0.98
	t-statistic	(0.10)	(0.61)	(3.16)*	(0.25)	(1.82)	(2.22)†	(0.08)	(3.20)*	(0.32)	(0.52)
Tangible Capital/ Assets	Survivors	−1.11	−2.74	−3.13	−1.74	−1.64	−0.82	−1.60	−1.30	−2.63	−3.19
	Closures	−1.81	−3.01	−4.23	−3.51	−2.35	−2.30	−7.44	−13.08	−6.27	0.84
	t-statistic	(1.83)	(0.57)	(1.83)	(2.16)†	(1.49)	(2.38)†	(4.93)*	(6.69)*	(1.11)	(1.72)

Note: * and † indicate significance at the 1 percent and 5 percent levels respectively.

the tangible capital to asset ratio declined at a significantly greater rate for the stock closures as compared to the stock survivors over most of the decade.

3 A STATISTICAL MODEL OF RISK-TAKING BEHAVIOR

The focus so far has been on the comparative differences in behavior between S&Ls that survived the 1980s and those that failed. The results presented in the preceding section provide some support for the view that weakly capitalized S&Ls engaged in greater risk-taking behavior. With more opportunities for engaging in riskier activities, a state charter is the charter type that one would expect to be most associated with riskier behavior.

This section presents a simple statistical model that attempts to take into account simultaneously several important factors so as to determine more adequately the effect of ownership structure, charter type, and survivor status on risk-taking behavior.[6] More specifically, the ratio of direct investment to total assets is used as a proxy for risk-taking behavior. This variable is then regressed upon a number of variables as follows:

$$DI_i = \alpha_0 + \alpha_1 D1_i + \alpha_2 D2_i + \alpha_3 FED_i + \alpha_4 STOCK_i + \alpha_5 TA_i + \alpha_6 TIS_i + e_i \tag{1}$$

where the variables are defined as in Table 8.

This regression equation was estimated using OLS based upon 36,791 cross-sectional, time-series observations. The empirical results are as follows:

$$\begin{aligned} DI = \underset{(2.50)}{0.77} \; &+ \underset{(41.34)}{0.07D1} \; - \underset{(-7.41)}{0.05D2} \; - \underset{(-10.79)}{0.35FED} \; + \underset{(33.46)}{1.23STOCK} \\ &+ \underset{(9.52)}{0.148TA} \; + \underset{(23.31)}{0.85TIS} \quad \bar{R}^2 = 0.13 \quad F = 927.98 \end{aligned} \tag{2}$$

where the estimated t-statistics appear in parentheses. The coefficient on D1 is positive, while the coefficient on D2 is negative. This means that weakly capitalized S&Ls were significantly more heavily involved in direct

[6] For an earlier application of this model to the state of Texas, see Barth, Hudson and Jahera (forthcoming).

TABLE 8
DEFINITIONS OF VARIABLES

DI	Ratio of direct investment to total assets.
D1	Dummy variable equal to 1 if the tangible capital-to-assets ratio is less than 3 percent, 0 otherwise, and then multiplied by the actual capital-to-asset ratio.
D2	Dummy variable equal to 1 if the tangible capital-to-assets ratio is greater than 3 percent, 0 otherwise, and then multiplied by the actual capital-to-asset ratio.
FED	Dummy variable equal to 1 if a federally chartered institution; 0 otherwise.
STOCK	Dummy variable equal to 1 if a stock institution; 0 otherwise.
TA	Total assets.
TIS	Dummy variable equal to 1 if an institution is tangible insolvent at any time during the sample period; 0 otherwise.
e	Random error term.

investment activity than the more strongly capitalized institutions, which is consistent with behavior that increases the value of the put option. This finding is reinforced by the positive coefficient on TIS, which indicates that S&Ls that became tangible insolvent during the period devoted a significantly larger share of their assets to direct investment. State chartered institutions were generally able to operate under less constraining regulations, including greater authority to engage in direct investment. In this regard, the negative sign on the FED dummy variable indicates that the federally chartered institutions devoted a significantly smaller proportion of their assets to direct investment. Given charter type, however, the stock S&Ls allocated a significantly larger share of their assets to direct investment than the mutual S&Ls. Finally, the larger the S&L—with large institutions tending to be stock institutions—the greater was the proportion of direct investment in total assets.

Since Texas S&Ls contributed disproportionately to the S&L debacle, a second regression equation was estimated. This equation included the domestic crude oil refiner acquisition cost ($/barrel) as a proxy for the severe adverse economic conditions affecting this state.[7] The addition of this variable should help control for the influence of Texas S&Ls on the results for the overall S&L industry. This particular variable reached a high of $34.33 per barrel in 1981 and then declined to $14.74 in 1988 before increasing to $17.87 in 1989. The empirical results obtained when this variable (OIL) was included are as follows:

$$\begin{aligned} DI = \; & \underset{(24.57)}{1.59} \; \underset{(55.46)}{+0.08D1} \; \underset{(-15.72)}{-0.05D2} \; \underset{(-11.76)}{-0.39FED} \; \underset{(31.76)}{+1.17STOCK} \\ & \underset{(9.02)}{+0.131TA} \; \underset{(24.07)}{+0.87TIS} \; \underset{(-14.98)}{-0.03OIL} \quad \bar{R}^2 = 0.14 \quad F = 832.26 \end{aligned} \tag{3}$$

where the estimated *t*-statistics appear in parentheses. The estimated coefficients and their statistical significance, when attempting to control for broader economic fluctuations, are quite similar to those reported in equation (2).[8] The relationship between the oil-price variable and the direct investment variable is inverse, indicating that as the Texas-oil-dependent economy weakened, S&Ls significantly increased their activity in direct investment. This finding suggests that greater risk-taking behavior occurred as opportunities diminished with deteriorating economic activity.

Overall, these empirical results indicate that ownership structure, capitalization, and charter type affect risk-taking behavior. These findings were unchanged when taking into account the oil price movements that so disrupted the Texas economy. Of course, much more work remains to be done before such findings can be considered conclusive. Although several factors have been identified here as influencing the risk-taking behavior of S&Ls, the more fundamental and unifying cause of the debacle may be the incentives associated with federal deposit insurance—particularly if such insurance induces inadequately capitalized stock-type S&Ls to engage in "excessive" risk-taking behavior when the opportunities arise.[9]

[7] Oil prices are from the *Annual Energy Review* (1991), published by the Energy Information Administration.

[8] Equation (2) was also estimated using other variables to control for overall economic activity, such as the change in oil prices, real oil prices and the office vacancy rate. The inclusion of these other alternative variables produced similar results.

[9] For additional empirical studies of risk-taking behavior by S&Ls, see Brickley and James (1986), Benston (1985), Barth, Bartholomew and Bradley (1990), and Gelbe and Shull (1990).

4 Summary and conclusions

The S&L industry suffered severely during the 1980s. It is now a much smaller and more diversified industry. Major legislation was enacted during the decade. However, the problems in the banking industry at the end of the decade led to still more legislation. In contrast to that of the early 1980s, the most recent legislation represents an attempt to re-regulate federally insured depository institutions. Yet the results of this and several other studies do not support the view that the S&L industry's problems were due to the deregulation at either the federal or state level in the early 1980s. Indeed, the evidence presented in this paper indicates that deregulation, if anything, only exacerbates risk-taking behavior, with the more basic determinants of such behavior being ownership structure and owner-contributed equity capital. In other words, the empirical results reported here support the view that incentives are more important for explaining S&L behavior than simply the range of activities in which S&Ls are permitted to engage.

In conclusion, there are important differences in behavior between mutual and stock S&Ls and, even more significantly in view of the moral hazard problem, between weakly and more strongly capitalized institutions. The empirical results presented here indicate that there were differences in behavior towards risk, but that the differences are consistent with the incentives that were provided by the economic and regulatory environment of the 1980s, with weakly capitalized and insolvent S&Ls engaging in higher-risk activities.

References

Barth, James R. 1991. *The Great Savings and Loan Debacle*. Washington, D.C.: American Enterprise Institute.

———, Philip F. Bartholomew and Michael G. Bradley 1990. "Determinants of Thrift Institutions Resolution Costs." *Journal of Finance* 45: 731–54.

———, Philip F. Bartholomew and Carol Labich 1990. "Moral Hazard and the Thrift Crisis: An Empirical Analysis." *Consumer Finance Law Quarterly Report* 44: 22–34.

———, R. Dan Brumbaugh, Jr. and Robert E. Litan 1992. *The Future of American Banking*. Armonk, NY: M.E. Sharpe.

______, R. Dan Brumbaugh, Jr., Daniel Sauerhaft and George H.K. Wang 1985. "Thrift Institution Failures: Causes and Policy Issues." *Proceedings of Conference on Bank Structure and Competition*, Federal Reserve Bank of Chicago: 184–216.

______, Daniel E. Page and R. Dan Brumbaugh, Jr. 1992. "Pitfalls in Using Market Prices to Assess the Financial Condition of Depository Institutions." *Journal of Real Estate Finance and Economics* 5: 151–66.

______, Carl D. Hudson and John S. Jahera, Jr. Forthcoming. "Risk Taking in the Texas S&L Industry: Charter and Ownership Effects." *The Financial Review*.

Benston, George J. 1985. *An Analysis of the Causes of Savings and Loan Association Failure*. Monograph Series in Finance and Economics, Salomon Brothers Center for the Study of Financial Institutions.

______. and R. Dan Brumbaugh, Jr. 1988. "On the Controversy Over Asset Restrictions for Thrift Institutions." *Housing Finance Review* 7: 18–27.

Brewer, Elijah 1990. "The Impact of Deposit Insurance on S&L Shareholders' Risk/Return Trade-offs." Conference on Bank Structure and Competition Proceedings, Federal Reserve Bank of Chicago: 96–140.

Brickley, James A. and Christopher M. James 1986. "Access to Deposit Insurance, Insolvency Rules and the Stock Returns of Financial Institutions." *Journal of Financial Economics* 16: 345–71.

Brumbaugh, R. Dan, Jr., 1988. *Thrifts Under Siege: Restoring Order to American Banking*. Cambridge: Ballinger Publishing Company.

Buser, Stephen A., Andrew H. Chen and Edward J. Kane 1981. "Federal Deposit Insurance, Regulatory Policy and Optimal Bank Capital." *Journal of Finance* 36: 51–60.

Craine, Roger and Richard W. Nelson 1990. "Can Depository Institutions Be Regulated as if They Were Margin Accounts?" Conference on Bank Structure and Competition Proceedings, Federal Reserve Bank of Chicago: 24–61.

Esty, Benjamin C. 1993. "Ownership Concentration and Risk-Taking in the S&L Industry." Unpublished working paper.

Furlong, Frederick T. and Michael C. Keeley 1989. "Capital Regulation and Bank Risk-Taking: A Note." *Journal of Banking and Finance* 13: 883–91.

Gelbe, Devra L. and Bernard Shull 1990. "FIRREA's Risk Control Theories: A Framework for Empirical Investigation." Unpublished paper.

Gunther, Jeffrey W. and Kenneth J. Robinson 1990. "Moral Hazard and Texas Banking in the 1980s: Was There a Connection?" *Financial Industry Studies*, Federal Reserve Bank of Dallas: 1–8.

Gup, Benton E., J. Thomas Lindley, James E. McNulty and James A. Verbrugge 1989. "The Performance of De Novo Thrift Institutions: Risk, Return, and Charter Type." Research Paper No. 156, Office of Policy and Economic Research, Federal Home Loan Bank Board, March.

Hadaway, Beverly L. and Samuel C. Hadaway 1981. "An Analysis of the Performance Characteristics of Converted Savings and Loan Associations." *Journal of Financial Research* 4: 195–206.

Kane, Edward J. 1989. *The S&L Insurance Mess: How Did It Happen.* Washington, D.C.: The Urban Institute Press.

Masulis, Ronald W. 1987. "Changes in Ownership Structure: Conversions of Mutual Savings and Loans to Stock Charter." *Journal of Financial Economics*: 29–59.

Merton, Robert C. 1977. "An Analytic Derivation of the Cost of Deposit Insurance and Loan Guarantees: An Application of Modern Option Pricing Theory." *Journal of Banking and Finance* 1: 3–11.

O'Keefe, John 1990. "The Texas Banking Crisis: Causes and Consequences 1980–1989." *FDIC Banking Review* 3: 1–34.

Ronn, Ehud I. and Avinash K. Verma 1986. "Pricing Risk-Adjusted Deposit Insurance: An Option-Based Model." *Journal of Finance* 41: 871–96.

Saunders, Anthony, Elizabeth Strock and Nickolaos G. Travlos 1990. "Ownership Structure, Deregulation and Bank Risk Taking." *Journal of Finance* 45: 643–54.

Teall, John L. 1993. "Shareholder Control and Financial Distress in the Thrift Industry." *Journal of Business Research* 26: 161–70.

Committee on Government Operations 1985. "Federal Regulation of Direct Investments by Savings and Loan Associations." Washington D.C.: U.S. House of Representatives, November 5.

U.S. Treasury 1991. "Modernizing the Financial System: Recommendations for Safer, More Competitive Banks." February.

Verbrugge, James A. and Steven J. Goldstein 1981. "Risk, Return, and Managerial Objectives: Some Evidence From the Savings and Loan Industry." *Journal of Financial Research* 4: 45–58.

Verbrugge, James A. and John S. Jahera, Jr. 1981. "Expense-Preference Behavior in the Savings and Loan Industry." *Journal of Money, Credit and Banking* 13: 465–75.

White, Lawrence J. 1991. *The S&L Debacle*. New York: Oxford University Press.

3

DEREGULATION GONE AWRY: MORAL HAZARD IN THE SAVINGS AND LOAN INDUSTRY

Rebel A. Cole, Joseph A. McKenzie
and Lawrence J. White

*Board of Governors of the Federal Reserve System;
Federal Housing Finance Board; and
Leonard N. Stern School of Business, New York University*

1 Introduction

The insolvencies of hundreds of thrift institutions (savings and loan associations and savings banks) in the late 1980s traumatized the worlds of both finance and politics. The estimated costs of honoring the federal deposit insurance guarantees on liabilities issued by these insolvent thrifts approach $200 billion on a present-value basis. A financial debacle of such proportions is a testament to the power of moral hazard in a market characterized by high leverage and limited liability.

This paper tests for evidence of moral hazard in the behavior of thrift owners and managers. It differs from previous tests for such behavior, including Benston (1985), Barth, Bartholomew, and Labich (1989), Hanweck and Crockett (1989), Barth, Bartholomew, and Bradley (1990), Cole (1990 and 1993), Demirgüç-Kunt (1990), and Hunter, Verbrugge, and Whidbee (1994), in that it employs a "structure–behavior–outcomes" ap-

The views expressed in this paper are those of the authors and not necessarily those of the Board of Governors of the Federal Reserve System or the Federal Housing Finance Board. The authors formerly were associated with the Federal Home Loan Bank Board, where White served as Board Member. Wayne Passmore, Julianne Nelson, Michael Long, Dana Jaffe, and seminar participants at Rutgers University, City University of New York, the National Bureau of Economic Research, The Centre for Economic Policy Research, and Wake Forest University provided helpful comments. An earlier version of this article was presented at the 1990 annual meeting of the Financial Management Association.

proach that surmounts many of the shortcomings afflicting earlier works.[1] Difficulties that have bedeviled previous efforts include the lack of appreciation of the difficulties of converting reported accounting values into usable economic variables and/or the failure to distinguish between the causes of insolvency and the determinants of the regulators' decisions to close institutions.

The product of this paper is a better understanding of both the causes and costs of thrift insolvencies. Improved understanding should enhance public-policy debates concerning not only the regulation and insurance of banks, thrifts, and credit unions, but also the larger issue of how to minimize the contingent liabilities imposed by federal financial guarantees.

The remainder of this paper is organized as follows: Section 2 presents the basic model and its general application to the thrift debacle of the 1980s. Section 3 discusses the specific application of the model, the econometric tests, and the data used for those tests. Section 4 provides the results of the tests, along with a discussion of the tests themselves. Section 5 provides a brief conclusion.

2 The model

The potential for moral-hazard behavior by the equity owners vis-à-vis the debt holders of a limited-liability corporation is now a widely understood phenomenon (Williamson, 1963; Jensen and Meckling, 1976; Fama, 1980; Fama and Jensen, 1983). The application of this principle to depository institutions, where federal agencies have been the guarantors to the major creditors (depositors), is now also widely understood (Merton, 1977 and 1978; Sharpe, 1978; Marcus and Shaked, 1984; Ronn and Verma, 1986). This approach to the behavior of the equity holders treats their ownership position as possessing the equivalent of a put option: at any time the equity owners can "put" the company to the creditors and walk away from their investment. The principle of limited liability means that the owners cannot be held responsible for losses to the debt holders beyond their equity investment. Accordingly, in the absence of constraints imposed by the creditors—such as "me-first" bond covenants—the owners prefer to engage in riskier *and* lower expected-value activities than they would

[1] This is similar to the structure–behavior–performance model that frequently is used to test hypotheses in the field of industrial organization. See, for example, Scherer and Ross (1990).

prefer if they had to absorb all losses (e.g., if there were no debt). Gains from positive outcomes accrue to the owners, but losses from negative outcomes are shared with creditors and are limited to the amount of equity investment. Recognizing the incentives inherent in such an arrangement, creditors of commercial firms typically insist upon agreements that restrain the actions of the equity holders and include the equivalent of a call option, so that the creditors at some point may "call" the company from the equity holders.

In the context of federally insured depository institutions, it is the government regulator that, through safety-and-soundness regulation, sets restrictions on the behavior of the depository's owners and sets the terms and the timing for the exercise of the call option (Brumbaugh and Hemel, 1984). This holds true because the uninsured liabilities of most banking firms are small in comparison to their insured liabilities, and because even nominally uninsured liabilities usually have been redeemed at par because of the "too-big-to-fail" policies of the deposit-insurance agencies. The timing of this call option's exercise, however, is influenced by the requirement that the government afford due process to the banking firm's equity holders.

It is well known that the value of the put option for the owners of a depository is a function of the market-value net worth of the depository;[2] the riskiness of the depository's activities as represented by the variance of its expected returns or by assets or activities that generate that variance; the stringency of the regulatory system, including both the formal rules (such as portfolio and activity restrictions, and the vigor of their enforcement); and the fee charged for deposit insurance.[3]

Subject to the constraints imposed by regulatory stringency and the deposit insurance regime, the equity holders will choose the portfolio

[2] This is equivalent to the subsidy element in the deposit insurance arrangement.

[3] This presentation follows the logic of Merton (1977) and Furlong and Keeley (1989). The analysis assumes that owners can easily increase or decrease the net worth of the institution by adding funds (through a capital contribution) or withdrawing funds (through a dividend payment or share repurchase). The net worth of the institution is thus a choice variable for the owners, subject to any regulatory or creditor constraints. In a two-period model, market conditions and the outcomes of other choices concerning risk-taking by owners will determine the second period's income, which owners can then capture through a change in net worth. Since the value of the put option incorporates this second-period outcome, the analysis of owners' choices with respect to the value of the put option is a sensible way to proceed.

configuration and level of net worth expected to maximize their utility, which is a function of the profitability of the depository and the value of the put option. The portfolio selected will have specific risk and return characteristics, and the *ex ante* risk of the portfolio will depend on the level of the depository's net worth and the degree of regulatory stringency. Note that the deposit insurance regime does not enter into the calculus so long as the premiums for deposit insurance are based on a flat-rate structure that is insensitive to the risks undertaken by any individual depository.[4]

From the perspective of the regulator, a depository's net worth is a crucial "outcome" variable. Of special concern are depositories with very low or negative net worth. The net worth of a depository at some future time t is equal to its current net worth plus net income (including both operating income and capital gains or losses), less any dividends paid out (including stock repurchases), plus any equity injections. Net income, dividends, and equity injections are likely to be functions of the interest rates and the regulatory structure during the previous period. Net income also will be a function of the risk level of the inherited portfolio, and (through capital gains or losses) any changes in interest rates or regulatory stringency that occur between times $t-1$ and t.

Based on the foregoing argument, we propose two hypotheses: first, the extent and depth of the thrift insolvencies of the late 1980s were directly caused by thrifts' risk-taking strategies in the early 1980s; and, second, that these strategic behaviors were in turn motivated by the initial structural conditions, such as low net worth and regulatory laxity, facing these thrifts at the beginning of the decade. These hypotheses can be summarized as a structure–behavior–outcomes model: *structure governs behavior, which in turn governs outcomes.*

The next section discusses the specific ways in which these hypotheses are tested.

3 Specific applications

The structure–behavior–outcomes model provides a framework for testing hypotheses concerning the moral-hazard behavior of thrift operators during the 1980s. This formulation avoids a number of the pitfalls that have

[4] Until the FDIC instituted risk-based deposit insurance premiums in 1992, premiums for banks and thrifts were levied at a fixed rate. Buser, Chen, and Kane (1981), however, argue that differences in regulatory scrutiny create de facto variable premiums.

weakened earlier efforts. In particular, it avoids using portfolio composition close to the date of failure, which reflects asset sales and writedowns, to make inferences about the cause and cost of failure.

In explicating our approach, we proceed "backwards": first outcomes; then behavior; and finally structure. Following this explanation, we describe the specific data and methodology used to test the moral hazard hypotheses.

Outcomes

The potential outcomes for the thrifts analyzed in this study are survival or failure. In the event of failure, the cost of liquidation is also an outcome of interest. Those thrifts that were (a) liquidated or placed with acquirers by the Federal Home Loan Bank Board during the period from 1986 through early 1989, as well as those that were (b) predicted by the Bank Board, as of early 1989, to be extremely likely candidates for liquidation or placement at a cost to the thrift deposit insurance fund, were deemed failures. There are 621 thrifts in this set—266 in group (a) and 355 in group (b).[5] Survival, for a thrift, means that, as of year-end 1989, the institution had tangible net worth equal to at least 3 percent of assets.[6] There are 1,654 thrifts in this category.[7]

This data set has a number of advantages over those used by previous research:

(1) The sample size is large, and the failure group is large relative to the size of the sample.

[5] For thrifts that were placed into the FHLBB's Management Consignment Program (MCP), placement in the program and ultimate resolution are not treated as independent events. This is important because the portfolio composition of a thrift at the time of its placement into the program was fundamentally different from that of the same institution at the time of its ultimate resolution. In a previous study of thrift resolution costs, Barth, Bartholomew, and Bradley (1990) treat the "resolution" of eight MCP thrifts as sixteen independent events, thereby biasing the coefficients of their explanatory variables. See Bisenius, Brumbaugh, and Rogers (1988) for a discussion of the Management Consignment Program.

[6] Tangible net worth is net worth under generally accepted accounting principles less intangible assets, most of which are goodwill with the remainder consisting chiefly of purchased loan servicing.

[7] Those institutions that were solely the acquirer-successors to thrifts that failed during the period 1986–1989 were excluded from the group of "healthy" thrifts, since we are interested in comparing failed thrifts with institutions that did not require disposal during those years.

(2) Virtually all of the failures were caused by asset-quality problems that were likely to be due to moral-hazard behavior rather than to the interest-rate risk problems that caused thrift insolvencies in the early 1980s and were largely beyond the control of the thrifts.
(3) The costs of these failures were estimated by the Federal Savings and Loan Insurance Corporation (FSLIC) using a consistent costing methodology and over a comparatively short time period.
(4) The "surviving"group of thrifts is relatively uncontaminated by likely failures.

In sum, the sample is large and inclusive, with sharply defined outcomes, so that there is a reasonable likelihood of success in determining the role of moral hazard in thrift failures, rather than just explaining the regulators' decisions to close, merge, or liquidate some thrifts among many insolvent or soon-to-be-insolvent candidates.[8]

The sample may contain some classification errors. The Bank Board's 1989 list of seriously troubled thrifts failed to identify a number of thrifts subsequently closed by regulators. Thus, the group of failures is underrepresented. Moreover, some of the "surviving" thrifts were closed after 1989, while a few of the "failing" thrifts have survived. In order to delineate the sample sharply, thrifts that are neither in the "failing" group nor in the well capitalized "surviving" group are excluded from the analysis.[9] On balance, however, the strengths of this sample far outweigh its drawbacks, so that it is most suitable for the purposes of the present study.

The outcomes consist of a binary representation for each thrift—survival or failure—along with the estimated liquidation costs to the deposit insurance fund for each of the failing thrifts, where the cost is expressed as a proportion of total liabilities.[10] Where placement with acquirers rather than liquidation occurred, estimated liquidation costs are used rather than the estimated costs of placements with acquirers so as to provide greater

[8] Cole (1993) analyzes and finds significant differences in the determinants of book-value insolvency and the determinants of regulatory closure.

[9] Excluded from the group of "healthy" thrifts are those institutions that were solely the acquirer-successors to thrifts that failed during the period 1986–1989, since the focus is on a comparison between the failed thrifts and thrifts that did not require disposal during those years.

[10] Total liabilities is superior to total assets as a deflator for this purpose because total assets reflect writedowns. In the extreme case, a total writedown of a single asset would result in an infinite ratio of liquidation cost to assets.

standardization for the cost variable and to avoid the necessity of including variables to explain the determinants of the cost reduction achieved through placements.[11]

A limitation of the cost data should be acknowledged. The actual disposal cost for an insolvent thrift is known only when its last asset is sold; for some thrifts, this last sale may not occur for as long as a decade after closure. These cost estimates, then, are forecasts based on a costing methodology developed by the FSLIC in the mid-1980s, incorporating its prior experiences with the disposal of insolvent thrifts. To the extent that actual market conditions changed after the FSLIC's methodology was developed (or that the methodology mischaracterized the FSLIC's experiences), actual costs will differ from estimated (forecasted) costs. In an important sense, then, the results reported in this chapter more directly concern the determinants of the FSLIC's cost estimates, rather than the determinants of the actual costs—because the latter were still unknown at the time of this study. To the extent that FSLIC's costing methodology was an accurate representation of its experiences and a reasonable forecast of its future costs, however, the results provide worthwhile evidence on the determinants of thrift failure costs.[12]

Behavior

The behavior of each thrift between year-end 1982 and year-end 1985 is represented by the compound annual growth rate of liabilities over these three years, by its portfolio allocation to major categories of its year-end 1985 balance sheet, and by some components of its expenses for the calendar year of 1985.

This choice of these dates is appropriate for the following reasons. During 1982, the second of the two major federal deregulation acts, the Garn–St Germain Depository Institutions Act, was passed.[13] Around this

[11] One such factor is the value of tax benefits granted to acquirers. See Kormendi *et al.* (1989). Other factors include potential economies of scale or scope that may arise as a result of a placement, and the value of the firm as a going concern due to expertise and preexisting customer relationships.

[12] Virtually all studies analyzing the costs of thrift and bank failures have been forced to use data derived from estimated rather than actual costs simply because actual cost data have not been available.

[13] The first act, the Depository Institutions Deregulation and Monetary Control Act, was passed in early 1980. For discussion of these acts and their provisions, see Garcia and Cargill (1985), White (1986), and White (1991, ch. 5).

time, a number of states enacted substantial deregulation measures for their state-chartered thrifts.[14] Year-end 1985 marks the end of a period of rapid growth for most thrifts and the last year of the FSLIC's "official" solvency.[15] Also, around this time a greatly expanded field staff of regulatory personnel was starting to scrutinize thrift portfolios more closely, and more stringent regulations began to restrict thrifts' behavior.[16] More importantly, this is a time *before* thrifts began to take substantial write-downs of bad assets.

This last point is crucial. Virtually all of the studies that have tried to relate thrift failures and/or failure costs to thrifts' portfolio choices have measured their asset compositions by their balance-sheet values either just prior to insolvency or just prior to closure. This is *after* substantial write-downs and asset sales have occurred. Data chosen in this manner are likely to yield biased and misleading results.

An example will illustrate this point: Suppose that, at time t, a thrift with net worth equal to 5 percent of assets invests 90 percent of its asset portfolio in asset A (e.g., conventional home mortgage loans) and 10 percent in asset B (e.g., commercial real estate). At time $t + 1$, examiners classify asset B as a total loss, forcing the thrift to write down its value to zero so that it disappears from the thrift's balance sheet; the thrift is now seriously insolvent, with net worth of -5.6 percent of assets. At time $t + 2$, regulators liquidate the thrift.

Any statistical efforts to relate the failures (or the costs of failures) of thrifts like this to balance-sheet compositions at either time $t + 2$ or time $t + 1$ will completely miss the asset that was the cause of the failure.[17] Only a "snapshot" of balance sheets at time t provides the proper basis for attributing the causes of the failures. Accordingly, this study focuses on three categories of behavioral indicators measured as of 1985.

The first category of behavioral variables is represented by the asset and liability portfolio allocations that thrifts reported on their year-end 1985 balance sheets. By this time, thrifts had ample opportunity to invest in

[14] In general, state-chartered thrifts have investment powers at least as liberal as those enjoyed by their federal-charter counterparts.

[15] Over the years 1982–88, the annual percentage growth rates for industry assets were as follows: 1982, 6.23; 1983, 17.10; 1984, 19.32; 1985, 9.47; 1986, 8.77; 1987, 7.48; and 1988, 7.97. Growth rates for thrifts in the state of Texas were considerably higher than for those located in the rest of the nation.

[16] For more detail on this period, see White (1991, ch. 6).

[17] Partial write-downs, of course, will mean under-representation of the assets that cause failure, which will bias parameter estimates.

previously prohibited asset classes so as to diversify their portfolios and achieve the superior risk-return mix that can come with diversification.[18] Alternatively, thrifts could use the new opportunity set for undertaking higher risk, moral-hazard-laden investments.

Most previous studies of thrift performance identify "nontraditional" thrift assets—land loans, nonresidential mortgages, commercial loans, direct real estate equity investments, other direct equity investments, and service corporation investments—as possible or likely sources of losses for thrifts (Benston, 1985; Benston and Koehn, 1988; Benston and Brumbaugh, 1988; McKenzie, Cole, and Brown, 1992; Cole, 1990 and 1993; Cole and McKenzie, 1994). Here, these same asset categories are used to test for moral-hazard behavior, but they are included in a superior form: They pre-date the reporting periods in which substantial write-downs were likely to occur.[19]

The specific portfolio vector includes all financial asset classes, expressed as proportions of total assets, except one- to four-family mortgages, mortgage-backed securities, and liquid assets. These latter asset classes are excluded because of their minimal credit risk. The included variables are:

(1) multifamily mortgage loans that are secured by residential properties with five or more units;
(2) nonresidential mortgage loans that are secured by commercial structures;
(3) land loans, including loans for the acquisition and development of land and also for raw land;
(4) unsecured commercial loans;
(5) consumer loans, such as automobile loans and credit card receivables;
(6) real estate held for investment or development purposes (this represents equity interests in real estate projects, and does not include the institution's offices);

[18] Cole and McKenzie (1994) explore the potential for asset diversification by thrifts during the 1980s.

[19] To test whether thrifts used these nontraditional assets for diversification as well as for moral-hazard risk-taking, the balance sheet variables were interacted with a dummy variable that took the value one if the thrift's year-end 1985 tangible net worth was greater than three percent and zero if otherwise. These interaction variables generally are not statistically significant, so they are not reported here.

(7) service corporation investment (service corporations are separately capitalized subsidiaries most often engaged in real estate development); and
(8) equity securities, excluding the thrift's stock in its regional Federal Home Loan Bank.

A second behavioral category is the expenses incurred during calendar year 1985. Specifically included in the model is the sum of directors', officers', and employees' expenses; furniture, fixtures, equipment, and automobile expenses; legal expenses; compensation expenses; and occupancy expenses (collectively referred to as expense-preference items). All are managerial choice variables that serve as potential indicators of expense-preference behavior. High levels of these expenses may indicate the presence of moral-hazard behavior benefiting owners and managers at the expense of creditors, including the deposit insurer (Jensen and Meckling, 1976; Verbrugge and Jahera, 1981; Fama and Jensen, 1982; Akella and Greenbaum, 1988; Blair and Placone, 1988; Kane, 1989; Cole, 1990 and 1993).

The third behavioral category is the extent of growth during the 1982–1985 period. Rapid growth is a likely indicator of moral-hazard behavior, since rapid growth provided thrift operators with the best avenue for taking advantage of the new opportunities that deregulation presented to them. Even under the best of circumstances, rapid growth places strains on an organization and increases the likelihood of costly errors. For thrifts facing expanded opportunities for investing in previously prohibited asset classes, the likelihood that rapid growth would lead to losses was exacerbated.[20]

Three measures of growth are analyzed. The first and primary measure is the percentage growth in total liabilities from year-end 1982 to year-end 1985. Two supplementary indicators of rapid growth are the proportions of a thrift's liabilities accounted for by deposits obtained through brokers, and by "jumbo" deposits of sizes greater than $100,000. Brokered deposits and reliance on wholesale funds do not by themselves cause failure, but they do enable a thrift to circumvent the constraints imposed by local retail deposit markets in implementing a rapid-growth, high-risk investment strategy.

Because the accumulation of goodwill might have been part of a rapid growth-by-merger strategy, goodwill also is included as an explanatory

[20] Growth through merger as well as through internal expansion is included because mergers can lead to the same type of strain on organizations.

variable. This permits a test to see if the "intangible" assets represented by goodwill had an effect on the likelihood of a thrift's failure. (Since the cost variable is the estimated cost of liquidation, goodwill assets should have imposed a dollar-for-dollar loss in the cost estimates.)

Structure

The structural characteristics chosen for analysis are represented by a set of variables focused primarily on year-end 1982. According to the model discussed in section 2, a thrift's net worth and regulatory environment should be major determinants of its risk-taking. Though the model is presented in terms of simultaneous risk-taking in response to the structural variables, actual behavior is unlikely to occur instantaneously. Consequently, choosing structural variables for year-end 1982 to explain subsequent behavior, measured as of 1985, and subsequent outcomes, measured as of 1986 through 1989, seems reasonable.

Further, measurement of a thrift's net worth at a point in time substantially earlier than its failure is more likely to capture a structural characteristic that could lead to moral-hazard behavior than is measurement at a point closer to the time of failure.[21] The latter measurement would more likely be an imperfect reflection of the insolvent thrift's eventual disposal cost rather than a predictor of likely moral-hazard behavior, especially since the regulatory regime (at least since 1986) considerably tightened its scrutiny and control over undercapitalized or insolvent thrifts.

Three variables are used to measure the effects of a thrift's market-value net worth. The first is its tangible net worth reported as of year-end 1982. The drawback to this measure is that it is based on historical cost accounting and does not include the decrease in market value of a thrift's portfolio of low-coupon mortgages due to the relatively high interest rates prevailing during 1982. To capture this element of market value, the thrift's net interest margin for the second half of 1982,—the difference between the interest it earned on its assets and the interest it paid on its liabilities—expressed as a ratio to assets, is also included in the model. This variable should indicate the severity of a thrift's interest-rate mismatch and thus provide an additional measure of its market-value net

[21] Most previous studies, including Benston (1985) and Barth, Bartholomew, and Bradley (1990), have taken data immediately prior to, or one or at most two years prior to, actual failure. Cole (1990, 1993) takes data from the last accounting period in which an institution reported positive GAAP net worth.

worth. A third variable included as a measure of market value is the thrift's size, expressed as the logarithm of year-end 1982 assets. This variable is included to proxy for the "franchise value" of a failed thrift, which is likely to be positively related to its asset size.

The risk profile of a thrift's chosen portfolio depends in part on the risk profile of its inherited portfolio. Moral-hazard-laden behavior is more evident in the *changes* in the riskiness of the portfolio than in degree of portfolio risk. One way to measure the initial portfolio risk is to calculate a summary measure of portfolio risk similar to the denominator of the ratio of capital to risk weighted assets adopted in 1990 by bank and thrift regulators in response to Section 301 of the Financial Institutions Reform, Recovery, and Enforcement Act of 1989 (FIRREA). This measure, the ratio of risk-weighted assets to total assets, is calculated using 1982 balance sheet data and the following set of risk weights: 0.00 for eligible liquid assets, 0.20 for other liquid assets (including mortgage-backed securities), 0.50 for one- to four-family mortgages, and 1.00 for other assets. These weights replicate those in the Basel Accords, which were developed much later than 1982 and may have been influenced by events in the 1980s. This variable, however, is a summary measure, albeit imperfect, of the riskiness of the portfolio before the period of asset deregulation and rapid growth.

Moral-hazard incentives also would be affected by the organizational form of the thrift. As late as 1980, 80 percent of all thrifts (accounting for 73 percent of all thrift assets) were mutual in organization, rather than stockholder-owned. In a mutual thrift, the managers are more concerned with protecting their jobs than maximizing the value of the firm because they cannot capture the full benefits from the favorable outcomes from risk-taking. Thus, the moral-hazard problem should be less severe for mutual thrifts than for stock thrifts. Publicly traded stock thrifts with professional managers who only share to a limited extent in the favorable outcomes, however, should behave more like mutuals than should closely held stock thrifts, where owners also serve as managers and can capture the full benefits of favorable outcomes. Further, the different (and, some have charged, appreciably more lax) regulatory regimes that applied to state-chartered thrifts could affect the moral-hazard incentives of both stock and mutual thrifts.

To model these differential effects, dummy variables are constructed to indicate state-chartered stock thrifts, state-chartered mutual thrifts, and federally chartered stock thrifts; the federally chartered mutual thrift category serves as the reference group. Also included in the model is a dummy variable indicating a publicly traded stock thrift.[22] These variables reflect organizational structure as of year-end 1982.

Another set of dummy variables is constructed to indicate thrifts located in Texas, California, and Florida. Thrifts chartered in theseS&Ls,in Texas, California and Florida states faced more liberal asset restrictions and experienced above-average failure rates. Also included in the model are dummy variables indicating state-chartered thrifts located in the three states. These six variables should provide evidence for assessing the competing hypotheses (a) that regional economic conditions contributed most to differential failure rates, and (b) that lax state regulation played the major role.

A final dummy variable is included in the model to indicate thrifts that were located in the Ninth Federal Home Loan Bank District, which includes the states of Arkansas, Louisiana, Mississippi, New Mexico, and Texas. This variable is included to test for any adverse consequences from that District Bank's move of its headquarters from Little Rock to Dallas in 1983, at which time almost all of the supervisory staff resigned so as to avoid moving from Little Rock. This move left the Ninth District with a very small and inexperienced supervisory staff during the period just after deregulation, when thrifts in that District embarked on strategies of rapid growth into newly permitted asset classes.

The data and the specific variables

The primary source of data is the semiannual (through 1983) and quarterly (since March 1984) thrift financial reports compiled by the Bank Board until its 1989 demise and since then by the Office of Thrift Supervision. This database provided all of the behavioral variables and most of the structural variables. The outcome variables were compiled by the staff of the FSLIC. The data on publicly traded thrifts were compiled by the Bank Board staff.

[22] Ideally, a variable to indicate whether a change of control of the thrift occurred in 1982 (e.g., bringing in a more aggressive entrepreneur) should be included; unfortunately, the relevant data were not available.

Specific tests

The structure–behavior–outcomes model provides a rich array of tests of the underlying hypotheses. The first test is for the relationship between outcomes and behavior:

$$\textit{Probability of Failure}_i = f(X_i) \qquad (1)$$

$$\textit{Liquidation Cost}_i = g(X_i, \textit{Fail86}_i, \textit{Fail87}_i, \textit{Fail88}_i) \qquad (2)$$

where *Probability of Failure*$_i$ and *Liquidation Cost*$_i$ represent the outcomes failure and expected liquidation cost, respectively; X_i is the vector of behavioral variables from Table 1;[23] and *Fail86*$_i$, *Fail87*$_i$ and *Fail88*$_i$ are dummy variables indicating whether the liquidation cost for the failed thrift was estimated during 1986, 1987, or 1988, respectively. These dummy variables are included to control for any differences in costing methodologies or discount-rate assumptions that the FSLIC might have used in these years, as compared with the omitted category (1989 cost estimates). These variables also could be measuring cost differences among thrifts that are not captured by the other variables.

Since *Probability of Failure*$_i$ is a binary dependent variable, the assumptions of ordinary least squares (OLS) regression analysis are not satisfied. In this situation, application of OLS results in biased and inconsistent parameter estimates. Unbiased and consistent parameter estimates of *Probability of Failure*$_i$ are obtained using a probit maximum-likelihood procedure.

OLS regression also may be inappropriate for estimation of *Liquidation Cost*$_i$. Unless the thrift institutions for which costs are available constitute a random sample of all thrifts, use of OLS (or some variant thereof) may result in biased coefficients. Clearly, a sample of thrift institutions that have failed or are expected to fail may not be representative of the universe of thrift institutions. If one can control for the non-random nature of the failed sample by a complete specification of all variables that determine the cost of liquidation, OLS still will produce unbiased and consistent parameter estimates. If there are unobserved variables that affect both the likelihood of closure and the cost of liquidation, however, the error terms in equations (1) and (2) will be correlated due to an overlap in omitted variables. Estimation procedures that ignore this correlation will produce biased coefficients for equation (2). Heckman (1979) proposes a two-step

[23] All of the tables for this chapter are displayed consecutively, starting after page 57.

procedure to compensate for this correlation in error terms. His procedure produces unbiased and consistent, but not fully efficient, parameter estimates. The joint estimation of equations (1) and (2) by the method of full-information maximum likelihood (FIML) suggested by Amemiya (1973), however, can be used to produce unbiased and asymptotically efficient parameter estimates.[24]

As a second test, one can "look through" behavior and test for the relationship between outcomes and structure:

$$\textit{Probability of Failure}_i = h(Z_i) \tag{3}$$

$$\textit{Liquidation Cost}_i = j(Z_i, \textit{Fail86}_i, \textit{Fail87}_i, \textit{Fail88}_i) \tag{4}$$

where Z_i is the vector of structural variables from Table 1. Again, the same methodological considerations apply to the estimation of equations (3) and (4).

Third, because neither the behavioral variables alone nor the structure variables alone may be capturing the full explanatory power of the data set, one can combine them:

$$\textit{Probability of Failure}_i = k(X_i, Z_i) \tag{5}$$

$$\textit{Liquidation Cost}_i = l(X_i, Z_i, \textit{Fail86}_i, \textit{Fail87}_i, \textit{Fail86}_i) \tag{6}$$

Fourth, one can test for the intervening relationships between behavior and structure. This can be done through individual OLS regressions where the individual behavioral variables are estimated as a function of the vector of structural variables:

$$x_i = m(Z_i), \tag{7}$$

[24] Heckman (1979) provides the original derivation of the selection model, while Maddala (1986) discusses many econometric issues related to the resolution cost estimation problem. Actual estimation was carried out using the LIMDEP statistical package developed by Greene (1989). The particular methodology used here is similar to that proposed by Amemiya (1973): consistent maximum-likelihood probit probability-of-failure estimates and least-square cost-of-liquidation estimates are used as starting values for the estimation of final parameter coefficients using a modification of the Davidon, Fletcher, and Powell algorithm. As Greene (1989) points out, obtaining convergence with this procedure often is problematic, especially with as many parameters as are estimated in this particular application. To facilitate convergence by reducing the number of parameters to be estimated, variables with p-values greater than 0.20 in the single-equation probit and OLS results are deleted from subsequent estimation of the simultaneous-equation FIML model.

where x_i is an individual behavioral variable. Discussion of the results from each of these four sets of tests appears in Section 4.

4 Results

Simple statistics

Table 1 provides the mean values of the model's outcome, behavioral, and structural variables for the entire sample of thrifts and, separately, for the "failing" and "surviving" groups of thrifts. Also presented are t-tests for significant differences in the mean values of the failing and surviving groups. Included for completeness in these comparisons of means are a number of asset and liability categories that are not included in the subsequent regression results. For each thrift, all of the continuous variables (except for *Size*, the log of total assets) have been scaled either by total liabilities or, more commonly, total assets. Overall, 27.3 percent of the sample thrifts (621 of 2,275) are classified as failures, and their mean estimated liquidation cost is 34.5 percent of year-end 1985 total liabilities.

Structural characteristics measured as of year-end 1982 show sharp contrasts in the failing and surviving groups. Failing thrifts reported significantly lower tangible net worth ratios and net interest margins, but significantly higher ratios of risk-weighted-asset ratios and levels of assets. State-charter and, to a lesser extent, federal-charter stock thrifts are significantly over-represented in the group of failing thrifts, which is supportive of the hypothesis that moral hazard incentives were affected by organizational form. Also significantly over-represented in the failing group are thrifts located in the Ninth FHLB District (41 percent of failing thrifts but only 16 percent of the entire sample) and thrifts located in Texas (30 percent of failing thrifts but only 10 percent of the entire sample). These results support the notion that the combination of a regional economic shock (the collapse in oil prices during 1982 and 1986) and a shortage of supervisory resources in the Ninth District FHLB greatly increased the incentives for moral hazard at thrifts located in the Southwest.

Differences in year-end 1985 asset portfolio allocations of the failing and surviving groups also are sharp. Failing institutions held higher proportions of all asset categories except one- to four-family mortgages and mortgage-backed securities. As compared with the surviving institutions, failing thrifts held twice the proportion of nonresidential mortgage loans, *nine* times the proportion of land loans, *eleven* times the proportion of equity real estate investment, *five* times the proportion of equity service corporation investment, and *eight* times the proportion of goodwill. The differences in means of the surviving and failing groups are significant at least at the 0.1 percent level for all asset categories except equity securities and junk bonds.[25] Thus, it is clear that failing thrifts invested earlier and more heavily in nontraditional assets, whereas surviving thrifts stuck to their core business of funding residential mortgages.

Differences in year-end 1985 liability portfolio allocations are similar. Relative to surviving thrifts, failing thrifts held almost twice the proportion of wholesale deposits, *six* times the proportion of brokered deposits, and twice the proportion of repurchase agreements. In addition, failing thrifts' liability growth during the 1983–1985 period was almost three times that of surviving institutions.

From year-end 1982 to year-end 1985, the average tangible net worth ratio of the failing institutions declined from 2.4 percent to negative 2.4 percent, a 480 basis point decline, whereas the surviving institutions lost only 30 basis points, from 5.5 percent to 5.2 percent.

Estimates of the probability of failure

Table 2 presents three sets of parameter estimates for the effects of the structural and behavioral variables on the probability of failure. In the second through fourth columns are single-equation OLS estimates of the failure model, which are presented for their intuitive clarity; in the fifth through seventh columns are single-equation probit estimates of the failure model; and in the last three columns are FIML estimates of the failure model, which is jointly estimated with the cost of liquidation model. Each set of estimates includes a specification including only structural variables, a specification including only behavioral variables, and a combined structure–behavior specification.

In each of the nine specifications, most of the explanatory variables have the hypothesized signs and are highly significant. In the structure-only specifications, the 1982 tangible net worth ratio is the most significant

[25] The junk bond variable presents a problem. The thrift industry's largest holder of junk bonds, by far, was Columbia Savings of Beverly Hills, and it was not included as a likely failure in the Bank Board's 1989 listing. Of course, Columbia Savings ultimately failed. The junk bond variable comes close to serving as a dummy variable for Columbia Savings, whose outcome was misclassified.

determinant of failure. Thrifts with lower net worth in 1982 were significantly more likely to fail during 1986–89, consistent with the hypothesis that moral hazard led the owners and managers of these undercapitalized thrifts to take more risks than did their better capitalized counterparts. Other variables significant in both the structure-only and the combined specifications include dummies indicating state-stock and federal-stock charters, Texas thrifts, and thrifts located in the Ninth FHLB District. The positive coefficients and high statistical significance of the two dummies indicating stock charter provide strong evidence that moral hazard was a greater problem at stock than at mutual thrifts. Thrifts located in Texas and in the Ninth FHLB District were significantly more likely to fail, consistent with the hypothesis that the supervision problems in that district significantly contributed to the disproportionate number of failures in the Southwest. None of the three dummy variables indicating state-chartered thrifts located in Texas, California, and Florida is consistently significant. These results indicate that, after controlling for the effects of other structural and behavioral characteristics (including stock organization), the effects of state chartering were not important in determining the likelihood of failure.[26]

The ratio of risk-weighted assets to total assets is positive and highly significant in the structure-only specifications, but is not significant in the combined specifications. This suggests that variation in the asset-portfolio variables better accounts for the effect of asset risk on the probability of failure than does the summary risk-weighted assets measure. Net interest margin is negatively related to failure and highly significant in the combined specification, but is only marginally significant in the structure-only specification.

In the behavior-only and the combined specifications, the asset-portfolio variables with the greatest influence on the probability of failure are the proportions of land loans, nonresidential mortgages, and goodwill: all are

[26] State regulatory regimes have been quite varied. Some (e.g., in the Northeast and Midwest) were generally considered more conservative than others (e.g., the Southwest and West). State-chartered thrifts in the Northeast were more likely to be mutuals; state-chartered thrifts in the Southwest and West were more likely to be stocks. Thus, the state-stock and state-mutual variables may be correlated with lax and stringent regulatory regimes, respectively; without an independent identification of the lax or the conservative nature of each state regime, however, it is difficult to be more definitive. These results do make clear, however, that one cannot condemn state regulation uniformly as adding to the thrift debacle.

positive and statistically significant at the 0.1 percent level. The proportions of commercial loans and equity real estate investments are also positive and are significant at the 1 percent level in both the behavior-only and the combined specifications.[27] These results provide additional evidence that moral hazard manifested itself in the form of excessively large portfolio portions allocated to non-traditional assets.

On the liability side, the proportion of brokered deposits is positive and significant in both specifications, and the liability growth rate over 1983–85 is positive and significant in the combined specification. These results, coupled with the strong positive and significant relationship between goodwill and failure, indicate that a strategy of rapid growth funded with volatile liabilities increased the probability of failure even after controlling for other structural and behavioral variables.

Finally, the ratio of expense-preference items to assets is positive and significant in the combined specification, providing evidence that excessive perquisite consumption by the owners and manager of failing thrifts significantly increased the likelihood of failure.

Specifications that include both the behavioral and the structural variables provide results that generally are consistent with the separate behavior-only and structure-only specifications. The overall explanatory power of the model rises when the full specification is employed, however, as evidenced by the increases in the log-likelihood, adjusted R^2, and pseudo R^2 statistics. The pseudo R^2 statistics indicate that the structure-only and behavior-only specifications explain about a third of the variation in the failure variable, whereas the combined specification explains almost half of this variation. All of these results provide strong support for the moral-hazard-behavior hypotheses.

The estimated costs of failure

Table 3 presents parameter estimates for the effects of the structural and behavioral variables on the expected cost of liquidation expressed as a proportion of year-end 1985 liabilities. Again, three sets of parameter estimates are presented. In the second through fourth columns are single-equation OLS estimates; in the last three columns are the FIML estimates;

[27] With the exception of Cole (1990, 1993), previous researchers have lumped real estate investment together with service corporation investment, confounding the effects of these asset classes. Benston (1985) and Barth, Bartholomew, and Bradley (1990), for example, report that direct investment was not a significant determinant of failure.

and in the fifth through seventh columns are OLS results corresponding to the pared-down FIML specifications. As with the failure results, each set of cost estimates includes a structure-only, a behavior-only, and a combined structure-behavior specification.

In general, all three sets of estimates are similar. Because of their theoretical superiority, the FIML results are the focus of discussion. Further, because the results of the combined specifications are generally quite consistent with the separate structure-only and behavior-only specifications, only the combined results are discussed in detail.

Only two of the structure variables—dummies indicating Texas state-chartered thrifts and thrifts located in the Ninth FHLB District—are significant in both the structure-only and the combined FIML specifications. Both are positive, indicating that, after controlling for other structural and behavioral variables, Ninth District thrifts were more costly to liquidate than thrifts located elsewhere, and that Texas state-chartered thrifts were even more costly to liquidate than other Ninth District thrifts. These results provide additional evidence strongly supportive of the hypothesized deleterious effects associated with the Ninth District FHLB's move from Little Rock to Dallas, and also suggest a breakdown in the supervision of state-chartered thrifts by the Texas S&L Commission.

Four additional structural variables are highly significant in the structure-only specification—*Risk-Weighted Assets*, *Tangible Net Worth*, and *State-Stock Charter* and *Federal-Stock Charter*. All but tangible net worth are positive, indicating positive associations with liquidation costs. The negative coefficient of tangible net worth provides additional support for the hypothesis that moral hazard was a more serious problem for undercapitalized thrifts, which subsequently took on more risk than their better capitalized counterparts and consequently were more costly to liquidate when they failed. The positive coefficients on the two stock-charter variables bolster the hypothesis that the moral-hazard problem was more severe at stock than at mutual thrifts and, in conjunction with the insignificance of the state mutual variable, tend to refute charges that state thrift regulators (other than in Texas) were unduly lax.

Two of the behavioral variables—*Land Loans* and *Service Corporation Investments*—are significant at the 0.01 percent level in both the behavior-only and combined FIML specifications. *Expense Preference Items* is significant in both specifications at the 5 percent level. All three of these behavioral variables have the expected positive sign, indicating that higher values are associated with higher expected liquidation costs. Three additional behavioral variables—*Nonresidential Mortgages*, *Commercial Loans*, and *Goodwill*—are statistically significant in the combined specification but not the behavior-only specification. All three are positive in the combined specification.

The magnitudes of the coefficients associated with the variables in Table 3 indicate the expected cost burden (i.e., the additional liquidation cost or, equivalently, the decrease in asset value) per dollar of liability incurred by these failing thrifts as of year-end 1985, after controlling for all other structural and behavioral variables. For example, in the combined FIML specification, the 0.139 coefficient on *FHLB District Nine Membership* indicates that failing Ninth District thrifts imposed an additional liquidation cost of 14 cents per dollar of liability, after controlling for other factors. The 0.153 coefficient on *Texas State Charter* indicates that Texas state-chartered thrifts imposed an additional liquidation cost of 15 cents per dollar of liability. The 1.018 coefficient on goodwill is not significantly different from one, consistent with the hypothesis that the goodwill of failing thrifts has no value in liquidations. None of the liability variables are significant in either of the specifications. Interestingly, this indicates that, after controlling for other structural and behavioral factors, rapid growth by other than a merger strategy did not significantly increase the cost of failure. Of the three dummy variables identifying the year in which the liquidation cost was estimated, only the 1988 dummy, which is positive, is statistically significant. This result implies that institutions whose liquidation costs were estimated during 1988 were expected to be more costly to liquidate than the structural and behavioral variables relevant to these thrifts would otherwise indicate.[28]

Comparison of the failure and cost models

Only one of the structure variables—*FHLB District Nine Membership*—is statistically significant in the combined specification of both the FIML failure and cost models. Four additional variables—*Risk-Weighted Assets*, *Tangible Net Worth*, *State-Stock Charter*, and *Federal-Stock Charter*—are

[28] It could be that the estimation methodology used in 1988 differed somehow from that of the years before or after, but since the same models and procedures were used, and the same staff did the analysis, this is unlikely.

significant in the structure-only specifications of both models. All of these variables except tangible net worth are positive.[29]

Five of the behavioral variables—*Nonresidential Mortgages*, *Land Loans*, *Commercial Loans*, *Goodwill*, and *Expense Preference Items*—have significant and positive signs in the combined specifications of both the FIML failure and cost models. In addition, the *Service Corporation Investments* variable is positive and significant in the behavior-only specification of both FIML models.

Was the thrift crisis a Southwestern regional phenomenon?

Because of the concentration of thrift failures and failure costs in the Southwest, some observers have dismissed the thrift crisis as a regional phenomenon. To see if the general findings of this study are driven by Southwestern institutions, the FIML model is reestimated using a sample that excludes thrifts located in the Ninth FHLB District. This reduces the sample size to 1,904 thrifts, of which 364 are classified as failures. The last four columns of Table 1 provide the mean values for this restricted sample and, separately, for the failing and surviving thrifts in the restricted sample, as well as t-tests for differences in the mean values of the failing and surviving groups. Comparisons of these statistics with the corresponding statistics for the unrestricted sample, which also appear in Table 1, reveal that the restricted sample is not qualitatively different from the unrestricted sample; i.e., the results hold for thrifts outside of the Southwest as well as for Southwestern thrifts.

Using this restricted sample, the FIML combined specification (including both structural and behavioral variables) is reestimated, and those results appear in columns 2 and 3 of Table 4. To facilitate comparisons, results for the FIML combined specification from Tables 2 and 3 are reproduced in columns 4 and 5 of Table 4. As with the descriptive statistics, a comparison of these results demonstrates that the estimates for the non-Southwestern sample are not qualitatively different than those for the full sample, although coefficients are somewhat different and t-statistics are somewhat lower. With the exception of the *Texas* and *Ninth FHLB District Membership* variables (which must, of course, be deleted from the

[29] Further research is needed to determine whether or not the insignificance of the risk-weighted asset variable in 1982 is collinear with 1985 asset allocation. Table 5 indicates that this variable is a significant determinant of a number of 1985 behavioral measures.

non-Southwestern specification) and the *Commercial Loans* and *Brokered Deposits* variables, each remaining variable that is statistically significant for the full sample also is significant in the restricted sample, and has the same sign. This holds for both the failure equation and the cost of liquidation equation. These results strongly refute arguments that the thrift crisis was strictly a Southwestern, regional phenomenon, and demonstrate that the fundamental findings of this study apply to the entire thrift population.

Behavior and structure

One basic hypothesis still to be tested is that a set of structural characteristics gave rise to certain behaviors. Table 5 provides evidence on these relationships, reporting regression results where the dependent variables are the individual portfolio characteristics as of 1985 and the independent variables are the structural characteristics as of 1982. For expositional simplicity, only coefficients significant at least at the 5 percent level are reported, but all relationships are estimated with the full vector of structural characteristics. The small mean values of the dependent variables (presented in Table 1) must be considered in interpreting these results, in that some of the reported coefficients on the regional and structural dummy variables are a multiple of this mean.

There are several general conclusions. First, institutions with higher levels of capital and lower levels of risk-weighted assets in 1982 invested proportionately much less in nontraditional assets. Tangible net worth is negative and significant in explaining five of ten asset categories and insignificant in the remaining five, whereas the risk-weighted assets variable is positive and significant in explaining seven of ten asset categories and insignificant in the remaining three. Well capitalized institutions also relied much less heavily on volatile deposits liabilities (i.e., wholesale deposits, brokered deposits, and repurchase agreements) in funding their operations. Second, stock-charter institutions invested greater proportions of their assets in these nontraditional asset categories and used wholesale funds to a greater extent than did mutual institutions. The state-stock variable is positive and significant in explaining eight of ten asset categories and all three volatile liability categories, while the federal stock variable is positive and significant in explaining six asset categories as well as wholesale deposits.

Third, institutions located in the Ninth FHLB District invested more heavily in most nontraditional assets and depended more heavily on brokered and jumbo deposits than did institutions in the other eleven FHLB Districts. The Ninth FHLB District variable is positive and significant in explaining nonresidential mortgages, land loans, unsecured commercial loans, and consumer loans, as well as wholesale and brokered deposits.

Fourth, larger institutions invested more heavily in nontraditional assets. Asset size is significant in explaining eight of the ten asset categories, and seven are positive relationships.

Overall, these results are generally consistent with the earlier behavior-outcomes and structure-outcomes results.

5 Conclusions

This article uses a structure–behavior–outcomes paradigm to model the experience of the thrift industry during the 1980s, and then tests this model using data and methodology that avoid many of the problems that have weakened the findings of earlier studies. The results provide strong support for the hypothesis that moral-hazard-laden behavior was a critical factor explaining the failures and liquidation costs of more than 600 thrifts during the late 1980s. The results also provide a clearer picture of the ways in which this behavior manifested itself.

In general, the results indicate that the net worth and organizational structures of thrifts as measured in 1982 were important determinants of the subsequent behaviors of these institutions in the period until 1985, and of outcomes in the period 1986–1989. Further, it appears that the proximate causes of the failures and liquidation costs of the hundreds of thrifts closed during this latter period were (with some exceptions) their investments in nontraditional assets that, for the most part, had been proscribed prior to deregulation in the period 1980–82. It does appear that there was a regional aspect to the thrift crisis; failures and failure costs were especially severe among the thrifts in the Southwest. Further analysis, however, reveals that the model and results apply almost as strongly to thrifts outside of the Southwest.

These results lend force to the policies mandated by FIRREA and FDICIA, requiring depository institutions to maintain higher levels of capital and tying both capital levels and deposit insurance premiums to the riskiness of a depository's asset portfolio. They also support efforts to ensure that such institutions are adequately examined, and promptly closed when determined to be critically undercapitalized.

Further research should be able to refine the hypotheses and methods presented here. The approach of specifying structure, behavior, and outcomes separately, and of collecting the data and testing the hypotheses in ways consistent with this specification, offers a useful means of understanding the experience of the thrift industry during the 1980s.

References

Acharya, S. and J.-F. Dreyfus 1989. "Optimal Bank Reorganization Policies and the Pricing of Federal Deposit Insurance." *Journal of Finance* 44: 1313–1333.

Akella, S. and S. Greenbaum 1988. "Savings and Loan Ownership Structure and Expense-Preference." *Journal of Banking and Finance* 12: 419–37.

Altman, E. 1977. "Predicting Performance in the Savings and Loan Industry." *Journal of Monetary Economics* 10: 443–66.

Amemiya, T. 1973. "Regression Analysis where the Dependent Variable is Truncated Normal." *Econometrica* 41: 997–1016.

Arshadi, N. and E. Lawrence 1987. "An Empirical Examination of New Bank Performance." *Journal of Banking and Finance* 11: 33–48.

Barth, J., P. Bartholomew and C. Labich 1989. "Moral Hazard and the Thrift Crisis: An Analysis of the 1988 Resolutions." In *Banking System Risk: Charting a New Course*, Chicago: Federal Reserve Bank of Chicago: 344–84.

Barth, J., P. Bartholomew, and M. Bradley 1990. "The Determinants of Thrift Resolution Costs." *Journal of Finance* 45: 731–54.

Benston, G. 1985. "An Analysis of the Causes of Savings and Loan Association Failures." New York University, Graduate School of Business Administration, Salomon Brothers Center for the Study of Financial Institutions, Monograph Series in Finance and Economics, Nos. 4/5.

______. and R. D. Brumbaugh 1988. "On the Controversy over Asset Restrictions for Thrift Institutions." *Housing Finance Review* 7: 361–9.

______. and M. Koehn 1988. "Capital Dissipation, Deregulation, and the Insolvency of Thrifts." Paper presented at the Annual Meetings of the American Finance Association, New York.

Bisenius, D., R.D. Brumbaugh and R. Rogers 1988. "Insolvent Thrifts, Agency Issues, and the Management Consignment Program." Federal

Home Loan Bank Board, Office of Policy and Economic Research, Working Paper No. 141.

Blair, D. and D. Placone 1988. "Expense-Preference Behavior, Agency Costs, and Firm Organization: The Savings and Loan Industry." *Journal of Economics and Business* 40: 1–15.

Brumbaugh, R. D. and E. Hemel 1984. "Federal Deposit Insurance as a Call Option: Implications for Depository Institutions." Federal Home Loan Bank Board, Office of Policy and Economic Research, Working Paper No. 116.

Buser, S., A. Chen and E. Kane 1981. "Federal Deposit Insurance, Regulatory Policy, and Optimal Bank Capital." *Journal of Finance* 36: 775–87.

Cole, R. 1990. "Agency Conflicts and Thrift Resolution Costs." Federal Reserve Bank of Dallas, Financial Industry Studies Department, Working Paper No. 1–90, July.

______. 1993. "When Are Thrifts Closed: An Agency-Theoretic Model." *Journal of Financial Services Research* 7: 287–307.

______. and J. McKenzie 1994. "Thrift Asset-Class Returns and the Efficient Diversification of Thrift Institution Portfolios." *Journal of the American Real Estate and Urban Economics Association* 22: 95–116.

Cordell, L., G. MacDonald and M. Wohar 1993. "Corporate Ownership and the Thrift Crisis." *Journal of Law and Economics* 36: 719–56.

Demirgüç-Kunt, A. 1991. "Principal–Agent Problems in Commercial-Bank Failure Decisions." Federal Reserve Bank of Cleveland, Working Paper 9106.

Dhrymes, P. 1974. *Econometrics: Statistical Foundations and Applications.* New York: Springer-Verlag.

Fama, E. 1980. "Agency Problems and the Theory of the Firm." *Journal of Political Economy* 88: 288–307.

______. and M. Jensen 1983. "Separation of Ownership and Control." *Journal of Law and Economics* 26: 301–25.

Flannery, M. 1982. "Deposit Insurance Creates a Need for Bank Regulation." *Business Review*, Federal Reserve Bank of Philadelphia, January/February: 17–27.

______. 1989. "Pricing Deposit Insurance When Insurer Measures Risk with Error." *Banking System Risk: Charting a New Course*, Chicago: Federal Reserve Bank of Chicago: 70–100.

Furlong, F. and M. Keeley 1989. "Capital Regulation and Bank Risk-Taking: A Note." *Journal of Banking and Finance* 3: 883–91.

Garcia, G. and T. Cargill 1985. *Financial Reform in the 1980s*. Stanford: Hoover Institution.

Greene, W. 1989. *LIMDEP Version 5.1*. New York, March.

Hanweck, G. and J. Crockett 1989. "A Theoretical and Empirical Analysis of the Incentives for 'Go-for-Broke' Behavior by Thrift Management and Regulatory Implications for Risk-Based Capital Requirements and Federal Deposit Insurance Premia as Incentives for Risk-Taking Control." Mimeo, George Mason University.

Heckman, J. 1979. "Sample Selection Bias as a Specification Error." *Econometrica* 47: 153–61.

Hunter, W., J. Verbrugge and D. Whidbee 1994. "Risk Taking in De Novo Savings and Loans in the 1980s." *Journal of Financial Services Research* 8, forthcoming.

Jensen, M. and W. Meckling 1976. "Theory of the Firm: Managerial Behavior, Agency Costs, and Ownership Structure." *Journal of Financial Economics* 3: 305–60.

Kane, E. 1981. "Reregulation, Savings and Loan Diversification, and the Flow of Housing Finance." In *Savings and Loan Asset Management Under Deregulation*, San Francisco: Federal Home Loan Bank of San Francisco.

______. 1983. "The Role of Government in the Thrift Industry's Net-Worth Crisis." In *Financial Services: The Changing Institutions and Government Policy*, G. Benston, ed., Engelwood Cliffs, N.J.: Prentice Hall: 156–84.

______. 1986. "Appearance and Reality in Deposit Insurance Reform." *Journal of Banking and Finance* 10: 175–188.

______. 1989. *The S&L Insurance Mess: How Did It Happen?* Washington, D.C.: The Urban Institute Press.

Karaken, J. and N. Wallace 1978. "Deposit Insurance and Bank Regulation: A Partial Equilibrium Exposition." *Journal of Business* 51: 413–38.

Kormendi, R., V. Bernard, C. Pirrong and E. Snyder 1989. "Crisis Resolution in the Thrift Industry: Beyond the December Deals." *Report of the Mid-America Institute Task Force on the Thrift Crisis*, March.

Kummer, D., N. Arshadi and E. Lawrence 1989. "Incentive Problems in Bank Insider Borrowing." *Journal of Financial Services Research* 3: 17–31.

Maddala, G. 1983. *Limited-Dependent and Qualitative Variables in Econometrics*. Cambridge: Cambridge University Press.

———. 1986. "Econometric Issues in the Empirical Analysis of Thrift Institutions' Insolvency and Failure." Federal Home Loan Bank Board, Office of Policy and Economic Research, Invited Research Working Paper No. 56.

Marcus, A. and I. Shaked 1984. "The Valuation of FDIC Deposit Insurance Using Option-Pricing Estimates." *Journal of Money, Credit, and Banking* 16: 447–60.

McKenzie, J., R. Cole and R. Brown 1992. "Moral Hazard, Portfolio Allocation, and Asset Returns for Thrift Institutions." *Journal of Financial Services Research* 5: 315–39.

Merton, R. 1977. "An Analytic Derivation of the Cost of Deposit Insurance and Loan Guarantees: An Application of Modern Option Pricing Theory." *Journal of Banking and Finance* 1: 3–11.

———. 1978. "On the Cost of Deposit Insurance When There Are Surveillance Costs." *Journal of Business* 51: 439–52.

Myers, S. and N. Majluf 1984. "Corporate Financing and Investment Decisions When Firms Have Information That Investors Do Not Have." *Journal of Financial Economics* 13: 187–222.

Narayanan, M. 1985. "Managerial Incentives for Short-Term Results." *Journal of Finance* 40: 1469–84.

Pantalone, C. and M. Platt 1987. "Predicting Failures of Savings and Loan Associations." *Journal of the American Real Estate and Urban Economics Association* 15: 46–64.

Pennacchi, G. 1987. "Alternative Forms of Deposit Insurance: Pricing and Bank Incentive Issues." *Journal of Banking and Finance* 11: 291–312.

Pyle, D. 1983. "Pricing Deposit Insurance: The Effects of Mismeasurement." Federal Reserve Bank of San Francisco and University of California at Berkeley, October.

Ronn, E. and A. Verma 1986. "Pricing Risk-Adjusted Deposit Insurance: An Option-Based Model." *Journal of Finance* 41: 871–95.

Rudolph, P. and B. Hamden 1988. "An Analysis of Post-Deregulation Savings and Loan Failures." *Journal of the American Real Estate and Urban Economics Association* 16: 17–33.

Scherer, F. and D. Ross 1990. *Industrial Market Structure and Economic Performance*. Third Ed., Boston: Houghton-Mifflin.

Sharpe, W. 1978. "Bank Capital Adequacy, Deposit Insurance, and Security Values." *Journal of Financial and Quantitative Analysis* 13: 701–10.

Simonson, D., J. Stowe and C. Watson 1983. "A Canonical Correlation Analysis of Commercial Bank Asset/Liability Structure." *Journal of Financial and Quantitative Analysis* 18: 125–38.

Strunk, N. and F. Case 1988. *Where Deregulation Went Wrong: A Look at the Causes Behind Savings and Loan Failures in the 1980s*. Washington, D.C.: U.S. League of Savings Institutions.

Verbrugge, J. and J. Jahera 1981. "Expense Preference Behavior in the Savings and Loan Industry." *Journal of Money, Credit and Banking* 13: 465–76.

White, L. 1986. "The Partial Deregulation of Banks and Other Depository Institutions." In L. Weiss and M. Klass, eds., *Regulatory Reform: What Actually Happened*, Boston: Little, Brown.

———. 1991. *The S&L Debacle: Public Policy Lessons for Bank and Thrift Regulation*. New York: Oxford University Press.

Williamson, O. 1963. "Managerial Discretion and Business Behavior." *American Economic Review* 53: 1032–57.

TABLE 1

UNIVARIATE STATISTICS FOR VARIABLES USED TO EXPLAIN THE PROBABILITY OF FAILURE AND THE COST OF LIQUIDATION FOR THRIFTS

Variable	All FHLB Districts				All FHLB Districts Except District Nine			
	All Thrifts	Failing Thrifts	Surviving Thrifts	*t*-stat[a]	All Thrifts	Failing Thrifts	Surviving Thrifts	*t*-stat[a]
Number of Thrifts	2,275	621	1,654	–	1,904	364	1,540	–
Cost of Liquidation[b]	–	0.345	–	–	–	0.217	–	–
Liquidation cost ($m)	–	128	–	–	–	89	–	–
Structural Variables[c]								
Risk-Weighted Assets[d]	0.624	0.643	0.617	*−7.11*	0.619	0.663	0.615	*3.94*
Tangible Net Worth[d]	0.047	0.024	0.055	*−10.02*	0.049	0.022	0.055	*−7.62*
Net Interest Margin[d]	0.003	0.001	0.004	*−3.79*	0.003	0.0006	0.0041	*−3.71*
Net Income[d]	−0.003	−0.002	−0.004	*2.21*	−0.004	−0.0036	−0.0038	*0.17*

Total Assets ($m)	174	224	155	*2.67*	290	514	237	*3.01*
Federal Mutual Charter	0.480	0.385	0.516	*−5.69*	0.519	0.492	0.526	*1.17*
Federal Stock Charter	0.026	0.045	0.019	*2.94*	0.026	0.060	0.018	*3.26*
State Mutual Charter	0.309	0.138	0.372	*−12.80*	0.334	0.151	0.377	*−10.03*
State Stock Charter	0.185	0.432	0.093	*16.05*	0.121	0.297	0.079	*8.72*
Texas	0.097	0.304	0.019	*15.21*	–	–	–	–
Texas State Charter	0.080	0.259	0.012	*13.88*	–	–	–	–
Florida	0.027	0.039	0.023	*1.83*	0.033	0.066	0.025	*3.03*
Florida State Charter	0.007	0.016	0.004	*2.37*	0.008	0.027	0.004	*2.70*
California	0.048	0.069	0.041	*2.55*	0.058	0.118	0.044	*4.21*
Calif. State Charter	0.029	0.047	0.022	*2.63*	0.035	0.080	0.024	*3.78*
Publicly Traded	0.016	0.023	0.014	*1.30*	0.017	0.033	0.014	*1.97*
FHLB Ninth District Membership	0.163	0.414	0.069	*16.63*	–	–	–	–

Notes: [a]Approximate t-statistic for significance of difference of means between failing and surviving thrifts. [b]Proportion of total liabilities as of December 31, 1985. [c]Structural characteristics as of December 31, 1982. [d]Proportion of total assets as of December 31, 1985.

TABLE 1 (contd.)

UNIVARIATE STATISTICS FOR VARIABLES USED TO EXPLAIN THE PROBABILITY OF FAILURE AND THE COST OF LIQUIDATION FOR THRIFTS

Variable	All FHLB Districts				All FHLB Districts Except District Nine			
	All Thrifts	Failing Thrifts	Surviving Thrifts	*t*-stat[a]	All Thrifts	Failing Thrifts	Surviving Thrifts	*t*-stat[a]
Behavioral Variables								
Single-Family Mortgages[b]	0.528	0.395	0.578	*−24.73*	0.552	0.435	0.580	*−16.61*
Multifamily Mortgages[b]	0.047	0.072	0.037	*10.36*	0.044	0.068	0.038	*7.40*
Nonresidential Mortgages[b]	0.080	0.132	0.061	*17.23*	0.073	0.125	0.060	*12.39*
Land Loans[b]	0.026	0.074	0.008	*14.13*	0.013	0.038	0.008	*8.01*
Mortgage-Backed Securities[b]	0.064	0.055	0.067	*−3.34*	0.068	0.069	0.068	*0.24*
Commercial Loans[b]	0.010	0.020	0.006	*9.27*	0.007	0.016	0.005	*7.98*
Consumer Loans[b]	0.043	0.056	0.038	*6.29*	0.038	0.047	0.036	*3.52*
Real Estate Owned[b]	0.010	0.026	0.004	*12.11*	0.007	0.022	0.004	*9.67*

Real Estate Investments[b]	0.004	0.011	0.001	*7.02*	0.003	0.009	0.001	*4.59*
Service Corp. Investments[b]	0.008	0.020	0.004	*8.46*	0.006	0.017	0.004	*5.79*
Equity Securities[b]	0.0004	0.0006	0.0004	*0.72*	0.0005	0.0007	0.0004	*0.80*
Junk Bonds[b]	0.0007	0.0013	0.0005	*1.82*	0.0007	0.0012	0.0006	*1.41*
Goodwill[b]	0.006	0.016	0.002	*10.97*	0.004	0.016	0.002	*7.98*
Delinquent Loans[b]	0.026	0.051	0.016	*12.83*	0.022	0.048	0.016	*10.56*
Foreclosures[b]	0.011	0.027	0.005	*10.80*	0.007	0.019	0.004	*7.36*
Tangible Net Worth[b]	0.032	−0.024	0.052	*23.03*	0.036	−0.032	0.052	*−18.46*
Expense-Preference Items[b]	0.014	0.015	0.013	*5.87*	0.013	0.015	0.013	*4.50*
Total Deposits[c]	0.933	0.888	0.950	*−14.20*	0.935	0.875	0.950	*−13.15*
Retail Deposits[c]	0.865	0.791	0.893	*−16.92*	0.875	0.894	0.793	*−13.64*
Wholesale Deposits[c]	0.065	0.095	0.054	*10.45*	0.058	0.080	0.052	*6.56*
Brokered Deposits[c]	0.013	0.031	0.005	*9.02*	0.010	0.031	0.005	*6.47*
Repurchase Agreements[c]	0.007	0.012	0.006	*3.77*	0.007	0.014	0.006	*3.89*
Liability-Growth Rate, 1983–85	0.180	0.334	0.123	*10.13*	0.153	0.282	0.123	*5.43*

Notes: [a]Approximate t-statistic for significance of difference of means between failing and surviving thrifts. [b]Proportion of total assets as of December 31, 1985. [c]Proportion of total liabilities as of December 31, 1985.

TABLE 2
ESTIMATES OF THE DETERMINANTS OF THE PROBABILITY OF THRIFT FAILURE[a]

Variable	Ordinary Least Squares			Single-Equation Probit			FIML Probit[b]		
	Structure	Behavior	Both	Structure	Behavior	Both	Structure	Behavior	Both
Constant	−0.234 (−2.11)	−0.035 (−1.83)	−0.019 (−0.18)	−2.878 (−6.03)	−1.832 (−19.74)	−2.514 (−4.198)	−2.601 (−6.62)	−1.774 (−25.15)	−1.704 (−15.37)
Structural Variables[c]									
Risk-Weighted Assets[d]	0.670 (5.73)		0.019 (0.17)	2.680 (5.44)		0.457 (0.76)	2.325 (6.24)		[e]
Tangible Net Worth[d]	−2.157 (−12.15)		−1.767 (−9.81)	−7.541 (−10.19)		−8.559 (−8.25)	−5.395 (−12.32)		−8.726 (−10.40)
Net Interest Margin	−1.214 (−1.58)		−3.171 (−4.33)	−5.635 (−1.75)		−19.320 (−4.60)	−4.566 (−1.94)		−19.343 (−5.77)
State-Stock Charter	0.270 (9.28)		0.106 (3.86)	0.919 (8.27)		0.405 (3.03)	1.017 (11.41)		0.367 (3.08)
State-Mutual Charter	−0.051 (−2.83)		−0.028 (−1.71)	−0.280 (−3.31)		−0.186 (−1.94)	−0.054 (−1.27)		−0.178 (−1.74)
Federal-Stock Charter	0.279 (5.31)		0.157 (3.24)	0.899 (4.59)		0.613 (2.75)	0.771 (4.10)		0.520 (2.30)
Texas	0.311 (4.75)		0.316 (5.31)	0.861 (3.44)		0.943 (3.28)	0.765 (5.84)		1.018 (4.84)

Texas State Charter	−0.033		−0.119	0.194		0.104	e		e
	(−0.49)		(−1.89)	(0.70)		(0.33)			
California	0.020		−0.072	0.056		−0.265	e		e
	(0.34)		(−1.34)	(0.25)		(−1.05)			
Calif. State Charter	0.195		0.030	0.706		0.015	0.218		e
	(2.50)		(0.41)	(2.39)		(0.04)	(1.86)		
Florida	0.082		0.005	0.318		−0.017	0.172		e
	(1.50)		(0.11)	(1.54)		(−0.07)	(1.32)		
Florida State Charter	0.189		0.081	0.441		−0.133	e		e
	(1.74)		(0.82)	(1.11)		(−0.29)			
Size (Log of Assets)	0.008		0.004	0.047		0.045	0.027		e
	(1.11)		(0.60)	(1.53)		(1.19)	(0.94)		
Publicly Traded Stock	−0.188		−0.138	−0.646		−0.777	0.024		−0.686
	(−2.79)		(−2.24)	(−2.54)		(−2.70)	(0.16)		(−2.61)
FHLB Ninth District Membership	0.185		0.097	0.611		0.344	0.764		0.337
	(5.94)		(3.36)	(5.14)		(2.39)	(7.47)		(2.24)

Notes: [a]Estimates of the probability of failure during 1986–1989. For each variable, the first row presents the parameter estimate and the second row presents its t-statistic. [b]FIML probit results are estimated jointly with the parameters of an equation explaining expected liquidation costs as a proportion of year-end 1985 total liabilities, using a variation of the sample-selection-bias correction suggested by Heckman (1979). [c]Structural characteristics as of December 31, 1982. [d]Proportion of total assets as of December 31, 1982. [e]Variables with p-values greater than 0.20 in the single-equation probit results have been deleted to facilitate convergence of this procedure.

TABLE 2 (contd.)

ESTIMATES OF THE DETERMINANTS OF THE PROBABILITY OF THRIFT FAILURE[a]

Variable	Ordinary Least Squares			Single-Equation Probit			FIML Probit[b]		
	Structure	Behavior	Both	Structure	Behavior	Both	Structure	Behavior	Both
Behavioral Variables									
Multifamily Mortgages[c]		0.479 (3.60)	0.281 (2.19)		1.691 (2.90)	0.974 (1.45)		1.813 (3.18)	1.002 (1.49)
Nonresidential Mortgages[c]		1.368 (12.08)	1.016 (9.29)		5.073 (9.65)	4.149 (6.97)		4.864 (9.37)	4.216 (7.06)
Land Loans[c]		1.453 (12.46)	0.621 (5.14)		6.818 (9.17)	3.905 (4.72)		7.508 (24.44)	4.069 (9.46)
Commercial Loans[c]		1.535 (4.65)	1.105 (3.57)		5.827 (3.55)	5.243 (2.95)		5.939 (3.85)	5.466 (3.58)
Consumer Loans[c]		0.997 (6.62)	0.305 (2.06)		3.722 (5.82)	1.106 (1.48)		3.702 (6.12)	1.313 (1.91)
Real Estate Investments[c]		2.172 (5.60)	1.538 (4.05)		10.093 (4.22)	8.681 (3.52)		10.466 (6.83)	8.413 (4.49)
Service Corp. Investments[c]		1.034 (3.42)	0.253 (0.87)		5.820 (3.10)	2.352 (1.15)		5.115 (3.57)	[e]

Equity Securities[c]		0.961	0.503		2.318	−5.053		e	e
		(0.54)	(0.30)		(0.32)	(−0.62)			
Goodwill[c]		4.196	2.306		14.911	6.914		14.784	7.634
		(10.80)	(6.01)		(8.29)	(3.17)		(12.15)	(5.07)
Liability Growth, 1983–85		0.034	0.233		0.113	1.535		e	1.411
		(1.26)	(7.86)		(0.91)	(6.75)			(7.32)
Brokered Deposits[d]		0.744	0.752		1.508	1.488		1.890	1.560
		(4.39)	(4.69)		(2.28)	(2.04)		(4.52)	(2.94)
Wholesale Deposits[d]		0.173	−0.133		0.495	−0.694		e	e
		(1.47)	(−1.17)		(0.95)	(−1.16)			
Expense-Preference Items[c]		0.909	6.011		0.498	25.439		e	20.920
		(0.72)	(4.61)		(0.09)	(3.69)			(3.83)
R^2[f]	0.35	0.38	0.47	0.31	0.35	0.46			
F-Statistic	82.26	107.14	72.86						
Log-Likelihood				−920	−873	−717	−830	−727	−587

Notes: [a]Estimates of the probability of failure during 1986–1989. For each variable, the first row presents the parameter estimate and the second row presents its *t*-statistic. [b]FIML probit results are estimated jointly with the parameters of an equation explaining expected liquidation costs as a proportion of year-end 1985 total liabilities, using a variation of the sample-selection-bias correction suggested by Heckman (1979). [c]Structural characteristics as of December 31, 1982. [d]Proportion of total assets as of December 31, 1982. [e]Variables with *p*-values greater than 0.20 in the single-equation probit results have been deleted to facilitate convergence of this procedure. [f]Adjusted R^2 for OLS results; McFadden's pseudo-R^2 for probit results.

TABLE 3

ESTIMATES OF THE DETERMINANTS OF THRIFT LIQUIDATION COSTS[a]

Variable	Ordinary Least Squares			Ordinary Least Squares			FIML Probit[b]		
	Structure	Behavior	Both	Structure	Behavior	Both	Structure	Behavior	Both
Constant	0.211 (1.79)	−0.053 (1.92)	0.252 (2.18)	0.247 (2.20)	0.053 (1.99)	0.060 (1.97)	−0.658 (−5.60)	0.278 (4.63)	0.243 (2.27)
Structural Variables[c]									
Risk-Weighted Assets[d]	0.175 (1.56)		0.042 (0.40)	0.173 (1.60)			0.551 (5.23)		e
Tangible Net Worth[d]	−0.278 (−1.73)		−0.136 (−0.83)	−0.244 (−1.75)			−1.731 (−14.27)		e
Net Interest Margin[d]	0.339 (0.45)		−0.210 (−0.29)				e		e
State-Stock Charter	0.082 (2.82)		0.021 (0.79)	0.090 (3.86)			0.323 (12.84)		e
State-Mutual Charter	−0.001 (−0.03)		0.000 (0.01)				e		e
Federal-Stock Charter	0.105 (2.23)		0.058 (1.34)	0.097 (2.21)		0.038 (0.98)	0.247 (4.44)		0.038 (0.68)
Texas	−0.005 (−0.09)		0.025 (0.53)				e		e

Texas State Charter	0.178 (3.35)		0.124 (2.58)	0.168 (5.00)		0.156 (5.59)	0.171 (4.57)		0.153 (5.03)
California	0.023 (0.36)		−0.035 (−0.59)				e		e
Calif. State Charter	0.020 (0.25)		−0.042 (−0.56)				e		e
Florida	−0.017 (−0.27)		−0.044 (−0.77)				e		e
Florida State Charter	0.054 (0.56)		0.008 (0.10)				e		e
Size (Log of Assets)	−0.015 (−1.80)		−0.021 (−2.69)	−0.018 (−2.37)		−0.018 (−2.90)	0.007 (0.77)		−0.018 (−2.50)
Publicly Traded	−0.077 (−1.15)		−0.071 (−1.16)				e		e
FHLB District Nine Membership	0.170 (5.42)		0.119 (4.10)	0.165 (6.25)		0.092 (5.22)	0.337 (10.55)		0.139 (5.11)

Notes: [a]Estimates of expected liquidation costs as a percentage of year-end 1985 total liabilities for thrifts failing during 1986–1989. For each variable, the first row presents the parameter estimate and the second row presents its *t*-statistic. [b]FIML probit results are estimated jointly with the parameters of an equation explaining the probability of failure, using a variation of the sample-selection-bias correction suggested by Heckman (1979). [c]Structural characteristics as of December 31, 1982. [d]Proportion of total assets as of December 31, 1982. [e]Variables with *t*-statistics less than 1.0 in absolute magnitude have been deleted to facilitate convergence of this procedure.

TABLE 3 (contd.)

ESTIMATES OF THE DETERMINANTS OF THRIFT LIQUIDATION COSTS[a]

Variable	Ordinary Least Squares			Ordinary Least Squares			FIML Probit[b]		
	Structure	Behavior	Both	Structure	Behavior	Both	Structure	Behavior	Both
Behavioral Variables									
Multifamily Mortgages[c]		0.235	0.166		0.251	0.145		0.010	0.145
		(1.85)	(1.46)		(1.99)	(1.33)		(0.73)	(1.20)
Nonresidential Mortgages[c]		0.279	0.283		0.282	0.265		−0.073	0.265
		(2.76)	(3.09)		(2.82)	(3.04)		(−0.48)	(2.57)
Land Loans[c]		1.036	0.556		1.057	0.541		0.780	0.541
		(12.19)	(6.70)		(12.74)	(6.84)		(8.29)	(8.07)
Commercial Loans[c]		0.548	0.571		0.593	0.542		0.209	0.542
		(2.11)	(2.47)		(2.32)	(2.44)		(0.69)	(2.13)
Consumer Loans[c]		0.539	−0.008		0.554			0.263	[e]
		(3.47)	(−0.06)		(3.58)			(1.32)	
Real Estate Investments[c]		0.627	0.515		0.619	0.335		0.193	0.335
		(2.27)	(1.96)		(2.26)	(1.41)		(0.69)	(1.15)
Service Corp. Investments[c]		1.303	1.349		1.378	1.218		1.092	1.217
		(5.97)	(6.69)		(6.70)	(6.70)		(7.24)	(10.83)
Equity Securities[c]		0.585	0.721					[e]	[e]
		(0.36)	(0.48)						

Goodwill[c]		1.061	0.934		1.059	1.019		0.249	1.018
		(3.61)	(3.36)		(3.62)	(3.92)		(0.78)	(3.97)
Liability Growth, 1983–85		0.005	0.011					e	e
		(0.25)	(0.47)						
Brokered Deposits[d]		0.118	0.217			0.182		e	0.181
		(0.85)	(1.72)			(1.51)			(1.48)
Wholesale Deposits[d]		0.087	−0.076					e	e
		(0.82)	(−0.78)						
Expense-Preference Items[c]		2.551	3.032		2.793	2.424		2.535	2.424
		(2.06)	(2.47)		(2.31)	(2.19)		(2.08)	(2.16)
1986 Failure	0.009	−0.046	−0.015				e	e	e
	(0.21)	(−1.10)	(−0.39)						
1987 Failure	−0.000	−0.062	−0.028		−0.059		e	−0.052	e
	(−0.01)	(−1.60)	(−0.82)		(−1.55)			(−0.88)	
1988 Failure	0.119	0.082	0.086	0.119	0.085	0.092	0.059	0.085	0.092
	(5.84)	(3.96)	(4.61)	(6.11)	(4.17)	(5.22)	(4.83)	(3.86)	(5.11)
Correlation of error terms[f]							0.993	−0.514	−0.001
							(406.24)	(−5.22)	(−0.01)
R^2	0.40	0.37	0.52	0.41	0.38	0.53			
F-Statistic	24.13	24.19	23.00	54.65	35.05	50.66			

Notes: [a]Estimates of expected liquidation costs as a percentage of year-end 1985 total liabilities for thrifts failing during 1986–1989; *t*-statistics in parentheses. [b]See note b to Table 3. [c]Proportion of total assets as of December 31, 1982. [d]Proportion of total liabilities as of December 31, 1982. [e]Variables with *p*-values greater than 0.20 in the single-equation results were deleted to facilitate convergence of this procedure. [f]Estimated correlation between the error terms in the failure and cost equations.

TABLE 4
FIML ESTIMATES OF THE DETERMINANTS OF THRIFT FAILURE AND THRIFT LIQUIDATION COSTS[a]

Variable	All FHLB Districts Except District Nine: Failure	All FHLB Districts Except District Nine: Liquidation Cost	All FHLB Districts: Failure	All FHLB Districts: Liquidation Cost
Constant	−1.604 (−13.27)	0.243 (2.85)	−1.704 (−15.37)	0.243 (2.27)
Structural Variables[b]				
Tangible Net Worth[c]	−8.294 (−8.39)		−8.726 (−10.40)	
Net Interest Margin[c]	−16.770 (−4.12)		−19.343 (−5.77)	
State-Stock Charter	0.449 (3.28)		0.367 (3.08)	
State-Mutual Charter	−0.211 (−1.95)		−0.178 (−1.74)	
Federal-Stock Charter	0.553 (2.39)	0.011 (0.34)	0.520 (2.30)	0.038 (0.68)
Texas			0.765 (5.84)	
Texas State Charter				0.153 (5.03)
Size (Log of Assets)		−0.014 (−2.42)		−0.018 (−2.50)
Publicly Traded	−0.692 (−2.57)		−0.686 (−2.61)	
FHLB District Nine Membership			0.337 (2.24)	0.139 (4.14)

Notes: [a]FIML results obtained by jointly estimating an equation explaining the probability of thrift failure during 1986–1989 and an equation explaining the expected liquidation cost for these thrifts expressed as a proportion of year-end 1985 total liabilities, using a variation of the sample-selection-bias correction suggested by Heckman (1979); *t*-statistics shown in parentheses. [b]Structural characteristics as of December 1982. [c]Proportion of total assets as of December 1982.

TABLE 4 (contd.)

Variable	All FHLB Districts Except District Nine		All FHLB Districts	
	Failure	Liquidation Cost	Failure	Liquidation Cost
Behavioral Variables				
Multifamily Mortgages[b]	0.828	−0.104	1.002	0.145
	(1.13)	(−0.97)	(1.49)	(1.20)
Nonresidential Mortgages[b]	3.928	0.274	4.216	0.265
	(5.95)	(2.95)	(7.06)	(2.57)
Land Loans[b]	3.662	0.581	4.069	0.541
	(7.99)	(7.11)	(9.46)	(8.07)
Commercial Loans[b]	7.713	0.376	5.466	0.542
	(3.68)	(1.17)	(3.58)	(2.13)
Consumer Loans[b]	1.651		1.313	
	(1.97)		(1.91)	
Real Estate Investments[b]	9.389	0.263	8.413	0.335
	(4.33)	(1.18)	(4.49)	(1.15)
Service Corp. Investments[b]		0.705		1.217
		(4.04)		(10.83)
Goodwill[b]	9.164	0.735	7.634	1.018
	(5.70)	(2.62)	(5.07)	(3.97)
Liability Growth, 1983–85	1.200		1.411	
	(5.56)		(7.32)	
Brokered Deposits[c]	1.645	0.151	1.560	0.181
	(2.80)	(2.12)	(2.94)	(1.48)
Expense-Preference Items[b]	13.687	1.919	20.920	2.424
	(2.35)	(2.81)	(3.83)	(2.16)
1988 Failure		0.108		0.092
		(7.31)		(5.11)
Correlation of error terms		−0.109		−0.001
		(−0.50)		(−0.01)
Sample Size	1,904	364	2,275	621

See notes on facing page.

TABLE 5
1985 Behavioral Variables as Functions of
1982 Structural Variables (OLS Estimates)[a]

	Behavioral					
Structural Variables[b]	Multi-family Mort-gages[c]	Non-resid-ential Morts.[c]	Land Loans[c]	Comm. Loans[c]	Con-sumer Loans[c]	Real Estate Invest-ment[c]
Intercept	−0.168	−0.112		−0.026		−0.021
Risk-Weighted Assets[e]	0.177	0.252		0.029	0.132	0.180
Tangible Net Worth[e]		−0.224		−0.047	−0.133	
Net Interest Margin[e]				0.187	0.269	−0.129
State-Stock Charter	0.015	0.025	0.033	0.010		0.003
State-Mutual Charter		−0.016				
Federal-Stock Charter	0.019	0.026	0.034	0.012		
Texas			0.046	−0.013		
Texas State Charter			0.040			0.011
California	0.056					
Calif. State Charter		0.050				0.039
Florida		0.022		0.007		
Florida State Charter	0.043		0.045			
Size (Log of Assets)	0.009	0.003		0.001	−0.003	0.001
Publicly Traded	−0.024					−0.010
FHLB District Nine Membership		0.028	0.017	0.012	0.020	
Adjusted R^2	0.15	0.20	0.29	0.09	0.09	0.15
F-Statistic	26.76	38.09	62.33	15.26	16.58	28.73

Notes: [a]All 2,275 sample institutions are included in these regressions. Only coefficients significant at least at the 5 percent level are reported. [b]Structural characteristics as of

TABLE 5 (contd.)
1985 BEHAVIORAL VARIABLES AS FUNCTIONS OF 1982 STRUCTURAL VARIABLES (OLS ESTIMATES)[a]

Variables							
Service Corp. Investment[c]	Equity Investment[c]	Goodwill[c]	Wholesale Deposits[d]	Brokered Deposits[d]	Repo Agreements[d]	Liability Growth, 1983–85	Expense-preference Items[c]
−0.036		−0.025			−0.044	−0.166	0.022
0.034		0.022		0.029	−0.032	0.588	
−0.032		−0.112	−0.143	−0.069	−0.036	1.534	−0.020
−0.155	−0.028	0.120	0.656		0.244	1.909	0.153
0.011	0.001	0.008	0.035	0.029	0.075	0.165	0.003
			−0.007			−0.032	
	0.002	0.010	0.046			0.058	0.002
0.015		0.012		−0.018		0.109	
0.009	0.002		0.024	0.046		0.088	0.005
0.021		0.014		−0.023		0.019	−0.003
			0.053			0.131	0.002
0.021	0.003	0.015	0.079			0.115	
0.002		0.002			0.006	−0.014	−0.001
0.010	0.004	−0.009		0.025	0.040		
			0.033	0.012		0.061	
0.14	0.04	0.16	.020	0.10	0.12	0.34	0.20
26.66	7.56	30.90	38.91	17.79	20.88	78.22	39.33

December 31, 1982. [c]Proportion of total assets as of December 31, 1985. [d]Proportion of total liabilities as of December 31, 1985. [e]Proportion of total assets as of December 31, 1982.

4

UNDERLYING DETERMINANTS OF CLOSED-BANK RESOLUTION COSTS

William P. Osterberg and James B. Thomson

Federal Reserve Bank of Cleveland

1 Introduction

THE LAST DECADE was marked by a record rate of post-depression bank failures. From 1982 through the end of 1992, 1,429 banks were closed, accounting for 71 percent of those closed since the inception of the Federal Deposit Insurance Corporation (FDIC) in 1934. Even more striking, however, were the record losses that were posted. The cost to the FDIC of resolving bank failures averaged 21 percent of total closed-bank assets from 1986 through 1992. By comparison, Benston *et al.* (1986) report that losses to depositors due to the bank failures of 1930–33 represented only about 0.81 percent of total failed bank assets.

In response to the record number of bank closings, and the skyrocketing costs of resolving nonviable banks, Congress enacted the Federal Deposit Insurance Corporation Improvement Act of 1991 (FDICIA). The main provisions of FDICIA sought to limit the degree of discretion of bank regulators in dealing with troubled depository institutions. The most notable of these provisions include prompt corrective action and limitations on the Federal Reserve's discount window.[1] With these legal constraints on forbearance Congress hoped to reduce the ultimate costs of resolving closed banks.

The degree to which FDICIA will meet its goals will critically depend on the correlation between book measures of net worth (the relevant measure

The authors thank Christopher Pike and Sandra Sterk for outstanding research support. The views in this paper are those of the authors and not necessarily those of the Federal Reserve Bank of Cleveland or the Federal Reserve Board of Governors.

[1] For a discussion of prompt corrective action, see Carnell (1993) and Pike and Thomson (1992). For a discussion of FDICIA's discount window provisions, see Todd (1993).

of net worth for prompt corrective action) and economic net worth (relevant for determining losses). Therefore, FDICIA-mandated closure rules will be effective only if they are binding on regulators, that is, if they force earlier closings than do unconstrained closure rules. What matters here, of course, is the lag between the realization of losses on assets and their recognition by book-based regulatory accounting systems.

This paper looks at the underlying determinants of bank resolution costs, and provides some evidence of a significant lag between the realization and recognition of losses on bank assets. Our approach is in the spirit of James (1991) and Bovenzi and Murton (1988) in that we model resolution costs as a function of problem assets, risky assets, and core deposits. We depart from those early studies in three ways. First, our research is more current: We look at FDIC commercial banks closed between 1986 and 1992, while James's sample includes banks closed from 1985 through the middle of 1988. Second, our measures of problem assets are taken from the Federal Financial Institutions Examination Council's (FFIEC) Quarterly Report of Income and Condition (call reports). James uses confidential examination data. Finally, we extend our basic specification, which is analogous to that of James, to include proxies for fraud, off-balance-sheet risk, brokered deposits, and both regional and size effects. All of these variables are found to be significant determinants of closed-bank resolution costs. Several alternative specifications are rejected by the data.

2 Three faces of closed-bank resolution costs

The ultimate cost of resolving an insolvent bank derives from three sources. First, there are the losses that reflect the underlying insolvency of the bank. These losses are the realization of the downside risk associated with a bank's investment and financing decisions. On an economist's extended balance-sheet, these losses equal the negative market net worth of the firm (excluding the value of government guarantees). When looking at a historical cost accounting balance sheet, these losses will initially be unbooked losses. Net unbooked losses are likely to be correlated with the bank's capital, its problem assets, the risk structure of its balance sheet, and its off-balance-sheet activities.

The second component of resolution costs is the losses related to forbearance.[2] Forbearance arises because, as Kane (1986) argues, bank regulators face constraints regarding information, funding, administrative and legal issues, and political considerations in dealing with insolvent banks. As a result, regulators adopt socially suboptimal closure rules. Forbearance losses are those incurred after the depository is no longer economically viable but before it is closed.[3]

Finally, there are the costs associated with receivership, including administrative and legal expenses. For example, expenses for the FDIC's division of liquidation averaged 8.3 percent of collections in 1991 (see the FDIC's 1991 *Annual Report*).[4] Moreover, at the end of 1992, the FDIC's estimated contingent liability for unresolved legal cases was $404 million. Costs of receivership also include losses that arise from the inefficient asset salvage operation of the receiver (see Kane, 1990).

In practice, it is difficult to separate resolution cost into its three components. To do so would require a model that predicts economic insolvency, a model of the regulatory closure rule, and clean estimates of the FDIC's marginal receivership cost associated with closing each bank. While Thomson's (1992) two-step model of the closure decision extends the bank failure literature by explicitly separating economic insolvency from the closure rule, there is considerable work still to be done on measuring and predicting insolvency and on modeling regulatory closure rules.[5] Furthermore, few case-specific data on receivership costs are available, let alone data on the marginal receivership cost for each closed institution. Ultimately, therefore, we are left with estimating a resolution cost equation that includes all three types of resolution costs in the dependent variable.

[2] Although the costs of forbearance have not been explicitly calculated for banks, DeGennaro and Thomson (1995) find that these costs were considerable for thrifts.

[3] Allen and Saunders (1993) model deposit insurance as a callable perpetual put option. The value of forbearance is the difference between the value of the call option under unconstrained regulatory closure rules and its value under constrained closure rules.

[4] James (1991, Table 1) reports that administrative and legal expenses associated with bank closings were 9.96 percent of failed bank assets in 1985 and 1986. James's expense numbers are substantially higher than the FDIC's total administrative and legal expenses, which were 3.6 percent of failed bank assets for those years (see the FDIC's 1986 *Annual Report*). They are, however, similar to the FDIC's division of liquidation expenses as a percentage of recoveries on receivership assets held by the FDIC for 1985 and 1986.

[5] For a review of the bank failure literature, see Demirgüç-Kunt (1989).

3 The data and empirical model

The sample includes all commercial banks insured by the FDIC and the Bank Insurance Fund (BIF) that were closed, or required FDIC financial assistance to remain open, from January 1, 1986 through December 31, 1992. Quarterly balance sheet and income data for these banks are from the FFIEC's call reports from March 31, 1984 through December 31, 1992. Closure data, expected resolution cost (to the FDIC), and resolution type, are from FDIC (1993).

We started with an empirical model similar to that in James (1991) by relating resolution costs (loss on assets in James) to sources of unbooked gains and losses on the bank's extended balance sheet. Unlike James, however, who had access to confidential data on asset quality and individual receivership cases, our proxies for unbooked gains and losses are constructed from balance sheet data reported on the quarterly call report.

Table 1 gives a complete list of the variables that we analyze in the study. RESCOST is the FDIC's estimated resolution cost as published by the FDIC (1993, appendix A). UNCOL is a proxy for problem assets not reported by the bank. As Bovenzi and Murton (1988) note, distressed banks have incentives to cover up the number of problem assets in their portfolios. One method for doing this is to book income on a nonperforming loan to prevent it from being classified as past due or nonaccruing. Therefore, UNCOL should be positively correlated with unbooked losses. Book equity plus reserves, CAP, represents the cushion between the value of assets and the promised payments to debt holders.

PD30 (loans past due 30 days), PDNA and OREO are initial proxy variables for asset quality. Given that the primary source of unbooked losses is losses on the asset portfolio, on-book problem assets should be a good proxy for these unbooked losses. CORE controls for the franchise (charter) value associated with core deposits (Keeley, 1990) and is a source of unbooked gains. Buser,inxxBuser Chen, and Kane (1981) argue that the FDIC will close banks in a manner that preserves the value of the charter in order to minimize its losses. ICORE is included in the model to control for the loss of the charter when the FDIC chooses liquidation as its resolution option.[6] NCRASST is included as a proxy for portfolio risk.

[6] The FDIC has three basic choices in handling a troubled bank. First, it can liquidate the bank by selling its assets and paying off the deposits. Second, it can sell the closed bank to another financial institution. By selling the bank, the FDIC can preserve the value

TABLE 1 (contd. on next page)
DEFINITIONS OF VARIABLES

Variable	Sign[a]	Description
RESCOST	n.a.	Estimated resolution cost to the FDIC. See FDIC (1993, appendix A).
UNCOL	+	Interest income earned on loans that is uncollected.
CAP	−	Equity capital plus the loan loss reserve and allocated risk transfer reserve.
PD30	+	Loans 30 days past due.
PDNA	+	Loans 90 days past due or nonaccruing.
OREO	+	Other real estate owned.
INSLNS	+	Loans to insiders.
NCRASST	+	Risky assets not included in the totals for OREO, PD30 (loans 30 days past due but still accruing), PDNA, or INSLNS.
OBSLN	?	Total notional value of loan commitments, loan sales, and standby letters of credit reported. (OBS = OBSLN + OBSOTHER)
OBSOTHER	?	Total notional value of other off-balance-sheet items reported by banks.
CORE	−	Core deposits: measured as domestic deposits under $100,000.
ICORE	+	Equal to CORE if the bank was resolved via a payout, 0 otherwise.
BRKDEP	−	Brokered deposits.
TOTASS	n.a.	Total on-balance-sheet assets.

Initially, then, to be as close to James (1991) as possible, we estimate the following equation by weighted least squares, where the regressors are dated four to six months before the closure date.

$$\text{RESCOST} = \alpha_0 + \alpha_1\text{OREO} + \alpha_2\text{PD30} + \alpha_3\text{PDNA} + \alpha_4\text{CORE}$$
$$+\alpha_5\text{ICORE} + \alpha_6\text{UNCOL} + \alpha_7\text{CAP} + \alpha_8\text{NCRASST} + \epsilon \quad (1)$$

of its charter and thereby reduce the resolution costs by the amount of the premium the acquirer is willing to pay for this intangible asset. Finally, the FDIC can seek to preserve the charter's value through a direct capital infusion, known as open bank assistance. For a more thorough discussion of FDIC closed-bank resolution options, see Caliguire and Thomson (1987).

TABLE 1 (contd.)
DEFINITIONS OF VARIABLES

Variable	Sign[a]	Description
Size Dummy Variables		
DSZ1	?	= 1 if TOTASS ≤ $50 million, 0 otherwise;
DSZ2	?	= 1 if $50 million < TOTASS ≤ $100 million, 0 otherwise;
DSZ3	?	= 1 if $100 million < TOTASS ≤ $500 million, 0 otherwise;
DSZ4	?	= 1 if $500 million < TOTASS ≤ $1 billion, 0 otherwise;
DSZ5	?	= 1 if $1 billion < TOTASS ≤ $5 billion, 0 otherwise;
DSZ6	?	= 1 if $5 billion < TOTASS, 0 otherwise.
Regional Dummy Variables (defined by Federal Reserve District)		
DUMSE	?	= 1 if the bank is in the Richmond or Atlanta Fed District;
DUMMW	?	= 1 if the bank is in the Cleveland, Chicago, or St. Louis Fed District;
DUMSW	?	= 1 if the bank is in the Dallas Fed District;
DUMHP	?	= 1 if the bank is in the Minneapolis or Kansas City Fed District;
DUMWE	?	= 1 if the bank is in the San Francisco Fed District;
DUMNE	?	= 1 if the bank is in the Boston, New York, or Philadelphia Fed District.

Note: [a]Expected sign for the regression coefficient in equations (1), (3), or (4).

We then test several alternative specifications relating to the inclusion of off-balance-sheet items (OBSLN, OBSOTHER), insider loans, and brokered deposits. We also test for whether to lump together PD30 and PDNA, OBSLNS and OBSOTHER. For the resulting specification, we then test for differences across size categories and regions. Regarding the size categories, we looked at differences across filer types (filer type is related to size) and across the size categories defined by the dummies DSZ1–DSZ6. Regarding regional effects, we examined differences across the regions defined by the regional dummies in the table, and also tested for the inclusion of three variables capturing regional variation in banking conditions.

Next, we perform both stepwise and backwards regressions that consider the entire list of variables discussed above. Finally, we estimate the resulting specification for the five cases when the regressors are dated four to six months before closure, six to nine months before closure, 12 to 15 months before closure, 24 to 27 months before closure, and 36 to 39 months before closure.

The average resolution cost (RESCOST) for banks in the sample was $19.813 million, or 21 percent of failed bank assets. Table 2 presents sample statistics for the regressors for five fixed time intervals before closure. From Table 2, we see that the average size of banks closed was $141 million in assets. Moreover, looking at TOTASS across the subsamples, we find that these banks shrank considerably in the year prior to closure.[7] A similar pattern is exhibited by these banks' loan portfolios and their off-balance-sheet exposure. As one would expect, both capital and asset quality deteriorate in the last year before closure. Because balance-sheet items are unreliable immediately before closure, we confine our initial focus to the specification where the regressors are lagged four to six months prior to closure.

4 Empirical results

Following James (1991), equation (1) is estimated using weighted least squares, where the observations are weighted by one over the square root of total assets, with all regressors dated four to six months prior to closure. The results are displayed as equation (2).

$$\begin{aligned}\widehat{RESCOST} = {} & \underset{(380.512)^*}{1033.395} + \underset{(0.060)^*}{0.522OREO} + \underset{(0.177)^*}{0.511PD30} + \underset{(0.047)^*}{0.456PDNA} \\ & - \underset{(0.008)^*}{0.019CORE} + \underset{(0.009)^*}{0.045ICORE} + \underset{(0.934)^*}{11.107UNCOL} - \underset{(0.077)^*}{1.315CAP} \\ & + \underset{(0.017)^*}{0.071NCRASST} \qquad \bar{R}^2 = 0.798 \quad N = 1{,}121 \end{aligned} \tag{2}$$

[7] Data reported in the last two panels of Table 2 do not include observations on some of the failures occurring in 1986 and 1987. Therefore, while the data suggest that these banks may have shrunk for up to three years prior to closure, differences in the sample across time make it difficult to interpret differences in these means.

TABLE 2
DESCRIPTIVE STATISTICS

	Months elapsed between Call Report and Closure					
	4 to 6		6 to 9		12 to 15	
	Mean	Std. Dev.	Mean	Std. Dev.	Mean	Std. Dev.
UNCOL	1036.43	5392.33	1127.52	5760.97	1327.60	6984.65
CAP	6937.79	57056.24	8818.37	64394.29	10585.24	66705.51
PD30	3928.39	19263.24	4188.67	22391.39	3481.84	15329.59
PDNA	11270.03	90909.14	11939.58	88814.22	8873.49	61538.64
OREO	5709.82	28811.49	5078.02	25045.40	3467.07	16504.32
INSLNS	767.69	5668.06	713.62	4439.21	1059.62	8820.36
NCRASST	73605.04	465766.59	81677.75	528614.53	92411.51	594871.05
OBSLN	34650.27	399339.59	37405.97	425070.17	43226.11	466151.18
OBSOTHER	11286.60	324105.11	14239.04	423253.16	20061.68	606373.60
CORE	92437.49	4444252.96	95622.14	463226.33	91186.95	438577.07
ICORE	15901.86	15901.86	16464.47	110579.12	16225.10	113233.20
DSZ6	0.0045	0.07	0.004	0.07	0.004	0.07
DSZ1	0.68	0.47	0.67	0.47	0.65	0.48
DSZ2	0.14	0.35	0.15	0.36	0.15	0.36
DSZ3	0.14	0.35	0.15	0.35	0.16	0.37
BRKDEP	4694.15	43598.76	4610.01	49753.35	3517.04	34087.87
DUMNE	0.06	0.24	0.06	0.24	0.06	0.24
DSZ4	0.02	0.14	0.02	0.14	0.02	0.14
DUMSW	0.47	0.50	0.47	0.50	0.06	0.23
TOTASS	141.38	830.64	152.19	907.92	162.27	981.47

TABLE 2 (contd.)
DESCRIPTIVE STATISTICS

	Months elapsed between Call Report and Closure			
	24 to 27		36 to 39	
	Mean	Std. Dev.	Mean	Std. Dev.
UNCOL	1378.56	6711.86	1560.55	7203.13
CAP	11405.26	57830.37	13271.86	63164.40
PD30	2704.28	12345.26	2588.19	12146.05
PDNA	4967.40	23375.61	4106.26	23131.93
OREO	2013.55	13453.74	1194.81	7864.23
INSLNS	802.35	3693.26	1108.97	5818.52
NCRASST	105044.06	658903.91	124144.50	694599.59
OBSLN	47598.87	444994.26	60994.96	489308.60
OBSOTHER	15176.29	434189.43	8593.10	201572.07
CORE	87175.40	405181.39	95799.57	443397.02
ICORE	16270.28	130926.38	16231.59	125773.46
DSZ6	0.007	0.08	0.009	0.10
DSZ1	0.63	0.48	0.61	0.49
DSZ2	0.17	0.38	0.18	0.38
DSZ3	0.16	0.37	0.17	0.37
BRKDEP	3832.19	43363.88	4577.47	57103.85
DUMNE	0.06	0.24	0.07	0.26
DSZ4	0.02	0.13	0.02	0.16
DUMSW	0.49	0.50	0.53	0.50
TOTASS	168.52	961.47	193.56	1016.77

Sources: FFIEC Reports of Income and Condition and authors' calculations.

(Standard errors are in parentheses; * indicates statistical significance at the 1 percent level.) The results show that, on average, loans 30 days past due (PD30) and loans that are past due 90 days or are nonaccruing (PDNA) increase resolution costs by 51 cents and 46 cents on the dollar, respectively. Also, as expected, holdings of other real estate owned (OREO) and other risky assets (NCRASST) raise the costs of resolution. Each dollar of core deposits reduces resolution costs by 1.9 cents. As in James, the positive and significant coefficient on ICORE suggests that the bank's charter value is lost when the institution is resolved through liquidation.

The coefficient on UNCOL is consistent with the view that distressed banks use this item to hide growing asset-quality problems. Bovenzi and Murton (1988) note that income earned but not collected can arise from legitimate activities such as investments in real estate, where both the principal and interest are paid at maturity. However, we doubt that the magnitude of the estimated coefficient can be explained completely by such legitimate activities.

In James (1991), the coefficient on capital in the loss-on-assets equation is expected to be equal to zero if there are no unbooked gains or losses on assets. Here, on the other hand, since the dependent variable is resolution cost, we expect the coefficient on CAP to equal −1 in the absence of unbooked gains and losses. The estimated coefficient on CAP is both negative and significantly different from −1. Thus, we are in agreement with James in finding evidence of net unbooked losses.

We then consider adding, separately, the variables OBS, INSLNS, and BRKDEP. Standard F-tests imply that OBS and INSLNS belong in our specification ($F_{2,1109} = 202.420$), but do not validate the addition of BRKDEP to OBS and INSLNS ($F_{1,1108} = 1.713$). F-tests also suggest that we split OBS into its components, OBSLNS and OBSOTHER ($F_{1,1109} = 83.458$) and that we do not aggregate PD30 and PDNA into a composite bad loans category ($F_{1,1109} = 7.145$). With these modifications, the following estimates are obtained.

$$
\begin{aligned}
\widehat{\text{RESCOST}} = \; & \underset{(345.404)}{329.181} + \underset{(0.056)^*}{0.493}\text{OREO} - \underset{(0.172)^*}{0.462}\text{PD30} + \underset{(0.052)^*}{0.807}\text{PDNA} \\
& - \underset{(0.009)^*}{0.053}\text{CORE} + \underset{(0.008)^*}{0.046}\text{ICORE} + \underset{(0.907)^*}{5.735}\text{UNCOL} - \underset{(0.073)^*}{1.053}\text{CAP} \\
& + \underset{(0.021)^*}{0.248}\text{NCRASST} - \underset{(0.016)^*}{0.186}\text{OBSLN} - \underset{(0.007)^*}{0.054}\text{OBSOTHER} \\
& + \underset{(0.267)^*}{2.783}\text{INSLNS} \qquad \bar{R}^2 = 0.814 \quad N = 1{,}121 \qquad (3)
\end{aligned}
$$

(Again, standard errors are in parentheses and the asterisks indicate statistical significance at the 1 percent level.) Note that the coefficients on both categories of off-balance-sheet items are negative and significant. In the case of off-balance-sheet loan items (OBSLN), such as loan commitments and letters of credit, we can interpret the negative coefficient as indicating market discipline. For OBSOTHER, a negative coefficient is consistent with derivative securities being used to hedge against on-balance-sheet risk.[8]

The coefficient on loans to insiders (INSLNS) is expected to be negative if the bank relaxed credit standards in making such loans. However, under this explanation we would not expect the coefficient to exceed one, as is the case here. This is consistent with Thomson's (1991, 1992) interpretation of INSLNS as a proxy for fraud.[9]

The augmented specification (3) is next estimated separately by filer type, referring to the FFIEC form submitted. The four categories are: (1) banks with domestic and foreign offices; (2) banks with only domestic offices and total assets no more than $100 million; (3) banks with only domestic offices and total assets between $100 million and $300 million; and (4) banks with only domestic offices and total assets over $300 million. Using another F-test, we reject the restriction that the coefficients are equal across filer types ($F_{36,1073} = 16.434$). Since filer type does not exactly correspond to size, we also estimate the same specification for each of the dummy variable categories, DSZ1–DSZ6. We reject the restriction that the coefficients are equal across these size categories ($F_{33,110} = 4.401$).[10] We then estimate the same specification for all banks, but with the size dummies included as regressors. To avoid the dummy variables trap, we must exclude either the intercept or one of the dummies.[11]

We follow a similar procedure regarding regional effects. We first estimate equation (3) separately for each region, where the regions are specified by the dummy variables DUMSE, DUMHP, DUMSW, DUMWE, DUMMW, and DUMOTH. We reject the restriction that the coefficients are equal across regions ($F_{60,1109} = 16.486$).[12] Then we estimate the same specification for the sample as a whole, with five of the regional dum-

[8] See Avery and Berger (1991), Boot and Thakor (1991), and Koppenhaver and Stover (1991).

[9] Graham and Horner (1988) find that fraud was a significant factor in the failure of 35 percent of national banks closed between 1979 and 1987.

[10] This test statistic was calculated for the restriction that the coefficients are equal across the four categories: DSZ1 = 1, DSZ2 = 1, DSZ3 = 1, and all other banks.

[11] Because the size category for DSZ6 includes only five banks, including that dummy implies almost perfect collinearity. Also, OBSOTHER is not reported for the smallest banks (DSZ1 = 1).

[12] The specification is different for DUMMW = 1 because OBSOTHER is missing.

mies (including DUMNE) on the right-hand side, along with a common intercept.

It is well known that such a specification may be sensitive to the order in which variables are entered, so we next analyze the total list of variables using both stepwise and backward regression. At this point, we also include in the list three variables that may capture variation in regional economic conditions—BF, BFLIAB, and PCI. Because the backward regression procedure starts with the full list of potential regressors, we must leave out one of the size dummies (DSZ1) and one of the regional dummies (DUMOTH). At this point, we also examine the collinearity diagnostics suggested by Belsley, Kuh, and Welsch (1980). We deem a component harmful in terms of multicollinearity when its condition index is over 30. We also deem the standard error of a particular coefficient estimate to be unacceptably degraded if a high proportion of its variance is associated with a component with a high condition index.

The results from the stepwise and backward regressions are broadly similar. All of the non-dummy variables belong, with the exception of the three regional conditions measures (BF, BFLIAB, and PCI) and PD30. Also, BRKDEP now appears in the final specification even though our original test suggested its exclusion. There are some differences between the two procedures regarding the regional and size dummies. With the backward regressions, all of the size and regional dummies are kept. The collinearity diagnostics for each procedure did indicate that the final component induced harmful collinearity. However, as all *t*-statistics implied significance at the 1 percent level we did not redo the backward and stepwise procedures with a reduced list of regressors. The final specification of the model as indicated by the stepwise procedure (using data for the four to six month time horizon) is as follows:

$$\begin{aligned}\text{RESCOST} = {} & \alpha_0 + \alpha_1\text{UNCOL} + \alpha_2\text{CAP} + \alpha_3\text{PDNA} + \alpha_4\text{OREO} \\ & + \alpha_5\text{INSLNS} + \alpha_6\text{NCRASST} + \alpha_7\text{OBSLN} + \alpha_8\text{OBSOTHER} \\ & + \alpha_9\text{CORE} + \alpha_{10}\text{ICORE} + \alpha_{11}\text{DSZ6} + \alpha_{12}\text{DSZ1} + \alpha_{13}\text{DSZ2} + \alpha_{14}\text{DSZ3} \\ & + \alpha_{15}\text{BRKDEP} + \alpha_{16}\text{DUMNE} + \alpha_{17}\text{DSZ4} + \alpha_{18}\text{DUMSW} + \epsilon. \qquad (4)\end{aligned}$$

In Table 3, we report the weighted least squares results for equation (4) when that specification is run for various horizons (i.e., the regressors are lagged to various degrees).

TABLE 3 (contd. on next page)
WLS RESULTS FOR EQUATION (4)[a]

	Months elapsed between Call Report and Failure				
	4 to 6	6 to 9	12 to 15	24 to 27	36 to 39
α_0	69842 (13394)*,[b]	81400 (12977)*	134598 (13996)*	18846 (14748)	29201 (16965)*
UNCOL	4.376 (0.893)*	3.288 (0.855)*	2.967 (0.811)*	2.122 (0.881)*	2.080 (1.143)*
CAP	−1.165 (0.072)*	−1.107 (0.089)*	−1.046 (0.122)*	−0.278 (0.198)	−0.749 (0.250)*
PDNA	0.786 (0.049)*	0.940 (0.050)*	1.393 (0.090)*	1.013 (0.137)*	1.280 (0.226)*
OREO	0.453 (0.0560)*	0.480 (0.059)*	0.689 (0.073)*	0.813 (0.0815)*	0.936 (0.1589)*
INSLNS	1.775 (0.276)*	1.329 (0.286)*	0.012 (0.091)*	1.132 (0.240)*	1.111 (0.194)*
NCRASST	0.202 (0.020)*	0.258 (0.023)*	0.301 (0.026)*	0.102 (0.030)*	0.131 (0.027)*
OBSLN	−0.158 (0.016)*	−0.179 (0.021)*	−0.177 (0.020)*	0.191 (0.022)*	0.213 (0.019)*
OBSOTHER	−0.038 (0.007)*	−0.031 (0.005)*	−0.071 (0.004)*	−0.100 (0.007)*	−0.180 (0.015)*
CORE	−0.088 (0.010)*	−0.134 (0.010)*	−0.233 (0.012)*	−0.104 (0.019)*	−0.093 (0.018)*
ICORE	0.062 (0.010)*	0.041 (0.010)*	0.052 (0.010)*	−0.051 (0.010)*	−0.049 (0.012)*

Overall, the results using data drawn from four to six months prior to closure are consistent with equations (2) and (3). The coefficients on UNCOL, PDNA, OREO, INSLNS, ICORE, and NCRASST are positive and significant, while the coefficients on CAP, CORE, OBSLN, and OBSOTHER are negative and significant. Moreover, while there are some minor differences in the size of the coefficients across equations, qualitatively the results are the same as those for the specifications employed in (2) and (3).

TABLE 3 (contd.)
WLS Results for Equation (4)[a]

	Months elapsed between Call Report and Failure				
	4 to 6	6 to 9	12 to 15	24 to 27	36 to 39
DSZ6	466982 (51538)*	489923 (53678)*	586938 (51844)*	−314809 (50229)*	−409859 (58407)*
DSZ1	−69250 (13290)*	81400 (12977)*	130498 (13996)*	−16740 (14641)	−26551 (16818)
DSZ2	−65659 (13039)*	−75640 (12649)*	−122915 (13611)*	−11992 (14449)	−21597 (16556)
DSZ3	−56594 (12484)*	−66183 (12109)*	−106014 (13092)*	1067.4 (13918)	−9081.3 (15949)
BRKDEP	−0.095 (0.034)*	−0.071 (0.034)*	−0.220 (0.049)*	−0.345 (0.097)*	−0.203 (0.082)*
DUMNE	5856.9 (1692.8)*	6777.7 (1714.7)*	10253 (1792.6)*	14426 (1991.0)*	19096 (2137.5)*
DSZ4	−34555 (11588)*	−40628 (11289)*	−73158 (12207)*	−8425.7 (13245)	3374.5 (14747)
DUMSW	1345.0 (593.1)*	1241.1 (608.3)*	1884.2 (641.4)*	956.4 (755.2)	1319.5 (878.6)

Notes: Sample includes all FDIC-insured banks that failed from January 1986 through December 1992. Data are from the FFIEC Quarterly Reports of Condition and Income from January 1984 through December 1992 and from the FDIC (1993). [a]Observations are weighted by one over the square root of total assets. [b]Standard errors are in parentheses. *Significantly different from zero at the 1 percent significance level.

The coefficient on brokered deposits is negative and significant, suggesting that banks' reliance on money markets for funding reduces ultimate resolution costs. One could interpret this result as a sign of market discipline. Another possible conclusion is that troubled banks that are heavily reliant on brokered funds are more likely to be subject to prompt closure. This interpretation is consistent with Thomson's (1992) model of the regulatory closure decision.

The coefficients on the size dummies are consistent with a direct relationship between the fixed costs associated with resolving a closed bank and the bank's asset size. Finally, the positive and significant coefficients on DUMNE and DUMSW indicate that the depressed economies in the Northeast and Southwest contributed significantly to the costs of resolving failed banks in those regions.

Interpretation of the results for equation (4) estimated using data from more than six months before closing is not as straightforward as the four-to-six-month results. However, a cursory look at each coefficient across the five different subsamples indicates regulatory forbearance. Our ability to explain expected resolution costs at time of closure using data from up to 39 months before closure suggests that banks closed between 1986 and 1992 were insolvent long before their doors were shut. Moreover, the pattern of individual regression coefficients across time-to-closure subsamples indicates an increase in unbooked losses the further one gets from the closure date. For example, the coefficients on PDNA and OREO rise monotonically with the time-to-closure horizon.

5 Conclusion

In this paper we have extended previous examinations of the determinants of bank-failure resolution costs. We examine the balance sheet determinants of the FDIC's estimated cost of resolution and confirm most of the findings of James (1991), who looked at loss on assets and used confidential examiner reports. Unlike James, however, we find no evidence that our capital variable reflects net unbooked losses in addition to the other variables included in the analysis.[13] In addition, we find a role for insider loans, off-balance-sheet items, and both regional and size dummies.

When we extend the interval between the observation of the banks' balance sheets and the time of closure, we find that the balance-sheet data can still explain a high percentage of the resolution costs. This suggests that regulators may have practiced forbearance.

Our research can be extended in several directions. First, modeling the regulators' closure decisions by adding an equation to predict closure would allow us to focus more carefully on the role of forbearance in explaining resolution costs. Second, examining the determinants of resolution type

[13] We do find evidence of unbooked losses in our capital variable when we estimate our base model—i.e., equation (1), which was motivated by James (1991)—but we cannot reject the hypothesis that the coefficient on the capital variable equals -1 once off-balance-sheet items and insider loans are included in the model, as in equations (3) and (4).

would further allow us to disentangle the influences of balance-sheet items and regulatory response. These changes would also permit further identification of the roles of insider loans and off-balance-sheet items.

References

Allen, L. and A. Saunders 1993. "Forbearance and the Valuation of Deposit Insurance as a Callable Perpetual Put." *Journal of Banking and Finance* 16 (June): 629–43.

Avery, R. B. and A. N. Berger 1991. "Loan Commitments and Bank Risk Exposure." *Journal of Banking and Finance* 15 (September): 173–92.

Barth, J. R., P. F. Bartholomew and M. G. Bradley 1990. "Determinants of Thrift Institution Resolution Costs." *Journal of Finance* 45 (July): 731–54.

Belsley, D., E. Kuh and R. Welsch 1980. *Regression Diagnostics*. New York: John Wiley & Sons.

Benston, G. J., R. A. Eisenbeis, P. M. Horvitz, E. J. Kane and G. G. Kaufman 1986. *Perspectives on Sound and Safe Banking: Past, Present, and Future*. Cambridge, MA: MIT Press.

Blalock, J. B., T. J. Curry and P. J. Elmer 1991. "Resolution Costs of Thrift Failures." *FDIC Banking Review* 4 (Spring/Summer): 15–26.

Boot, A. W. A. and A. V. Thakor 1991. "Off-Balance Sheet Liabilities, Deposit Insurance and Capital Requirements." *Journal of Banking and Finance* 15 (September): 825–46.

Bovenzi, J. F. and A. J. Murton 1988. "Resolution Costs of Bank Failures." *FDIC Banking Review* 1 (Fall): 1–11.

Brown, R. A. and S. Epstein 1992. "Resolution Costs of Bank Failures: An Update of the Historical Loss Model." *FDIC Banking Review* 5 (Spring/Summer): 1–16.

Buser, S. A., A. H. Chen and E. J. Kane 1981. "Federal Deposit Insurance, Regulatory Policy, and Optimal Bank Capital." *Journal of Finance* 36 (September): 775–87.

Caliguire, D. B. and J. B. Thomson 1987. "FDIC Policies for Dealing with Failed and Troubled Institutions." *Economic Commentary*, Federal Reserve Bank of Cleveland, October 1.

Carnell, R. S. 1993. "A Partial Antidote to Perverse Incentives: The FDIC Improvement Act of 1991." *Annual Review of Banking and Law* 12: 317–71.

DeGennaro, R. P. and J. B. Thomson 1995. "Capital Forbearance and Thrifts: Examining the Costs of Regulatory Gambling." *Journal of Financial Services Research* 8 (forthcoming).

Demirgüç-Kunt, A. 1989. "Deposit-Institution Failures: A Review of the Empirical Literature." *Economic Review* (4th quarter), Federal Reserve Bank of Cleveland: 2–18.

Federal Deposit Insurance Corporation 1993. "Failed Bank Cost Analysis: 1986–1992." Washington, D.C. (FDIC).

Graham, F. C. and J. E. Horner 1988. "Bank Failure: An Evaluation of the Factors Contributing to the Failure of National Banks." *Proceedings from a Conference on Bank Structure and Competition*, Federal Reserve Bank of Chicago (May): 405–35.

James, C. 1991. "The Losses Realized in Bank Failures." *Journal of Finance* 46 (September): 1223–42.

Kane, E. J. 1986. "Appearance and Reality in Deposit Insurance Reform." *Journal of Banking and Finance* 10: 175–88.

______. 1990. "Principal-Agent Problems in S&L Salvage." *Journal of Finance* 45 (July): 755–64.

Keeley, M. C. 1990. "Deposit Insurance, Risk, and Market Power in Banking." *American Economic Review* 80 (December): 1183–1200.

Koppenhaver, G. D. and R. D. Stover 1991. "Standby Letters of Credit and Bank Capital: Evidence of Market Discipline." *Proceedings from a Conference on Bank Structure and Competition*, Federal Reserve Bank of Chicago (May): 373–94.

Pike, C. J. and J. B. Thomson 1992. "FDICIA's Prompt Corrective Action Provisions." Federal Reserve Bank of Cleveland *Economic Commentary* (September 1).

Randall, R. E. 1993. "Lessons from New England Bank Failures." *New England Economic Review* (May/June): 13–50.

Thomson, J. B. 1991. "Predicting Bank Failures in the 1980s." *Economic Review* 1st Quarter, Federal Reserve Bank of Cleveland: 9–20.

______. 1992. "Modeling the Bank Regulator's Closure Option: A Two-Step Logit Regression Approach." *Journal of Financial Services Research* 6: 5–23.

Todd, W. F. 1993. "Discount Window Provisions of the Federal Deposit Insurance Corporation Improvement Act of 1991." *Banking Policy Report* (March 1).

5

FEDERAL RESERVE LENDING TO BANKS THAT FAILED: IMPLICATIONS FOR THE BANK INSURANCE FUND

R. Alton Gilbert

Federal Reserve Bank of St. Louis

DEBATE that led to passage of the Federal Deposit Insurance Corporation Improvement Act (FDICIA) in 1991 focused on changes in public policy to reduce losses of the deposit insurance funds. One aspect of public policy subject to such scrutiny was lending by the Federal Reserve to troubled banks. Analysis prepared by Congressional staff indicated that over 300 of the banks that failed in 1985–91 were borrowing from the Fed when they failed, and that 90 percent of the banks that borrowed for extended periods of time eventually failed.[1] Other evidence caused the authors of that Congressional staff study to conclude that Fed credit extended the life of borrowers that ultimately failed. Critics of Fed lending practices concluded on the basis of this evidence that lending to troubled banks increased losses to the Bank Insurance Fund (BIF).[2] This concern led to constraints on Federal Reserve lending to troubled banks in FDICIA (see the next section below).

Restrictions on Federal Reserve lending to troubled banks raise several issues, including the proper role of the discount window and the necessary freedom of action for a central bank in limiting systemic impacts of problems in the operation of a banking system. Failures of banks have systemic impacts if they cause other banks to fail. This article focuses on the more

The author thanks Kenneth Spong and Walker Todd for helpful information and insights. The views of the author do not necessarily reflect the views of the Federal Reserve Bank of St. Louis or the Federal Reserve System.

[1] See U.S. House of Representatives (1991c).

[2] See Garsson (1991), Rehm (1991), Starobin (1991) and Todd (1991, 1992). The FDIC insures the deposits of banks and savings and loan associations but maintains BIF as a separate fund for commercial banks and mutual savings banks. Banks pay insurance premiums into BIF, which then covers any losses when banks fail.

narrow issue of whether Federal Reserve lending to troubled banks in recent years raised the losses of BIF. Critics of Fed lending practices have emphasized anecdotal evidence from a few bank failure cases, particularly the failures of the Bank of New England and the Madison National Bank.[3] This article, in contrast, examines whether the record of Fed lending to many failed banks supports the arguments of the critics.

The evidence in this study indicates that loans from the Fed to many of the failed banks in their last year were concentrated near the time of failure and were allocated to the banks with the greatest liquidity needs. The evidence does not support the argument that Federal Reserve lending to troubled banks increased the losses of the FDIC.

1 Restrictions on Federal Reserve lending under FDICIA

FDICIA restricts Federal Reserve lending to banks that do not meet the minimum capital requirements. For purposes of various provisions of FDICIA, a bank that fails to meet each of the minimum capital requirements is classified as *undercapitalized*. A bank is classified as *critically undercapitalized* if its tangible equity is less than two percent of its total assets.

The Federal Reserve may be liable to the FDIC for losses resulting from loans to critically undercapitalized banks. If the Federal Reserve lends to a bank for more than five days after it becomes critically undercapitalized, and a deposit insurance fund incurs a loss greater than would have been incurred in the absence of the loan, the Board of Governors will be liable to the FDIC for part of the loss.

FDICIA restricts Federal Reserve lending to an undercapitalized bank to no more than 60 days in any 120-day period, unless the head of the appropriate federal supervisory agency or the chairman of the Board of Governors certifies the bank's viability. A certification of viability is a determination that, in light of the economic conditions and circumstances in the local market, the bank is not critically undercapitalized, is not expected to become critically undercapitalized and is not expected to be placed in conservatorship or receivership. If a certification of viability is made, the Reserve Bank may lend to the bank for 60 more days. A new determination is required every 60 days. If the Federal Reserve extends credit to an

[3] See Schwartz (1992), Todd (1992) and comments by policymakers in Rehm (1991). For hearings on the failures of these banks, see U.S. House of Representatives (1991a and 1991b).

undercapitalized bank beyond the 60 day limit without a certificate of viability, the bank will be classified as critically undercapitalized for purposes of Federal Reserve liability to the FDIC in case of bank failure.

2 Federal Reserve policy on lending to troubled banks prior to FDICIA

Prior to passage of FDICIA in 1991, the Federal Reserve had a general policy of lending only to banks considered viable by the government agencies that supervise banks.[4] In practice, however, that policy did not preclude loans to troubled banks for extended periods of time. Two of the large banks that received Fed credit for extended periods of time were the Franklin National Bank, in 1974, and the Continental Illinois National Bank, in 1984.[5]

In response to public criticism that the Federal Reserve had subsidized the Franklin National Bank, the Federal Reserve amended its lending regulations to establish a new, higher special discount rate for protracted emergency assistance to particular banks. Extended credit was made a separate category of discount window credit in 1980. Figure 1 indicates that, at times, most discount window lending has been extended credit. Prior to passage of FDICIA in the fall of 1991, there were no legal constraints on the size or duration of Federal Reserve lending to troubled banks.

3 The debate over lending to troubled banks

Public discussion that led to passage of limits in FDICIA on the authority of the Federal Reserve to lend to troubled banks involved two issues. The first issue, philosophical in nature, involved the proper purpose for lending. Walker Todd (1988, 1991, 1992), a leading contributor to this discussion, concluded that the proper role for the discount window is to lend for short periods of time to solvent banks that are temporarily insolvent. Todd described Federal Reserve lending to troubled banks for extended periods

[4] The federal agencies that supervise commercial banks are the Federal Reserve, the FDIC and the Office of the Comptroller of the Currency. State agencies also supervise state chartered banks. For a general description of bank supervision, see Gilbert (1993).

[5] For a history of Federal Reserve policies on discount window lending, see Schwartz (1992). Thrift institutions have had access to credit from the discount window since 1980, under provisions of the Monetary Control Act. This paper focuses on lending to commercial banks. For convenience, all depository institutions are called banks.

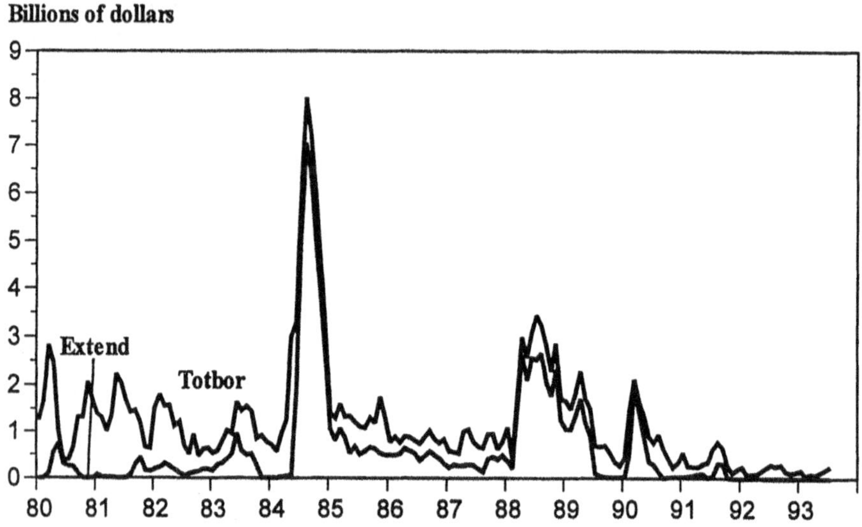

FIGURE 1: TOTAL AND EXTENDED CREDIT BORROWINGS

of time as the substitution of credit from the Federal Reserve for capital of the banks, which he considered inappropriate use of the discount window.

The second issue involved the implications of Federal Reserve lending practices for BIF losses. This second issue appears to have been more important to Congress than the philosophical issues raised by Todd, because BIF losses may affect the budget of the federal government. For that reason, this article focuses on the second issue in the debate, the implications of Fed lending practices for BIF.

Critics of Fed lending practices cited two reasons why lending to troubled banks may have increased BIF losses. First, credit from the Federal Reserve may have given the borrowers extra time to assume additional risk. Banks may have increased risk through rapid growth of their assets, in desperate gambles to regain financial strength, or through actions to benefit shareholders, such as paying dividends.

The second argument involved reductions in uninsured deposits at borrowers. Deposits often decline when the public becomes aware of a bank's troubles, but deposits in denominations above the insurance limit of $100,000 per account tend to fall more rapidly than fully insured deposits. Banks that borrowed from the Federal Reserve near the time of their failure may have had larger reductions in their uninsured deposits than the nonborrowers because the borrowers could fund declines in their uninsured deposits with Federal Reserve credit.

Implications of declines in uninsured deposits for the losses to BIF in bank failure cases depend on the methods used by the FDIC to resolve failed bank cases.[6] The simplest method is liquidation, in which the failed bank is closed, the FDIC pays insured depositors in full, and the FDIC over time pays the uninsured depositors a fraction of their deposits, which depends on the value of the failed bank's assets. If the value of the assets is less than the value of the liabilities, the FDIC and the uninsured depositors share as losses the gap between the value of assets and liabilities. A decline in uninsured deposits raises the cost to BIF if a case is resolved through liquidation, since a decline in uninsured deposits forces the FDIC to absorb more of the shortfall of the value of assets below liabilities.

In cases resolved through transfer of insured deposits, banks bid for the deposit accounts of a failed bank in denominations below the insurance limit. The winning bidder assumes the insured deposit accounts of the failed bank, and the FDIC makes a cash payment to the winning bidder equal to the deposits, minus the premium paid by the winning bidder. The cost of a resolution arranged as a transfer of insured deposits tends to be lower than what the cost would have been under liquidation by the amount of the premium, net of administrative costs of arranging the resolution. The FDIC shares with the uninsured depositors any losses from resolving the failed bank. Declines in uninsured deposits have the same implications for BIF losses under liquidation and transfer of insured deposits.

During the years covered by this study, 1985–90, the FDIC resolved most bank failure cases through a third method called purchase and assumption (P&A). In a case resolved through P&A, the bank with the winning bid assumes all of the deposit liabilities of the failed bank and purchases some of its assets. The cash payment from the FDIC to the winning bidder equals all deposit liabilities (insured and uninsured), minus the value of assets purchased by the winning bidder, minus the premium. The FDIC does not share any of the losses with uninsured depositors in cases resolved through P&A, since the winning bidder assumes all of the deposit liabilities. Even in cases resolved through P&A, however, declines

[6] See the appendix to Gilbert (1992) for an analysis of the distribution of losses between the FDIC and uninsured depositors under alternative methods of resolving bank failure cases.

in uninsured deposits may increase BIF losses. In some cases, resolution costs might have been lower if the failed banks had been closed prior to the declines in uninsured deposits and resolved through liquidation or transfer of insured deposits.

The Evidence

The staff of the House Banking Committee in 1991 analyzed the implications of Federal Reserve lending to troubled banks for BIF losses, using data for all insured depository institutions that borrowed from the Federal Reserve from January 1, 1985, through May 10, 1991. The study concluded:

(1) Ninety percent of all institutions that received extended credit during this period subsequently failed.
(2) The Federal Reserve routinely extended credit to institutions with CAMEL ratings of 5 by their supervisory agencies (the rating that indicates imminent danger of failure).[7]
(3) Borrowers remained open for 10 to 12 months on average after being rated CAMEL 5 by their supervisory agencies. The study implies that the banks would not have stayed open that long after being rated CAMEL 5 without Federal Reserve credit.
(4) Borrowings increased dramatically as the condition of institutions deteriorated.
(5) The Federal Reserve took the highest quality assets as collateral when banks borrowed, in amounts substantially in excess of the loan amounts.
(6) Of the 530 failed institutions that borrowed from the Federal Reserve in the three-year period prior to their failure, 320 were borrowing at the time of their failure, with $8.3 billion in discount window credit outstanding.

[7] When government supervisors examine a bank, they give it ratings from 1 (the best) to 5 (the worst) on five aspects of its operations: Capital adequacy, Asset quality, Management, Earnings and Liquidity (CAMEL, for short). In addition, supervisors assign a composite CAMEL rating from 1 to 5, based on the ratings for these five components. Banks with composite ratings of 4 or 5 are classified as problem banks and subjected to relatively close supervision. Banks rated composite CAMEL 5 are in such poor condition that their supervisors consider them to be in imminent danger of failing.

This paper investigates the implications of these conclusions for BIF losses.

4 Borrowings by the sample of failed banks

This section presents information on Federal Reserve lending to a sample of banks that failed from 1985 to 1990. The number of bank failures per year was relatively large during that period. Including these years yields a large sample of failed banks. The sample ends in 1990 to avoid failures in periods in which Federal Reserve lending to troubled banks was influenced by the provisions in FDICIA. Since the content of FDICIA was discussed and debated throughout most of 1991, the sample ends with the failures in 1990. Note in Figure 1 that extended credit borrowings were relatively low throughout 1991 and have been zero or relatively small since November 1991, when FDICIA was enacted.

The sample is restricted to the failed banks that reported their deposits each week in their last year to the Federal Reserve, because the analysis involves deposit data in their last years. This restriction affects the size distribution of the banks in the sample. Relatively small banks report their deposit liabilities and vault cash for one week in a quarter, and their required reserves are set, based on their reports, for a quarter. The maximum asset size of the quarterly reporters was changed over the years 1985 to 1990.

Restricting the sample to those that reported deposit data to the Fed in each of their last 52 weeks reduces a potential sample of 815 failed banks to 318. Figure 2 presents the size distribution of the banks in the sample, based on their total assets as of failure date. Restricting the sample to banks that reported their deposits weekly for their last 52 weeks eliminates the very small banks. None of the banks in the sample had total assets below \$10 million, and only 19 of the 318 banks had total assets below \$20 million as of their failure date.

Results derived from this sample of 318 banks may not apply for smaller banks. In several ways, however, the observations on borrowings in the House Banking Committee study are similar to the patterns of borrowings by banks in this study. Also, among the 815 banks in the broader sample, ratios of BIF loss to total assets is not related systematically to asset size, and the distributions of banks by resolution methods are similar for the larger and smaller samples of banks.

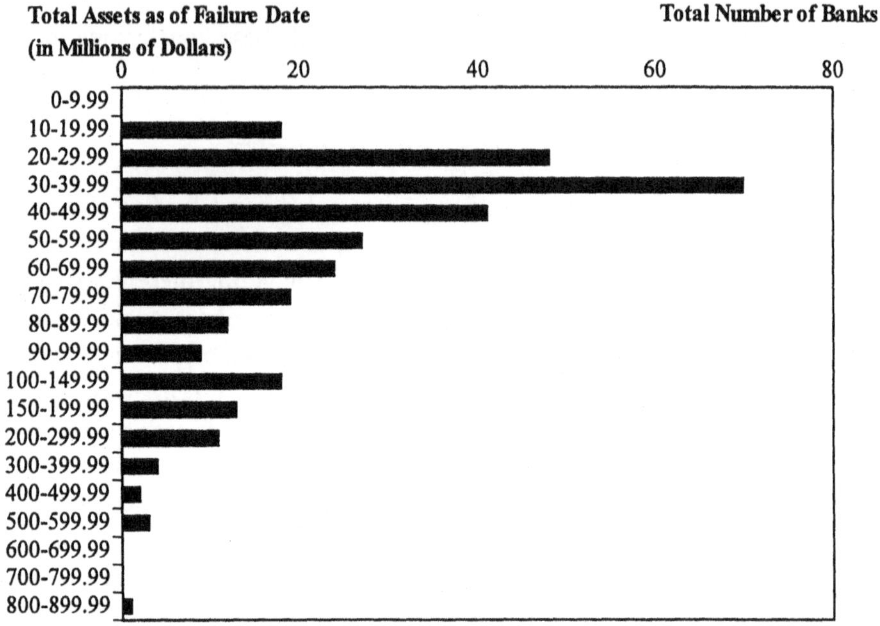

FIGURE 2: DISTRIBUTION OF BANKS IN THE SAMPLE BY TOTAL ASSETS AT FAILURE DATE

Table 1 presents the distribution of the 318 banks in the sample by year of failure and borrowings in their last 52 weeks. Failures of the banks occurred fairly uniformly over the 1985–90 period. About 58 percent of these banks borrowed in at least one of their last 52 weeks. Borrowings tended to be concentrated in the weeks just prior to failure. Of the 185 banks that borrowed in their last 52 weeks, 154 (83.2 percent) borrowed in at least one of their last 13 weeks. For the 318 banks as a group, about 54 percent of the total dollar amount of borrowings in their last 52 weeks occurred in their last 13 weeks. This observation confirms the conclusion in the staff study of the House Banking Committee that borrowings increased as the condition of the banks deteriorated.

Conclusions of the staff study of the House Banking Committee leave the impression that many failed banks borrowed for long periods prior to their failure. For instance, the observation that borrowers remained in operation 10 to 12 months on average as CAMEL-5 rated banks leaves the impression that credit from the discount window was essential for keeping the borrowers in operation during their last 10 to 12 months. This study indicates, in contrast, that only a small minority of the banks borrowed for at least half of their last year. Only 28 of the 318 banks (8.8 percent)

TABLE 1
DISTRIBUTION OF BANKS IN THE SAMPLE BY BORROWINGS FROM THE FEDERAL RESERVE IN THEIR LAST YEAR

Year of failure	Number of banks	Borrowed in their last 52 weeks (percent)	Borrowed in their last 13 weeks	Borrowed in at least 26 of their last 52 weeks
1985	50	26 (52.0)	24	4
1986	60	36 (60.0)	28	8
1987	60	43 (71.7)	39	6
1988	54	30 (55.6)	26	6
1989	44	26 (59.1)	18	2
1990	50	24 (48.0)	19	2
TOTAL	318	185 (58.2)	154	28

borrowed in at least 26 of their last 52 weeks.[8] The discount window may have become less accommodating to troubled banks in 1989–90; only four of the 94 banks that failed in those years borrowed in half or more of their last 52 weeks.

The sample of failed banks is distributed very unevenly across Federal Reserve Districts, with 88 percent of the banks located in Districts 6, 10, 11 and 12 (Table 2). These Districts also account for most of the banks that borrowed in their last 52 weeks. The banks that borrowed in half or more of their last 52 weeks were concentrated in Districts 10 (Kansas City) and 11 (Dallas), which may reflect differences in Reserve Bank lending practices. While the 12 districts follow the same general policies on lending, the staff of the district Reserve Banks have some freedom to follow different lending practices. Banks in the sample also differ substantially by the amount of their borrowings relative to the size of their total deposits. For most of the banks that borrowed from the Fed in their last year, average borrowings were small relative to their average total deposits. Over their last 52 weeks, for instance, 85 percent of the failed banks either didn't borrow from the Fed or their borrowings were less than 1 percent of their average total deposits (Table 3). In contrast, borrowings were large relative to total deposits at

[8] The extreme cases in this sample involved two banks in the Kansas City District that borrowed almost continuously for about two years and then failed.

TABLE 2
BORROWINGS BY FEDERAL RESERVE DISTRICT

Federal Reserve District	Number of banks	Borrowed in their last 52 weeks	Borrowed in their last 13 weeks	Borrowed in at least 26 of their last 52 weeks
1	4	2	1	0
2	7	3	1	0
3	0	0	0	0
4	3	2	1	0
5	0	0	0	0
6	36	22	19	2
7	14	6	4	2
8	2	1	1	0
9	7	2	2	0
10	66	46	37	10
11	148	85	75	12
12	31	16	13	2
TOTAL	318	185	154	28

a few of the banks. Borrowings of three banks exceeded 10 percent of their total deposits over their last 52 weeks. Ratios of borrowings to total deposits tended to be higher over the last 13 weeks than over longer periods prior to failure dates, since borrowings tended to rise and deposits decline as banks approached their failure dates. For instance, borrowings of 15 banks exceeded 10 percent of their total deposits over their last 13 weeks.

5 IMPLICATIONS OF BORROWINGS FOR THE BANK INSURANCE FUND

Analysis of the effects of Federal Reserve lending to troubled banks on the losses of BIF begins with comparisons in Table 4 of BIF losses associated with the failed banks that borrowed from the Federal Reserve and those that did not borrow in their last year. The mean BIF loss ratios in Table 4 for banks that did and did not borrow from the Fed in their last year are not adjusted for differences among the banks, other than borrowings, that might explain differences in BIF loss ratios, such as the condition of banks prior to borrowing or regional effects.

TABLE 3
DISTRIBUTION OF BANKS BY SIZE OF BORROWINGS RELATIVE TO AVERAGE TOTAL DEPOSITS

Range of ratios of borrowings to total deposits	Sum of borrowings divided by the sum of total deposits over the following periods ending on failure dates: Last 13 weeks: Number of banks	Last 13 weeks: Cumulative percent	Last 26 weeks: Number of banks	Last 26 weeks: Cumulative percent	Last 52 weeks: Number of banks	Last 52 weeks: Cumulative percent
Zero	164	51.75	149	46.86	133	41.82
$.000 < x \leq .001$	28	60.38	54	63.84	65	62.26
$.001 < x \leq .005$	29	69.50	29	72.96	52	78.62
$.005 < x \leq .010$	23	76.73	23	80.19	21	85.22
$.010 < x \leq .020$	20	83.02	22	87.11	23	92.45
$.020 < x \leq .050$	25	90.88	24	94.65	15	97.17
$.050 < x \leq .100$	14	95.28	10	97.80	6	99.06
$.100 < x \leq .200$	11	98.74	5	99.37	2	99.69
$.200 < x$	4	100	2	100	1	100

Mean BIF loss ratios are about 5 percentage points higher among the failed banks that borrowed from the Federal Reserve in their last year, and differences in the mean loss ratios are highly significant. The high *t*-statistics for differences in mean BIF less ratios indicate that there is only a very small chance that BIF loss ratios of the borrowers and nonborrowers were drawn from the same distribution.

The association between borrowings and BIF loss ratios in Table 4 do not necessarily indicate that Fed lending practices *caused* higher BIF losses. Perhaps the banks that borrowed from the Fed in their last year would have had higher BIF loss ratios than the other banks if the Fed had not loaned to them. Two observations raise doubts about the argument that loans by the Fed caused the higher BIF loss ratios among the borrowers. First, borrowings of most banks were concentrated near the time of their failure dates, long after they had assumed the risk that led to their failure. Second, if Federal Reserve lending caused the higher BIF loss ratios among the borrowers, we would expect the banks that borrowed the most relative to their deposit size to have the highest BIF loss ratios. This is not the case. Figures 3 and 4 present information on the association between BIF loss

TABLE 4
ASSOCIATION BETWEEN BIF LOSS RATIOS AND BORROWINGS BY FAILED BANKS

Group of banks based on borrowings from the Federal Reserve	Number of banks	Mean BIF loss ratio* (std. deviation in parentheses)	t-statistic for difference in means
Borrowings in last 13 weeks:			
Yes	154	0.3067 (0.1181)	
No	164	0.2514 (0.1253)	4.01
Borrowings in last 26 weeks:			
Yes	169	0.3079 (0.1228)	
No	149	0.2445 (0.1186)	4.73
Borrowings in last 52 weeks:			
Yes	185	0.3007 (0.1253)	
No	133	0.2468 (0.1175)	4.02

*The BIF loss ratio is the loss to BIF from a bank failure divided by the total assets of the failed bank as of its failure date.

ratios and ratios of borrowings to deposits among the banks that borrowed in their last year. Measuring borrowings over the last 13 weeks (Figure 3) and the last 52 weeks (Figure 4), there does not appear to be a positive association between BIF loss ratios and borrowings ratios.

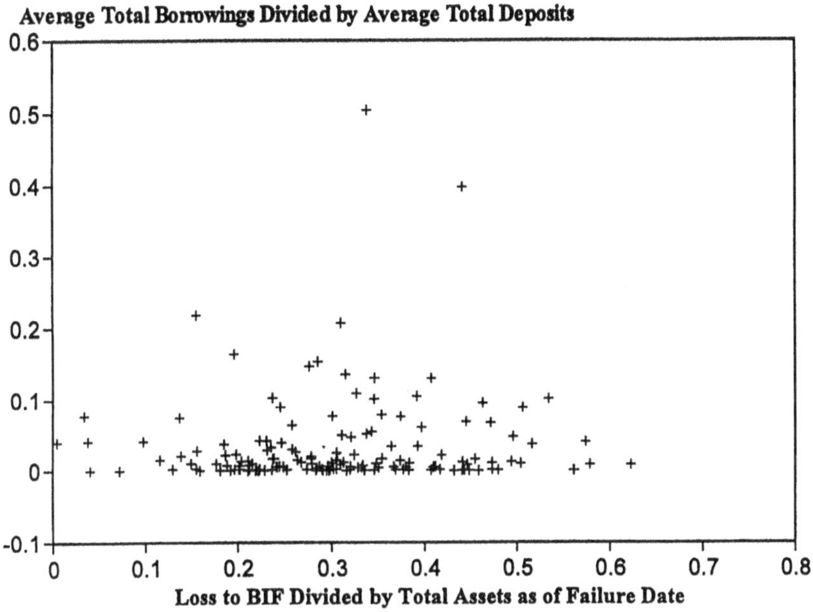

FIGURE 3: RELATIONSHIP BETWEEN BORROWINGS RATIOS AND BIF LOSS RATIOS: BANKS BORROWING IN LAST 13 WEEKS

The remainder of this section attempts to determine whether Fed lending practices caused the higher BIF loss ratios among the borrowers by investigating whether evidence supports the assumptions that underlie such a direction of causality.

Did Federal Reserve credit help keep problem banks open?

Credit from the Fed may have allowed the borrowers to remain open longer as troubled banks than the nonborrowers. Supported by Fed credit, the borrowers may have assumed additional risk just prior to their failure, resulting in larger losses to BIF when they failed. The study by the staff of the House Banking Committee emphasized such a link between borrowings and BIF losses. One of the key conclusions was that the failed banks which borrowed from the Federal Reserve in their last three years

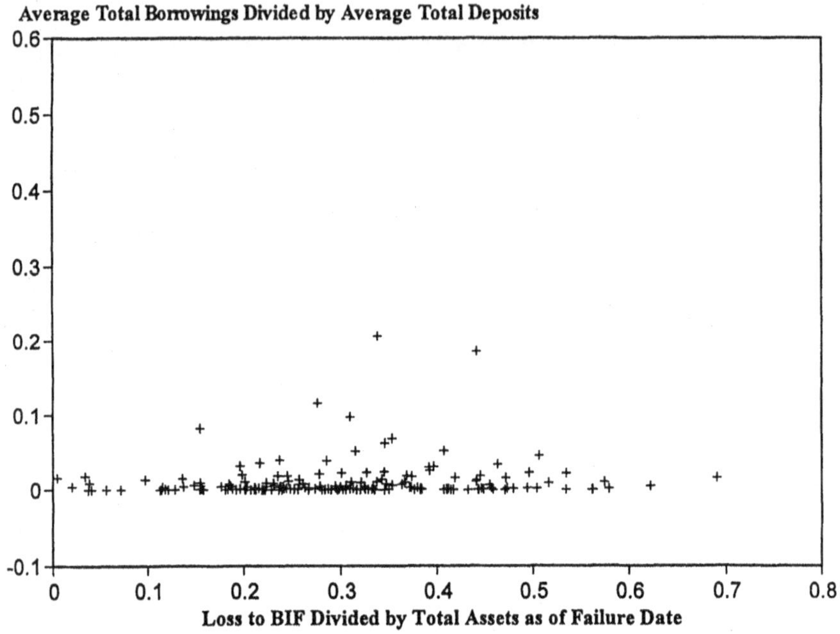

FIGURE 4: RELATIONSHIP BETWEEN BORROWINGS RATIOS AND BIF LOSS RATIOS: BANKS BORROWING IN LAST 52 WEEKS

remained open on average about 10 to 12 months after supervisors rated them as CAMEL 5. The study implies that these banks would have been closed earlier if the Federal Reserve had not provided credit.

There are two problems with such an inference. First, the study does not indicate when in their last three years these banks borrowed from the Federal Reserve. Suppose a bank borrowed for one day three years prior to its failure and was rated CAMEL 5 one year prior to failure. This case would be included among the observations supporting the inference that Federal Reserve credit helped some CAMEL 5 banks stay open for relatively long periods.

A second problem is a lack of comparison to the length of time that nonborrowers were rated CAMEL 5 prior to their failure dates. Tables 5 and 6 provide such a comparison. The sample of 318 failed banks is divided into two groups: those that borrowed from the Federal Reserve in their last 13 weeks and those that did not. Borrowings are observed over the last 13 weeks because any banks kept open only through access to Federal Reserve credit would have borrowed from the Federal Reserve near the time of their failure. Tables 5 and 6 present the distributions of these banks

TABLE 5
CUMULATIVE DISTRIBUTIONS OF BANKS
BY THE LENGTH OF TIME
THEY WERE CAMEL 4 OR 5 PRIOR TO FAILURE

	Borrowed from the Federal Reserve in their last 13 weeks:			
	Yes		No	
Months rated CAMEL 4 or 5: less than	Number of banks	percent	Number of banks	percent
1	5	3.2	6	3.7
2	11	7.1	10	6.1
5	15	9.7	13	7.9
10	27	17.5	27	16.5
15	47	30.5	52	31.7
20	72	46.8	77	47.0
25	96	62.3	105	64.0
30	111	72.1	120	73.2
36	130	84.4	135	82.3
36 or more	154	100.0	164	100.0
Median no. of months rated CAMEL 4 or 5	20.5		20	

by the length of time they were rated CAMEL 4 or 5, and rated CAMEL 5, respectively, prior to their failure. Banks with these ratings are classified as problem banks. It is relevant to know whether Federal Reserve credit helped such banks remain in operation for relatively long periods prior to their failure.

The distributions of banks by the number of months they were rated CAMEL 4 or 5 prior to their failure are almost identical for the borrowers and nonborrowers. The median number of months between the time the banks were rated problem banks and their failure was 20.5 months for the borrowers and 20 months for the nonborrowers.[9]

[9] The median is used, instead of the mean, because the few failed banks that remained open for long periods as problem banks could distort comparisons of means. For instance,

TABLE 6
CUMULATIVE DISTRIBUTIONS OF BANKS BY THE LENGTH OF TIME THEY WERE CAMEL 5 PRIOR TO FAILURE

	Borrowed from the Federal Reserve in their last 13 weeks:			
	Yes		No	
Months rated CAMEL 5: less than	Number of banks	percent	Number of banks	percent
1	15	9.7	22	3.7
2	30	19.5	40	6.1
5	46	29.9	63	7.9
10	77	50.0	102	16.5
15	111	72.1	130	31.7
20	135	87.7	146	47.0
25	148	96.1	153	64.0
30	152	98.7	158	73.2
36	153	99.4	162	82.3
36 or more	154	100.0	164	100.0
Median no. of months rated CAMEL 5	9.5		7	

The banks that borrowed in their last 13 weeks tended to be rated CAMEL 5 somewhat longer than the nonborrowers. The median period at this rating prior to failure was 9.5 months for borrowers, compared to 7 months for the nonborrowers.

Access to credit from the discount window, however, does not appear to have been the only factor determining how long the borrowers and nonborrowers rated CAMEL 5 remained in operation. If access to Fed credit had been the only factor, all of the borrowers would have had this rating for relatively long periods, and all of the nonborrowers for relatively short periods, prior to their failure. This was not the case. Periods that both borrowers and nonborrowers operated as CAMEL 5 ranged from less than one month to three years or more. About 20 percent of the borrowers were closed within two months of the time when their supervisors so rated them, whereas many of the nonborrowers remained in operation rated CAMEL 5 for much longer periods.

Suppose Tables 5 and 6 are interpreted as indicating that access to credit from the Federal Reserve allowed borrowers to remain in operation slightly longer as CAMEL-5 rated banks. What would this imply for losses to BIF? The idea that troubled banks should be closed promptly to keep them from taking actions that expose BIF to larger losses is based on the assumption that supervisors have been ineffective in preventing troubled banks from taking such actions. This author, however, has found evidence that supervisors have been effective in constraining the behavior of most of the troubled banks under their jurisdiction.

Some of the evidence reveals the behavior of banks while their capital ratios were below required levels or while supervisors rated them as problem banks. Supervisors attempt to limit asset growth, dividends and loans to officers and directors of the banks (the insiders) of undercapitalized and problem banks. Gilbert (1991) reported that large majorities of the banks that operated in 1985–89 for four or more consecutive quarters with capital ratios below the minimum capital requirement in effect at the time reduced their assets, refrained from paying dividends and had lower insider loans while undercapitalized. Gilbert (1992) found that the banks undercapitalized the longest prior to failure had the fastest declines in their total assets in their last year, and the group of banks undercapitalized the

among the 154 borrowers, three banks were rated CAMEL 4 or 5 for over 60 months prior to failure, and among the 164 nonborrowers, four banks were rated CAMEL 4 or 5 for over 60 months.

longest prior to their failure had the smallest percentage paying dividends in their last year. Gilbert (1993) found that banks reduced the growth rates of their assets and reduced their dividends when supervisors downgraded them to problem status.

Another study tests directly the association between the length of time prior to their failure that banks operated with capital ratios below the minimum required level and the losses to the deposit insurance fund resulting from their failures. Gilbert (1992) found no association between losses to the deposit insurance fund and the length of time banks were undercapitalized prior to their failure. Thus, if Federal Reserve lending practices allowed some CAMEL-5 rated banks to remain in operation slightly longer than the nonborrowers, it is not clear that those practices had any effect on BIF losses.

Behavior of the banks that borrowed

Conclusions about the behavior of most troubled banks may not apply to those that borrowed from the Fed near the time of their failure. Since these banks were privileged to have access to credit from the discount window near the time of their failure, they may have had other privileges not available to all troubled banks.

The articles cited above indicate that troubled banks subject to relatively close supervision tended to reduce their assets and refrain from paying dividends. Table 7 examines the deposit growth and dividends of borrowers and nonborrowers that were rated CAMEL 4 or 5 one year prior to their failure. Of these 238 banks, 96 did not borrow from the Fed in their last year, and the remaining 142 banks borrowed at least once in their last year. The 142 borrowers are divided into several groups, based on their average borrowings over their last year as a percentage of average total deposits over their last year. For each of the groups in Table 7, based on their borrowings ratios, the mean of the percentage change in total deposits in their last year was negative. The borrowers tended to have more rapid declines in total deposits in their last year than the nonborrowers, and those that borrowed more relative to the size of their total deposits tended to have faster rates of decline in total deposits than the banks with lower borrowings ratios. These observations are consistent with the view that the banks that borrowed most relative to their deposits had the greatest liquidity needs.

TABLE 7
DEPOSIT GROWTH AND DIVIDENDS OF BANKS RATED CAMEL 4 OR 5 OVER THEIR LAST YEAR

Range of ratios of borrowings to total deposits	Number of banks	Mean percentage change in total deposits	Banks paying dividends	Of banks paying dividends, mean of dividends as % of total assets
Zero	96	−12.1	14	0.12
$.000 < x \leq .001$	53	−13.1	3	0.04
$.001 < x \leq .005$	35	−17.2	6	0.09
$.005 < x \leq .010$	16	−20.2	3	0.05
$.010 < x \leq .020$	17	−19.5	2	0.03
$.020 < x \leq .050$	13	−27.3	0	n.a.
$.050 < x \leq .100$	5	−29.9	3	0.09
$.100 < x \leq .200$	2	−19.2	0	n.a.
$.200 < x$	1	−53.8	0	n.a.
	238		31	

About 13 percent of the banks rated CAMEL 4 or 5 in their last year paid dividends in their last year, and this percentage was about the same for the borrowers and nonborrowers. Dividends as a percentage of total assets, however, were smaller among the borrowers that paid dividends in their last year (mean of 0.07 percent) than among the nonborrowers that paid dividends in their last year (mean of 0.12 percent). Based on deposit growth and dividends, supervision of the problem banks that borrowed in their last year appears to have been at least as strict as the supervision of problem banks that did not borrow from the Fed.

Did borrowers have larger declines in uninsured deposits?

Evidence for one of the arguments that lending to troubled banks may have raised BIF losses is that the borrowers may have used credit from the Federal Reserve to fund withdrawals by depositors with balances in excess of $100,000 per account. Withdrawals by these depositors would raise the cost of resolving bank failures through methods other than P&A.

While it is not possible to observe uninsured deposits at short intervals, such as weekly or monthly, weekly data on deposits in denominations of $100,000 or more provide an approximation to data on uninsured deposits.[10] Table 8 indicates that for the banks that borrowed in their last year, the mean of the percentage change in large denomination time deposits over their last 52 weeks (negative 34.3 percent) was significantly different from the mean percentage change in other deposits (negative 9.6 percent). Large denomination time deposits of the banks that borrowed from the Fed in their last 26 weeks also declined more rapidly on average than their other deposits over their last 26 weeks (negative 26.2 percent compared to negative 8.6 percent).

This pattern of more rapid declines in large denomination time deposits than in other deposits at borrowers, however, is almost identical to the record for the banks that did not borrow from the Federal Reserve in their last year.[11] Credit from the Federal Reserve does not appear to have facilitated more rapid declines in large denomination time deposits at banks that borrowed from the Federal Reserve. These observations fail to support one of the arguments linking access to credit from the discount window and BIF losses: that declines in uninsured deposits near the time of failure were larger at borrowers than at nonborrowers.

Fed lending to troubled banks may have limited BIF losses by promoting orderly resolutions

Resolution of a failed bank through methods other than liquidation takes some time for the FDIC to arrange. The FDIC has to prepare a package of assets for bidders to examine, allow them time to assess its value, and arrange for transfer of the assets and liabilities to the winning bidder. Resolutions arranged as P&A tend to be less expensive to the FDIC than other types of resolutions.[12] Lending by the Federal Reserve may have allowed some banks to remain open while the FDIC worked to minimize resolutions costs.

One form of evidence that Federal Reserve lending facilitated orderly resolutions would be a lower percentage of liquidations among the banks that borrowed from the Federal Reserve near the time of their failure. Table 9 indicates that percentages of banks resolved by each of the three

[10] Deposit accounts in denominations of exactly $100,000 would be fully insured but included among the accounts in denominations of $100,000 or more.

[11] The t-statistics for differences between the mean growth rates of large denomination deposits at the borrowers and nonborrowers, measured over their last 26 weeks and over their last 52 weeks, are less than 0.2.

[12] See Gilbert (1992).

TABLE 8
DEPOSIT GROWTH IN THE LAST YEAR OF FAILED BANKS: BORROWERS AND NONBORROWERS

	Borrowed from the Fed in their last 52 weeks:	
	Yes	No
Mean percentage change in total deposits in their last:		
26 weeks	−13.0	−10.3
(*t*-statistic for difference in growth rates for borrowers and nonborrowers)	(−2.38)	
52 weeks	−17.3	−11.7
(*t*-statistic for difference in growth rates for borrowers and nonborrowers)	(−2.79)	
Mean percentage change in large time deposits in last 26 weeks	−26.2	−25.6
Mean percentage change in deposits other than large time deposits in last 26 weeks	−8.6	−7.0
t-statistics for differences in means of growth rates of large time deposits and other deposits	−9.01	−5.63
Mean percentage change in large time deposits in last 52 weeks	−34.3	−33.5
Mean percentage change in deposits other than large time deposits in last 52 weeks	−9.6	−6.0
t-statistics for differences in means of growth rates of large time deposits and other deposits	−6.83	−5.51

methods are about the same for the banks that borrowed in their last 13 weeks and those that did not.[13] These observations do not support the argument that Federal Reserve lending near the time of failure facilitated resolutions through methods other than liquidation.

TABLE 9
DISTRIBUTION OF FAILED BANKS BY BORROWINGS AND BY RESOLUTION METHOD

	Borrowed from the Federal Reserve in their last 13 weeks:			
	Yes		No	
Resolution method	Number	Percent	Number	Percent
Purchase and assumption	122	79.2	129	78.7
Transfer of insured deposits	23	14.9	24	14.6
Liquidation	9	5.8	11	6.7
TOTAL	154	100.0	164	100.0

Liquidations of failed banks might have been more common without Federal Reserve credit to troubled banks, since borrowers had more rapid declines in their total deposits in their last year than nonborrowers (Table 8). Without credit from the Federal Reserve, rapid deposit declines might have forced the FDIC to liquidate more banks. This argument, however, does not provide a strong defense for Federal Reserve lending to troubled banks, since the FDIC has authority to use its resources to keep troubled banks open until it can determine the least costly method of resolution. Options available to the FDIC include lending to troubled banks, injecting capital through open bank assistance, and operating failed banks as bridge banks while they search for buyers, as in the case of the Bank of New England.

[13] Results are similar to those in Table 9 if the division between the two groups of banks is based on borrowings in the 26 weeks ending in failure.

6 Conclusions

About 60 percent of the sample of banks that failed in 1985–90 borrowed from the Federal Reserve in their last 52 weeks. In addition, losses of the Bank Insurance Fund (BIF) were larger among the banks that borrowed from the Federal Reserve in their last year. The combination of these observations could be interpreted as evidence that the Federal Reserve engaged in a major operation of sustaining the life of troubled banks that eventually failed, and that the Federal Reserve increased BIF losses substantially by lending to many banks near the time of their failure.

This evidence, however, does not necessarily prove that Fed lending practices *caused* the higher BIF loss ratios of the borrowers. Perhaps the Fed made loans to banks which would have had relatively high BIF loss ratios with or without Fed loans. This article investigates whether evidence supports arguments that Fed lending causing larger BIF losses.

One argument is that Fed credit extended the life of the borrowers, giving troubled banks with little to lose, time to assume additional risk. The evidence does find that borrowers rated CAMEL 5 by government supervisors (in imminent danger of failing) remained open slightly longer than the nonborrowers. Additional evidence, however, indicates that the borrowers tended to have faster declines in total deposits and tended to pay smaller dividends than the nonborrowers. These observations on deposit growth and dividends are consistent with the view that the banks that borrowed from the Fed in their last year were under strict supervision appropriate for troubled banks.

The evidence does not support the argument that borrowers had relatively large declines in their uninsured deposits near the time of their failure, which would have raised the cost of resolution through methods other than purchase and assumption. Large denomination time deposits declined at about the same rates on average for borrowers and nonborrowers over their last 26 to 52 weeks.

It is possible to make an argument that, in many cases, Federal Reserve lending to failed banks helped limit BIF losses. In most cases, borrowings were concentrated in a few weeks just prior to failure. These loans may have allowed the banks to remain in operation, funding deposit withdrawals, while the FDIC worked to arrange resolutions less costly to BIF than liquidations. Evidence on resolution methods in the bank failure cases, however, does not support this interpretation. Percentages of failed bank cases resolved through purchase and assumption, transfer of insured deposits to other banks and liquidation were about the same for borrowers and other failed banks.

Overall, the evidence does not support the argument that Federal Reserve lending to failed banks affected the costs of bank failures to BIF.

References

Garsson, Robert M. 1991. "Gonzalez Says Fed Actions Fueled the Bank Fund's Losses." *American Banker*, June 12.

Gilbert, R. Alton 1991. "Supervision of Undercapitalized Banks: Is There a Case for Change?" Federal Reserve Bank of St. Louis *Review* (May/June): 16–30.

______. 1992. "The Effects of Legislating Prompt Corrective Action on the Bank Insurance Fund." Federal Reserve Bank of St. Louis *Review* (July/August): 3–22.

______. 1993. "Implications of Annual Examinations for the Bank Insurance Fund." Federal Reserve Bank of St. Louis *Review* (January/February): 35–52.

Rehm, Barbara A. 1991. "Lawmakers Attack Fed Lending: Discount Window Called Costly Prop for Shaky Banks." *American Banker*, May 13.

Schwartz, Anna J. 1992. "The Misuse of the Fed's Discount Window." Federal Reserve Bank of St. Louis *Review* (September/ October): 58–69.

Starobin, Paul 1991. "Out the Window." *National Journal* (June 22): 1557–62.

Todd, Walker F. 1988. "Lessons of the Past and Prospects for the Future in Lender of Last Resort Theory." *Proceedings of a Conference on Bank Structure and Competition*, Federal Reserve Bank of Chicago (May 11–13): 533–77.

______. 1991. "Banks are Not Special: the Federal Safety Net and Banking Powers." In Catherine England, ed., *Governing Banking's Future: Markets vs. Regulation*. Boston: Kluwer Academic Publishers: 79–105.

______. 1992. "FDICIA's Discount Window Provisions." Federal Reserve Bank of Cleveland *Economic Commentary* (December 15).

U.S. House of Representatives, Committee on Banking, Finance and Urban Affairs 1991a. *The Failure of the Bank of New England Corporation and Its Affiliate Banks*. Hearing, 102 Cong. 1 Sess. (Government Printing Office).

———. 1991b. *Failure of Madison National Bank* (Hearing). Washington, D.C.: Government Printing Office.

———. 1991c. "An Analysis of Federal Reserve Discount Window Loans to Failed Institutions." 102 Cong. 1 Sess. (June 11).

6

THE SAVINGS AND LOAN DEBACLE: MORAL HAZARD OR MARKET DISASTER?

Gregory A. Lilly

Elon College

1 Introduction

THE SAVINGS AND LOAN (S&L) industry is a good place to study the causes of depository institution failure for two reasons. First, in contrast to commercial banks, the traditional S&L is a relatively simple organization. Second, cause and effect cannot be determined without outcome variation, and the S&L industry provides plenty of variation in failure rates. Figure 1 plots the failure rate of federally insured S&Ls for the years 1934–1988. For comparison, the average failure rate during the four year period 1930–1933 is also shown.[1]

I shall follow tradition and break the recent episode of high failure rates into two parts, "the interest rate squeeze" of 1979–82 and "the debacle" of 1983–88.[2] As shown in Figure 1, the debacle corresponds with the highest average S&L failure rate since the early 1930s. What happened?

Most economists writing on the topic seem to agree on what happened and why. Despite some differences of emphasis and approach, recent books by three of the most active researchers in this field (Barth, 1991, Kane, 1989a, and White, 1991) tell a remarkably consistent story: federal deposit insurance is to blame. According to Barth (1991, p. 48), for instance, "it is important to focus on the specific role played by the structure of the federal deposit insurance system.... An assessment of available evidence

I would like to thank Allin Cottrell, Mike Lawlor, Karen Lilly, Tom Tiemann, and John Wood for their help.

[1] An institution is a failure if it is liquidated by the Federal Savings and Loan Insurance Corporation (FSLIC) or merged by the FSLIC with financial assistance.

[2] These terms are borrowed from White (1991), though I use them in a slightly different way.

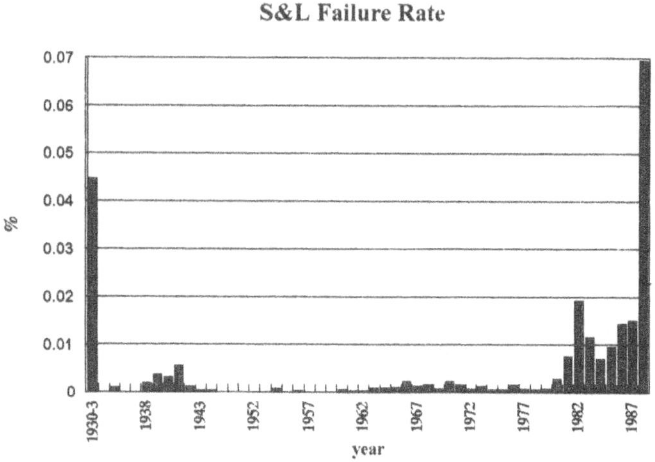

FIGURE 1
Data sources: Barth, Feid, Riedel and Tunis (1989); Barth, Bartholomew and Bradley (1990); Jaffee (1989)

indicates that federal deposit insurance itself is the unifying cause of the savings and loans' misfortunes."[3]

Given its focus on the role of insurance, the Barth–Kane–White explanation ultimately reduces to a story of moral hazard. The term "moral hazard" refers to the situation wherein the insured acts in his own self-interest and alters his behavior in response to the insurance contract, thereby increasing the likelihood that the insurer will incur a loss. Note that there are two necessary conditions for a moral hazard. The first is that the insured has a choice: at the time of the moral hazard, the insured must have the power to act so as to *not* increase the insurer's likelihood of loss. The second is that the insured *knows* that it has a choice. In other words, the word "moral" is there for a reason.

The Barth–Kane–White explanation does not have many challengers. Their story of moral hazard has quickly become professional orthodoxy. Assertions that the S&L debacle is a "classic example of a moral haz-

[3] R. C. Kormendi, V. L. Bernard, S. C. Pirrong, and E. A. Snyder explicitly make a similar claim; see Kormendi *et al.* (1989, p. 5).

ard problem" (Stiglitz, 1993, pp. 160–1) already appear in introductory textbooks. Is this quick acceptance due to incontrovertible empirical evidence in favor of the moral hazard explanation? I do not think so. The primary reason for the rapid ascent of the Barth–Kane–White explanation is, I think, ideological. The S&L debacle cries out for a villain: Who is to blame? In the popular press, this episode has become a story of what happens when government controls are lifted and greed is allowed to run rampant. Filtered through the typically "free-market" worldview of the economics profession, the popular account comes close to the claim that "the market" is to blame for the S&L debacle. Thus the embrace of the moral hazard explanation by economists. Barth, Kane, White, and others stress that although the S&L industry was deregulated, the regulatory structure left behind—that is, federal deposit insurance—was severely flawed. Hence "the market" was not able to work its magic; the remaining regulatory structure gave agents in the S&L industry the opportunity to avoid market discipline. In the words of Kane:

> Conventional wisdom holds that a firm becomes financially weak because of inept management, dishonest behavior, or unfavorable conditions in the markets the firm serves. The weakness we now observe in the [S&L] industry and FSLIC parody this view. Ironically, a root cause of much of the [S&L-] industry crisis is clever management. . . . Managerial cleverness lies in taking advantage of subsidies to risk-taking implicit in the way deposit insurance has been priced and administered by Congress and the FSLIC. (Kane, 1989a, pp. 5–6)

In this paper I wish to question the moral hazard explanation, and then to offer an alternative. I will therefore push the following three theses.

First, I suggest that we rehabilitate the conventional wisdom dismissed by Kane. Thus,

Thesis 1 *An S&L becomes insolvent because of "inept management, dishonest behavior, or unfavorable conditions in the markets the [S&L] serves."*

The conventional wisdom of Thesis 1 can explain the failures during the debacle. It can also explain the rest of Figure 1. The factors of managerial ineptitude and dishonesty operate, at all times, on the S&L industry. But these causes of failure randomly hit only a very small portion of the industry at any given time. If only these two factors are active, the S&L failure rate takes a random walk at a very low level. To explain the two spikes in Figure 1, we need to bring in the third cause of failure. On certain rare occasions there is extreme dislocation in the real estate and savings markets, which affects every S&L. Such dislocation occurred in the 1920s and '30s; it also occurred in the 1970s and '80s. When this third cause of failure becomes active we see a dramatic rise in the S&L failure rate.

We do not need to posit clever exploitation of deposit insurance by S&L managers in order to explain the data. Indeed, as you explore the data further, fundamental flaws in the moral hazard explanation begin to appear. Thus,

Thesis 2 *Deposit insurance is not the unifying cause of the S&L debacle.*

What can replace deposit insurance as the unifying cause? Well, what was the source of the chaotic conditions in the real estate and savings markets during the 1970s and '80s? I propose inflation, both experienced and expected. Thus,

Thesis 3 *The inflation experienced during the 1970s, and expected to continue during the '80s, is the unifying cause of the S&L debacle.*

The structure of the rest of the paper is as follows. Section 2 restates the moral hazard explanation as an explicit causal theory. In order to judge whether or not federal deposit insurance is "the unifying cause" of the S&L debacle, we need to characterize precisely both the moral hazard explanation and the notion of a cause. Section 3 challenges Barth, Kane, and White by developing Thesis 2. Four puzzles are presented which illustrate the poor fit between the moral hazard theory and aggregate data on the S&L industry. While this is not the place to fully develop Thesis 3 (or Thesis 1 for that matter), Section 4 contains a sketch of Thesis 3.

But before I begin, let me applaud the Barth–Kane–White explanation. It represents a bold, creative, and valuable systematization of a very complex reality. Bold systems are easy targets; they are also the only way we advance in our understanding.

2 The moral hazard explanation as a causal theory

"Causation" is here understood as a binary relation between pairs of well-formed formulas in the theory-language. Let the formula $F_i(x)$ stand for the claim that predicate F_i denotes (or applies to) object x. The expression

$$F_1(x) \rightarrow F_2(y)$$

means that *x*'s being denoted by F_1 is a cause of *y*'s being denoted by F_2 (or F_1-events cause F_2-events), and this expression is true if and only if

(1) $P(F_2(y)|F_1(x)) > P(F_2(y)|\text{not-}F_1(x))$, and

(2) $P(F_1(x)|F_2(y)) = P(F_1(x)|\text{not-}F_2(y))$, and

(3) There is no predicate F_3 in the theory-language such that

$$P[(F_2(y)|F_1(x))|F_3(z)] = P(F_2(y)|F_3(z)).$$[4]

Condition 1 says that F_1-events cause F_2-events if and only if $F_2(y)$ is more probable when $F_1(x)$ is true than when $F_1(x)$ is not true. Condition 2 says that the causal relation is antisymmetric—if F_1-events cause F_2-events, then F_2-events cannot cause F_1-events. Condition 3 prevents spurious correlations from being counted as cases of causation. If F_1-events and F_2-events are correlated as in condition 1, but this correlation is due to the fact that F_3-events are a common cause of both F_1 and F_2 events, condition 3 rules that this should not be taken as a case of causation of F_2 by F_1.

Theory construction

Constructing a causal theory involves two tasks—determining the theory-language, and determining the relevant causes.

Suppose the domain of reference for the moral hazard theory-language consists of just one type of object: S&Ls. The variables in the moral hazard theory (*x*, *y*, *z*, etc.) therefore range over the set of S&Ls. The following formulas illustrate the primitive 1-place predicates of the theory-language.

DI(*x*)	*x* offers deposit insurance and pays premiums that are unrelated to the risk of their portfolio.
IIR(*x*)	*x* faces interest rates that generally increased from 1977 to 1981.
LNW(*x*)	*x* has low net worth by 1982.
DRG(*x*)	*x* undergoes deregulation from 1980 to 1982.
STK(*x*)	*x* has stockholders.
IRT(*x*)	*x* engages in imprudent risk-taking.

[4] This definition of cause is found in Glymour *et al.* (1987, pp. 19–20).

More complex well-formed formulas are built by using the logical constants (and, not, and or) to concatenate the simple well-formed formulas.

Identifying the appropriate causal relations is the next step, recalling that in this section I am trying to state, as best I can, the Barth–Kane–White moral hazard explanation. Criticism will come in Section 3.

Interest rates, deposit insurance, and net worth

The traditional S&L specialized: it earned profits by attracting deposits from savers and then investing those funds in long-term, fixed-rate residential mortgages. Since the S&L industry was seen as a means of encouraging home ownership (a national goal, especially after World War II), its niche became a protected territory. The Federal Home Loan Bank (FHLB) system provided emergency liquidity during credit crunches. Owing to Regulation Q, S&L deposit rates were constrained by a ceiling, yet S&Ls were allowed to pay higher deposit rates than commercial banks. And in response to the experience of bank runs during the Depression, the FSLIC was created to guarantee the safety of S&L deposits, making the S&L savings account a more attractive investment.

For much of the postwar period, the industry was highly profitable. Meanwhile, few noticed that S&L intermediation—borrowing short to lend long—embodies interest rate risk.[5] A long-term, fixed-rate mortgage with an option to prepay can be viewed as a coupon bond with a known monthly coupon and an unknown maturity date and face value. Whenever interest rates rise, the market value of such assets falls.

Figures 2 and 3 show the postwar patterns of both long and short interest rates, using John Tukey's method of running medians (Tukey, 1977, pp. 210–12).[6] "The rough" is calculated by subtracting "the smooth" from

[5] A notable exception was Paul Samuelson (1945, 1969). Strangely, neither the industry nor the regulatory authorities developed Samuelson's insight. In response to a warning from Dwight Jaffee (1976) concerning maturity mismatches, an S&L executive said that "it is not completely clear as to the extent to which variations in maturity mix contribute to profitability problems in the savings and loan industry," and went on to question Jaffee's methodology (Roessner, 1976, pp. 105–6).

[6] Not only is this method a simple way to smooth, it also has several nice properties. First, the method uses a robust estimator of central location, the median. Second, few arbitrary decisions need be made by the researcher. The procedure is to take the original time series and compute the median for every three consecutive data points. Now compare the transformation (the medians of every three consecutive data points) with the original series. If they differ then do the same transformation (compute medians for every three consecutive data points) on the transformation. The algorithm terminates, yielding the

the actual data; thus the rough depicts the deviations from the general regularities.[7] Notice, in each case, the dramatic increase in interest rates during the period 1977–81; also notice the high volatility (as suggested by the rough) of interest rates in 1980 and 1981.

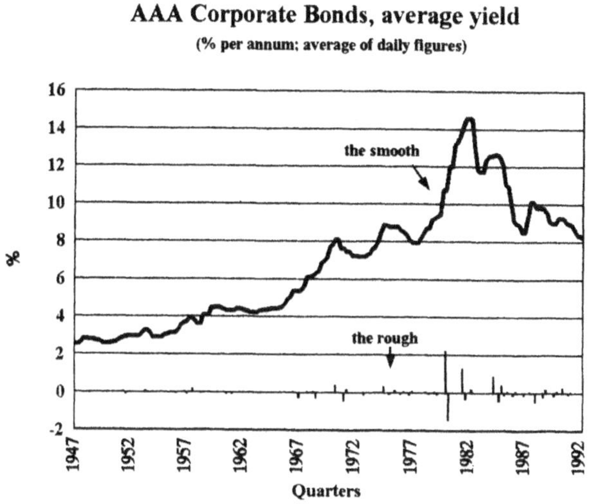

FIGURE 2
(Percent per annum; quarterly averages of daily rates)
Data source: Moody's Bond Survey

Given the form of S&L intermediation and the interest rate patterns of the late 1970s and early 1980s, it is no wonder that by 1982 an estimated 95 percent of S&Ls had either zero or negative market net worth (Brewer, 1989). When interest rates rise, costs—payments to depositors—rise faster than revenues—inflow from the mortgage portfolio. Profits and retained earnings take a beating.

The causal relation between high interest rates and low net worth is clear enough. How does deposit insurance fit in? The profitability of S&L

smooth, when the output of the transformation is equal to its input. Hence there is a "natural" stopping-point with Tukey's running medians: you smooth until it makes no more difference.

[7] Thus the actual data in Figures 2 and 3 can be recovered by just adding the rough to the smooth.

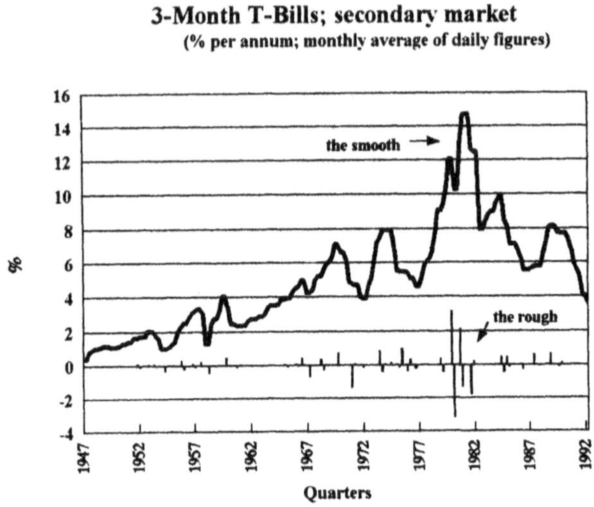

FIGURE 3

Data source: Federal Reserve Bulletin

intermediation is highly dependent on the course of interest rates, yet predicting interest rates is perilous at best. Why would agents who are risk-averse borrow short to lend long? Typically, the agents doing the S&L intermediation are betting with other people's money, but what about the agents funding the bets, i.e. the depositors? Since their funds are protected by deposit insurance, they have little reason to worry, even though they too are risk-averse. If the bets made by their S&L go sour, the FSLIC will reimburse the lost deposits later.

The predicate LNW has a time-aspect; it can only be true of 1982 S&Ls with low net worth. In a world of risk-averse agents and no deposit insurance, institutions engaging in S&L intermediation without sufficient net worth will not live long; their depositors need assurance. So if deposit insurance had not existed, the debacle would not have occurred in 1983–88. The massive failures would have occurred earlier, and there would have been fewer S&Ls with low net worth in 1982 simply because there would have been fewer S&Ls in 1982. Given the moral hazard story, the traditional S&L is not a viable organization in a free market composed of risk-averse agents. Deposit insurance is required to guarantee the very existence of an S&L; ergo the existence of deposit insurance (DI) is a cause of any 1982 S&L with low net worth.

To conclude the first stage of the explanation, deposit insurance and increasing interest rates are joint causes of low net worth as of 1982, or

$$\mathrm{DI}(x)\ \&\ \mathrm{IIR}(x) \rightarrow \mathrm{LNW}(x).$$

The mechanism producing this causal relation is based on two claims:

MH1 *Organizations engaging in S&L intermediation lose when interest rates increase for an extended period of time.*

MH2 *Agents and organizations are risk-averse.*

Organizational structure, deregulation, and risk-taking

Our next challenge is to understand how imprudent risk-taking (IRT) can be caused in a system where risk-aversion rules. The key, says White (1991, pp. 74–81) is to see how the *opportunities*, *capabilities* and *incentives* for S&L risk-taking increased at the beginning of the debacle.

Congress supplied the new opportunities. Concerned about the industry's very survival, Congress passed legislation (the Depository Institutions Deregulation and Monetary Control Act of 1980 and the Garn–St. Germain Act of 1982) which granted S&Ls greater power to manage their assets and liabilities. The hope was that S&Ls would diversify away from interest-rate risk by increasing their liability maturities and decreasing their asset maturities. The danger was that they would abuse their new powers by pursuing new activities that were previously outlawed. Thus DRG is a cause of IRT:

$$\mathrm{DRG}(x) \rightarrow \mathrm{IRT}(x),$$

and the mechanism producing this causal relation is based on this claim:

MH3 *In the early 1980s, S&Ls were given more choices; with these new choices they could do right (prudently diversify), or they could do wrong (either imprudently increase the scale of their old risk-taking, or imprudently engage in new kinds of risk-taking).*

To see how the incentives for S&L risk-taking increased in the early 1980s, we first need to recognize the difference between stock S&Ls

(STK(x)) and mutual S&Ls. A stock S&L is organized like any other modern corporation. The stockholders have sole claim on the residual cash flow of the organization. An S&L stockholder has limited liability, and is free to buy more shares, or sell currently owned shares. A particular stockholder may or may not be involved in the day-to-day affairs of the S&L, so a problematic ownership/control dichotomy can exist for any stock S&L.

Mutual S&Ls are quite different. According to Nicols

> a distinguishing characteristic of the mutual is the apparent omnipotence of management, which rarely accounts for its actions and policies as it must in the conventional stock corporation. Though the saver provides the funds which the association lends, he owns only his savings. Referred to as a member, he typically surrenders his proxy to management upon the opening of the account. Because there are no association owners to whom management must report, there are likewise no owners to whom profits or net earnings are distributed. (Nicols, 1972, p. 1)

Furthermore,

> the management of the [mutual] S&L association is only threatened in his position of complete autocracy by threats to solvency. The consequence is that management avoids undue exposure to risk. Risk increases vulnerability and is a threat to maintenance of control. (Nicols, 1972, p. 180)

Thus to the extent that stockholders do control their institutions, we should expect stock S&Ls to take more risks than mutuals. Stockholders want a decent return, and the associated risk can be offset via the diversification of equity holdings. Mutual S&L managers, who completely control their S&Ls, have no such luxury. Too many risks may lead to insolvency, which in turn may lead to the unemployment line. STK is therefore a cause of IRT:

$$\text{STK}(x) \rightarrow \text{IRT}(x),$$

and the mechanism producing this causal relation is based on this claim:

MH4 *Given their organizational structure, stock S&Ls take more risks (imprudent or not) than mutual S&Ls.*

While stock S&Ls have always had an incentive to take on risk, the interest rate squeeze produced another incentive. With net worth wiped out in the early 1980s, most S&Ls were technically insolvent. With little or nothing to lose, owners of stock S&Ls had a clear incentive to bet on long shots. If they lost, their investment would remain worthless, while the FSLIC would reimburse the depositors. If the stockholders won, their S&L would regain solvency, and they would pocket all the profit. So LNW is also a cause of IRT:

$$\text{LNW}(x) \rightarrow \text{IRT}(x),$$

and the mechanism producing this causal relation is based on the claim:

MH5 *When near or at insolvency, S&Ls—both mutual and stock—take more risks (imprudent or not); they have little or nothing to lose.*

We have talked about opportunities and incentives. What about capabilities? At the beginning of the debacle S&Ls had both the legal right and the incentive to increase their risk-taking, but did they have the power to do so? This is where deposit insurance fits in. The above-mentioned deregulation also enhanced S&L capabilities by making their savings deposits a more attractive investment. Two changes were made: the maximum insured deposit amount was increased from $40,000 to $100,000; and regulation Q was dismantled, allowing S&Ls to pay market rates in order to attract deposits. After these changes, the S&Ls had the power to accomplish the legal risk-taking that they wanted. Insured savings deposits would provide the funding no matter how imprudent the risks. Hence,

MH6 *S&Ls can attract unlimited funding, regardless of their portfolio risk, by offering insured deposits at (or above) market rates.*

To sum up, on the moral hazard explanation S&L failures are interpreted as the result of imprudent risk-taking. The challenge is to explain how imprudent risk-taking can occur when there is universal risk-aversion: the challenge is met via the six claims set out above as MH1–MH6. These factors produce the causal relations depicted in Figure 4.

Note the special role of deposit insurance in this explanation. Deposit insurance (DI) and the increasing interest rates of 1977–81 (IIR) combine to form the ultimate cause of imprudent risk-taking (IRT). But whereas interest rate levels are not controllable, the form of deposit insurance offered

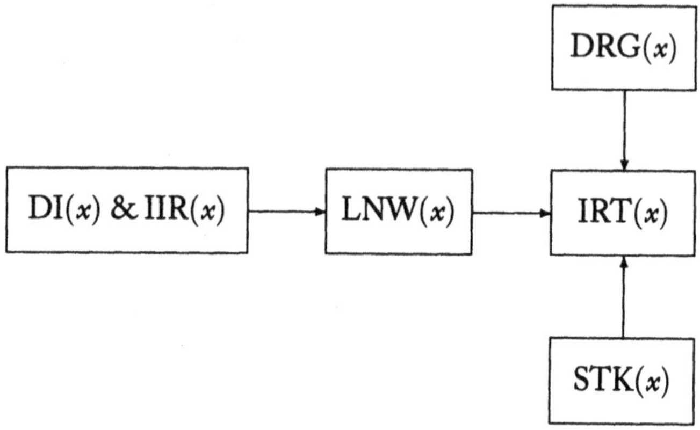

FIGURE 4: CAUSALITY IN THE MORAL HAZARD THEORY

is. Although deregulation (DRG), stock-organization (STK), and low net worth (LNW) are all contributing causes of imprudent risk-taking, without deposit insurance the S&Ls would have lacked the capacity to engage in IRT.

In this account the two necessary conditions for a moral hazard are satisfied. Deregulation gave the S&L industry the opportunity and capability to diversify. It was understood by all that the S&L industry needed to do a better job of avoiding interest rate risk. So at the beginning of the debacle, S&Ls had a choice, and they knew it!

3 FOUR PUZZLES FOR THE MORAL HAZARD EXPLANATION

My analysis is (I hope) in the tradition of Tukey's exploratory data analysis (see Tukey, 1977; Mosteller and Tukey, 1977). Since Tukey's ideas are not standard items in the econometrician's toolbox, I should say a word about them.

I will tend to emphasize data visualization, and de-emphasize probabilistic inference. Discovering patterns is our goal, rather than modeling randomness. Hence there will be more graphing and fitting, and less confidence intervals and hypothesis testing. Almost all of the fitting will employ linear regression, and much of the graphing will employ basic plots. The one plot that may be unfamiliar is Tukey's boxplot.

Figure 5 provides an example of three boxplots. Each plot is formed from a random sample of 200 data points, and each sample comes from a different distribution. One distribution is Gaussian with a mean of 0 and a standard deviation of 2.[8] Another is Gaussian with mean 0 and standard deviation 4. The third is derived by multiplying the Poisson with a mean of 1 by a uniformly distributed random variable (*a*) that takes a value between 0 and 3.

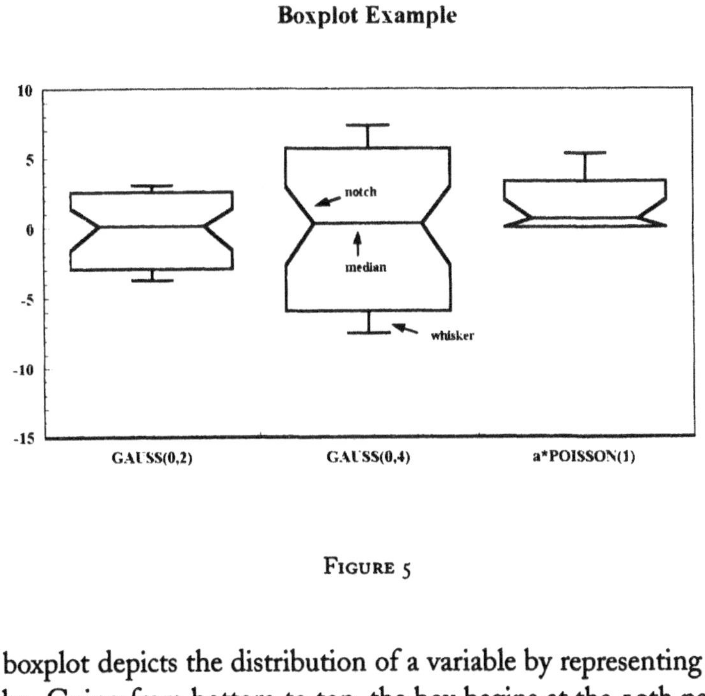

FIGURE 5

A boxplot depicts the distribution of a variable by representing its percentiles. Going from bottom to top, the box begins at the 10th percentile and ends at the 90th percentile. The horizontal line inside the box indicates the median. The notch in the box begins at the 25th percentile, or lower quartile Q1, and ends at the 75th percentile, or upper quartile Q2. The whiskers connect the box to the 5th and 95th percentiles.

[8] Tukey uses "Gaussian" rather than "normal" because after a lifetime of looking at real data he has concluded that real data are rarely normally distributed. Deviations from normality are important and frequently hard to detect (Mosteller and Tukey, 1977, ch. 1).

With one glance at a boxplot you can determine the location, spread and shape of the distribution in question. To determine location, find the line representing the median. To determine spread, notice either the height of the box, which will be the distance bounding the middle 80 percent of the data, or the height of the notch, which will be the interquartile range Q3–Q1. (In Figure 5, compare the boxplot of GAUSS(0,2) with the boxplot of GAUSS(0,4) in terms of box and notch heights.) To determine shape, notice if the median cuts the box into roughly equal parts, or if the whiskers are of roughly equal length. If so, then the distribution is symmetric, like the Gaussian examples; if not, the distribution is skewed, like the Poisson example in Figure 5.

Aggregation and behavior

Before developing the critique of the moral hazard explanation, let me justify an assumption I will make. I will talk as if the S&L industry (or some aggregate portion of it) is choosing or acting. Usually that is invalid since an aggregation cannot choose or act; only the appropriate components can. But if all the appropriate components are alike, the aggregate will behave just like the components. I think the assumption that all the appropriate components are alike is a good one in relation to the S&L industry. For evidence that the desire for uniformity was a strong force in the postwar S&L industry, consider the following.

> In general, the S&L business desires uniformity along sound lines. A greater consciousness of unity is present in the business now than ever before. There is also a feeling that every institution gains if the public finds that it can expect the same type of operation and same service from S&L associations whether they are across the street from each other, in different cities, or in different regions. A conviction has arisen that, if the S&L service is to achieve the popularity which it merits, it must represent essentially the same thing to all people. (Bodfish and Theobald, 1938, pp. 616–7)

These authors go on to talk about the role of conventions and textbooks in fostering uniformity in the S&L industry.

Puzzle 1: Why did most of the stock S&Ls refrain?

The moral hazard explanation seems very plausible; indeed it explains too much! The causes LNW and DRG were operating on just about every stock S&L in 1982, yet relatively few engaged in imprudent risk-taking. As White notes

> the legislative acts of 1980–1982 and the economic environment of the [S&L] industry at this time greatly enhanced the opportunities for [S&Ls] to take risks, their capabilities for funding those risk-taking opportunities, and their incentives for embarking on this strategy.... In retrospect, it is remarkable that so few [S&Ls]—numbering "only" in the hundreds—embarked on the risk-taking strategy that would lead to their demise ... and that most of the industry refrained. (White, 1991, p. 81)

We may conclude that either the moral hazard is incomplete—there is an important unidentified cause that prevented most stock S&Ls from taking imprudent risks beginning in 1982—or it is unsatisfactory.

Puzzle 2: Why did so many mutuals fail?

The problem just broached also arises with mutual S&Ls: Why did some of them engage in IRT, while most did not? But this question is not as damaging to the logic of the moral hazard explanation as the parallel question concerning stocks, since mutual organizations do not have the incentive structure presumed in the moral hazard account. If Nicols (1972) is right about the degree of risk aversion on the part of mutuals, the more important problem for the moral hazard explanation is that so many of these institutions failed during the debacle.[9]

One response might be that even mutuals will do IRT if their insolvency is about to be uncovered. Kane (1989b, p. 39) remarks that even the most conservative football coach will tell his quarterback to throw desperate "bombs" once their team is down by two touchdowns with three minutes left. Nevertheless, during the debacle many S&Ls that were insolvent by standard accounting measures were, by regulatory decision, kept open (White, 1991, pp. 82–7). This record of forbearance implies that the net worth regulations used by the FHLBB and FSLIC were soft and negotiable.

Given the choice, would a mutual S&L on the edge of insolvency take imprudent risks, or lobby for forbearance? I submit that most mutual S&Ls

[9] During the debacle there was never a year in which the percentage of failures that were mutuals fell below 50 percent. Meanwhile, the percentage of S&Ls that were mutuals fell from 76 percent in 1983 to 56 percent in 1988 (Barth, Bartholomew, and Bradley, 1989).

would consider think the latter option less costly. Now surely the regulators were smart enough to grant forbearance only at a price, namely, that the S&L agree to "good faith" tests (White, 1991, p. 139), which presumably means that the S&L would agree to forego imprudent risks as defined by the conventional wisdom of the time.

Would this forbearance "contract" be effective in mitigating the mutual S&L's incentive toward IRT? Let us return to Kane's football analogy. Suppose that when a team starts to play desperation football, the referees have the power to turn off the clock and postpone, indefinitely, the game's end. Would the losing coach have the incentive to continue his go-for-broke strategy? Throwing "bombs" with a poor chance of success is now costly; such a strategy wastes the opportunity to take the newly granted time and develop the slow but generally productive strategy of field position.

The loan equivalent of a football "bomb" is a loan with a high interest rate (due to a hefty risk premium) and a substantial up-front fee that the S&L can immediately record as income. This kind of loan looks good if the S&L needs the up-front fee now to ensure that it will be a going concern tomorrow. But mutuals lack any sort of stockholder pressure for net income, and with forbearance on the part of regulators there is little outside pressure for an immediate increase in net income. Thus the time horizon lengthens, and default risk regains its prominence.

With time pressure reduced, a risk-averse coach has less reason to resort to desperate play-calling. With regulatory pressure reduced, a risk-averse mutual S&L has less reason to resort to desperate risk-taking.

Puzzle 3: Did the industry engage in intentional IRT?

What exactly is imprudent risk-taking? The phrase itself implies that not all risk-taking is folly. Perhaps a good candidate for IRT would be a risk that lacks any sort of compensatory returns. Did the S&L industry take uncompensated risks during the debacle?

Let us follow tradition and define risk in terms of variability in the rate of return on net worth. What was the actual risk–return tradeoff experienced by the S&L industry, up to and including the debacle? Let us take the period 1950–1988 as our domain of observation. We begin by forming 35 rolling five-year periods: 1950–54, 1951–1955, and so on. Now for each year calculate the rate of return, and then compute the mean return for each five-year period. These means are measures of expected returns. In addition, for each five-year period calculate the standard deviation of the rate of return. These standard deviations are measures of total business risk. We expect, given risk aversion, to see a positively sloped curve in risk–return space. But Figure 6 shows that the S&L industry faced a negatively sloped risk–return tradeoff during the period 1950–1988. The linear regression confirms the strength of this relationship.

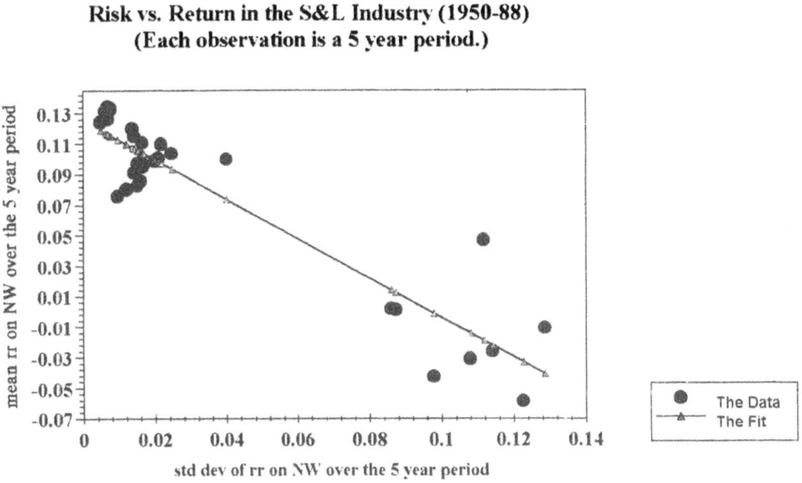

FIGURE 6
(rr on NW = rate of return on net worth)
Regression line: $\hat{y} = 0.125 - 1.288x$, $R^2 = .855$

It looks as if the S&L industry did in fact take some uncompensated risks. But when? Let us re-graph the data so that time is shown, as in Figure 7. Notice the abrupt change in pattern from the late 1970s onward—this later period appears to be a time of uncompensated risk-taking.

There are (at least) three fundamentally different ways of explaining Figures 6 and 7, two of them involving moral hazard. One moral hazard approach emphasizes (i) the traditionally strong mutual character of the industry, (ii) managerial preeminence over stockholders, and (iii) the industry tendency toward managerial uniformity. In this account stockholder pressure is weak and the explanatory burden is borne by the claim that once

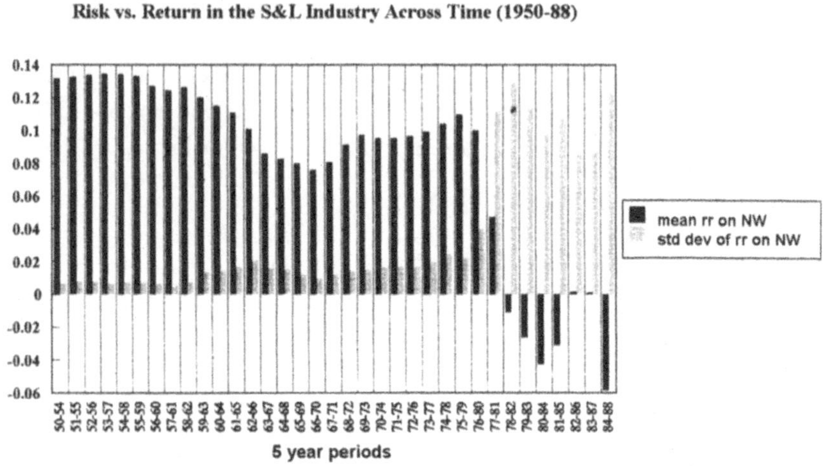

FIGURE 7

low net worth began to become a problem in the late 1970s the industry had nothing to lose by taking wild gambles.

Can we generate a graph like Figure 6 if we assume the industry went for broke during the debacle? Let us try a simple numerical example. Suppose the S&L industry's choice set consists of a safe option and a gambling option, each having four possible outcomes. The probabilities of the outcomes and the corresponding payoffs are presumed known. The safe option is:

\$0.3 billion	\$0.5 billion	\$0.7 billion	\$1 billion
(.2)	(.4)	(.3)	(.1)

where the payoffs are on the first row and the corresponding probabilities on the second. The gambling option is:

−\$2 billion	−\$1 billion	\$0 billion	\$6 billion
(.5)	(.2)	(.2)	(.1)

In terms of both risk and return, the gambling option is inferior to the safe option.[10] So why would a risk-averse industry, ruled by managers focused on survival, choose the gamble? Maybe the industry believes that an immediate \$6 billion injection to net worth is the only way to satisfy regulatory demands and insure at least temporary survival?

A simulation based on this example can produce a graph very much like Figure 6. Assume 38 years of choices between the safe and gambling options. For the first 32 years, the safe option is chosen because of tight regulatory control over choice and sufficient industry net worth. For the final six years, the gambling option is chosen because of lax regulatory control over choice and insufficient industry net worth, combined with strong regulatory pressure quickly to raise that net worth. When the resulting artificial data are processed as described above, they yield Figure 8.

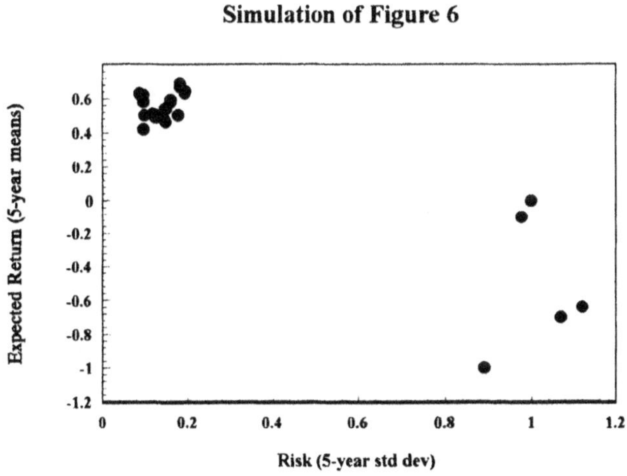

FIGURE 8

Thus the first type of moral hazard explanation can account for the shape of Figure 6. The explanation, however, conflicts with the facts. As already

[10] The expected value and standard deviation are \$0.57 billion and \$0.199 billion respectively for the safe option, and −\$0.6 billion and \$2.62 billion respectively for the gambling option.

noted, the FSLIC and FHLBB granted forbearance to the industry during the debacle. If managers and mutuals control the industry and they know the authorities are willing to give them time to recover, why would they—given their risk-aversion and desire to preserve the organization—continue the self-defeating strategy of going for broke?

A second possible moral hazard account emphasizes the role of S&L stockholders, assuming they exerted strong pressure during the debacle. Given their opportunities for diversification elsewhere, S&L stockholders should be risk-neutral. With their net worth already wiped out by the beginning of the debacle, stockholders would see no downside to exploiting forbearance and deposit insurance by accumulating insured deposits in order to invest in the gamble. If, in the numerical example above, the two outcomes resulting in losses are modified to reflect the zero payoffs the stockholders would actually face, the expected value of the gambling option is greater than that of the safe option. Risk-neutral S&L stockholders would therefore push for the gamble.

Before we test the latter account, let me offer a third explanation of Figures 6 and 7. This alternative is compatible with forbearance, does not utilize moral hazard, and makes no reference to deposit insurance.

While a negative correlation of risk and return is uncommon in the world of finance, the phenomenon regularly occurs in strategic management. In 1980, Edward Bowman took the 85 industries covered by the *Value Line Investment Survey* (comprising 1,572 companies), and computed for each company, over a nine-year period (1968–76), its mean rate of return and the corresponding standard deviation. His conclusion was that "fifty-six [industries] support the hypothesis of a negative risk–return correlation, twenty-one refute it, and eight are ties" (Bowman, 1980, p. 20). The most likely reason for the negative correlation is that good management is able to achieve both higher returns *and* less variability (Bowman, 1980, p. 25).

Suppose we accept Bowman's idea that in many industries strategic management skills are distributed along a quality index. Figures 6 and 7 then say that for the S&L industry as a whole, the distribution of strategic management skills varied across time. In particular, Figure 7 suggests that good S&L management was very rare during the 1980s. The conventional wisdom that S&Ls become insolvent because of "inept management, dishonest behavior, or unfavorable conditions in the markets the [S&L] serves" (Thesis 1 above) gives us a plausible reason why that was so. With unfavorable conditions in savings and real estate markets during the 1980s, it was much tougher to demonstrate good managerial skills. The regulators knew this and were willing to be patient *if* the S&Ls agreed not to take advantage of that patience. According to this alternative account, unfavorable market conditions made it difficult to know the right probabilities and payoffs. The gamble was not intentionally chosen, for no one understood it as such, *ex ante*.

Puzzle 4: Did deposit insurance provide a capability during the debacle?

We have two accounts which are compatible with the fact of forbearance and are able to explain the risk–return data. One is a moral hazard account which holds that insured deposits gave the industry a powerful capability that stockholders were anxious to use. The other talks about unfavorable market conditions and makes no mention of deposit insurance. Can evidence concerning S&L deposits during the debacle help us choose between the two accounts?

If one has a capability, one has the power to do X *when one wants to do X*. A capability implies some kind of control. In this section I want to argue that the typical S&L had little, if any, control over its insured deposits; thus any capability supplied by deposit insurance is weak, at best.

A traditional S&L "must have a dollar of cash on hand to make a dollar of loans" (Kendall, 1962, p. 87). What matters for the S&Ls' ability to grant loans is their net new deposits (NND)—defined by the FHLBB as "new deposits received less deposits withdrawn." One striking fact about the S&L debacle is the behavior of NND over both time and location, as shown in the boxplots of Figure 9. For geographical variation the S&L industry was divided into the twelve FHLB districts, and for eight years the aggregate NND in each district is collected and compared. Two interesting patterns emerge. There is extreme positive skewness in NND at the beginning of the debacle; and the median NND was quite low at all observations—the median is positive only three times, and the highest median value (in 1983) is around $1.8 billion. This $1.8 billion is the total of net new deposits in the Cincinnati FHLB district during 1983, when there were 370 S&Ls in that district. Figure 9 does not look like the picture of an industry shamelessly exploiting insured deposits for its funding.

So where was the funding coming from, if not from new insured deposits? One source that became increasingly important during the later stages of the debacle (when stock S&Ls become more prevalent) was what

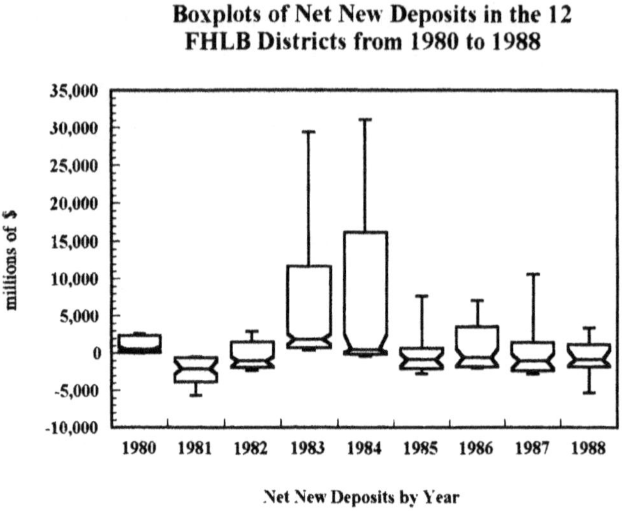

FIGURE 9
Data source: FHLBB

the FHLBB calls "other borrowed money," a category which includes "all borrowings other than FHLBank advances, principally reverse repurchase agreements, mortgage-backed bonds issued, commercial bank loans, commercial paper issued, overdrafts in transaction accounts, and all other borrowings."

Figure 10 shows just how important borrowed money (BM) became relative to NND. For the industry as a whole the sum of net increases in BM over 1980–88 was $155.63 billion, while the sum of NND was $94 billion for the same period. Why did S&Ls turn to other borrowed money if they could get cheaper funding through insured deposits? I suggest that they learned from experience that they could not control their insured deposits during the 1980s, and hence decided to pay the price for a more controllable funding source.

Consider the differential between the cost of funding through insured deposits and the cost of funding from other market sources. Let us define the deposit rate differential (DRD) as the difference between the average S&L deposit rate and a weighted average of market rates, where the weights

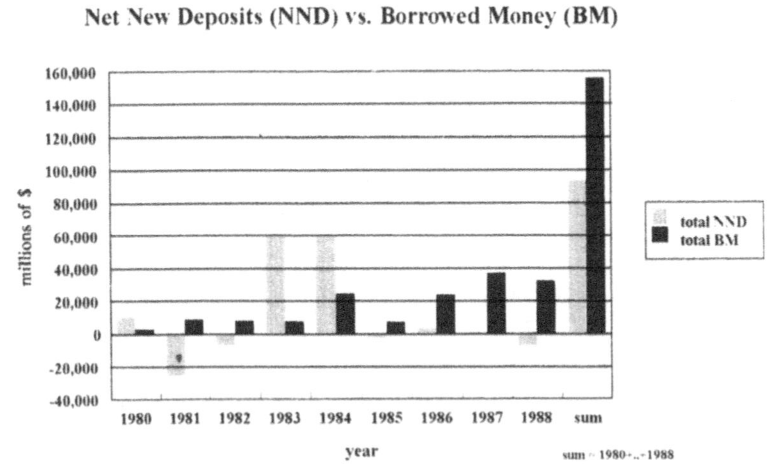

FIGURE 10
Data source: FHLBB

reflect the composite maturity on the liability side of the typical S&L balance sheet. Specifically, let

$$\text{DRD}_t = \text{S\&L deposit rate}_t - (0.3 \times \text{CBR}_t + 0.7 \times \text{CPR}_t)$$

where CBR is the corporate bond rate and CPR is the commercial paper rate.[11]

The behavior of DRD over time is graphed in Figure 11, which shows that S&L deposits are generally cheaper than market funding. In one year (1986) S&L deposit rates consistently beat the market index, yet this positive differential did not correspond with any great surge in NND, as can be seen in Figure 10. And note that while Figure 11 shows DRD becoming more and more negative in 1987–88, Figure 10 shows that BM was replacing NND at that time.

[11] The 1984 *Savings Institution Sourcebook* (published by the U.S. League of Savings) gives an average liability portfolio derived by aggregating FHLBB monthly supervisory reports. About 60 percent of the liabilities are either on demand or have a maturity of less

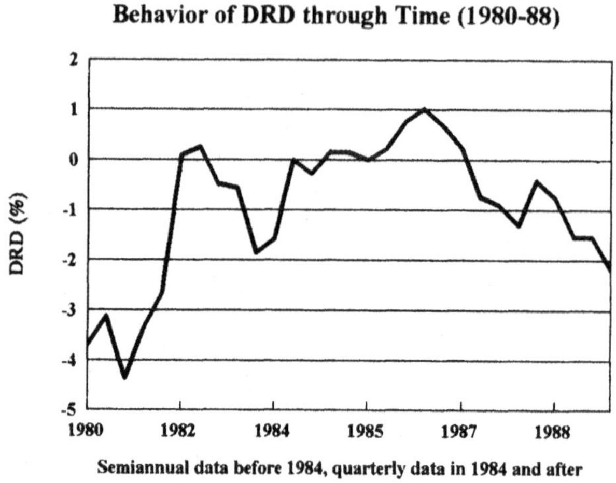

FIGURE 11:
Data sources: FHLBB, Moody's Bond Survey, *Federal Reserve Bulletin*

For further evidence that S&Ls had little control over their insured deposits see Figure 12, a scatterplot showing how changes in net new deposits are related to changes in the deposit rate differential. Also included in Figure 12 is a linear regression fit. The statistically significant relationship between these variables is as expected, but the relationship is far from close. In addition to substantial variability, the expected relationship fails to hold in eight of the 27 observations. Indeed, there are four periods in which DRD increases while NND is negative. Why would S&Ls intentionally choose to both increase their deposit costs and create a net deposit outflow? The evidence suggests that S&Ls lacked control over their insured deposits. This in turn implies that deposit insurance did not supply a capability to the industry.[12] Hence the second moral hazard account of the data shown in Figures 6 and 7 lacks support.

To sum up this section, four problems with the moral hazard explanation have been identified.

than two and a half years. 28 percent of the liabilities have a maturity greater than two and a half years. The remainder are $100,000-minimum CDs with unstated maturities.

[12] An uncontrollable capability is an oxymoron.

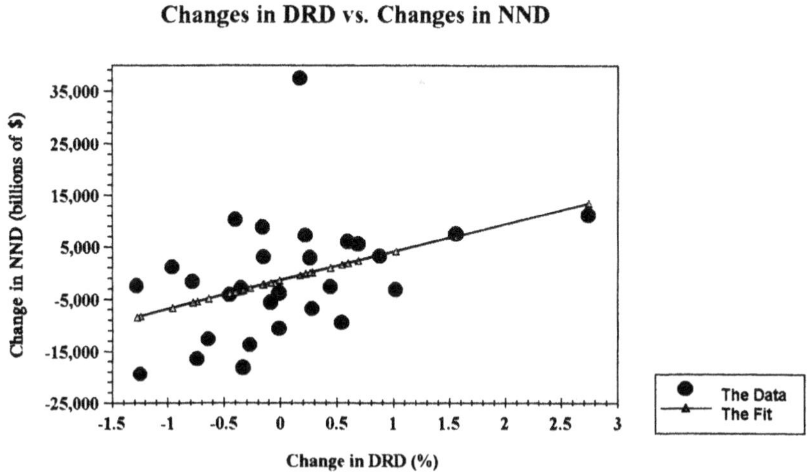

FIGURE 12

Regression line: $\hat{y} = -1390 + 5438x$, $R^2 = .162$, $t_x = 2.25$

(1) At least one proponent of the theory admits surprise at the relative lack of imprudent risk-taking during the debacle. It is especially puzzling that most stock S&Ls refrained from IRT. To fix this failing by assuming that the IRT was done by randomly distributed "bad apples" is to give up the moral hazard logic.

(2) There is no explanation of why so many mutual S&Ls failed. The structure, temper, and skills of the mutuals were just not conducive to intentional IRT. It is especially hard to understand why a mutual S&L would want to take imprudent risks when authorities were willing to exercise forbearance.

(3) If IRT is defined as *uncompensated* risk-taking, then IRT did occur at the industry level during the late 1970s and 1980s. And one can construct an account in which IRT is compatible with forbearance, but the price of this explanation is that the uncompensated risk-taking cannot be viewed as intentional. But moral hazard needs intent!

(4) The data say that insured deposits did not provide the powerful capability assumed by the stockholder-driven moral hazard explanation.

4 An alternative: inflation as the unifying cause

Two premises provide the foundation for an alternative explanation of the debacle. First, there was an implicit contract between the S&L industry and its regulators during the debacle.

P1 *The FHLBB and the FSLIC agreed to provide forbearance if the S&Ls promised not to intentionally increase the expected loss of the FSLIC. Most S&Ls tried their best to uphold that promise.*

As Figures 6 and 7 show, there was a lot of variability in rates of return for the industry during the late 1970s and '80s. This high variability was not, however, a sign of intentional risk-taking; rather it was due to a new environment that the S&Ls could neither control nor accurately predict. The crucial component of this new environment was actual and expected inflation. Thus the second premise is the statement set out as Thesis 3 above:

P2 *The actual and expected inflation of the 1970s and '80s is the ultimate cause of the high S&L failure rates during the debacle.*

Need I remind you of just how different inflation was during the 1970s?[13] Figure 13 gives a picture of inflation, measured as the quarterly change in the natural log of the CPI. Once again Tukey's method of running medians is used to smooth the time series. Figure 14 presents boxplots for inflation over various sub-periods in the postwar era. There are no apparent patterns with regard to spread and shape, but from 1953 to 1982 there is a definite trend toward an increasing location. Note in particular the difference between the boxplot for 1977–82 and that for 1983–88. I believe that few could have predicted the latter boxplot given the previous five plots in Figure 14. Surely most agents expected inflation over 1983–88 to be significantly higher than it was.

The challenge in this section is to show how premise P1 is consistent with the massive number of failures that occurred during the debacle. Here

[13] For evidence that 1970s inflation stumped even the best and brightest, see Solow (1979).

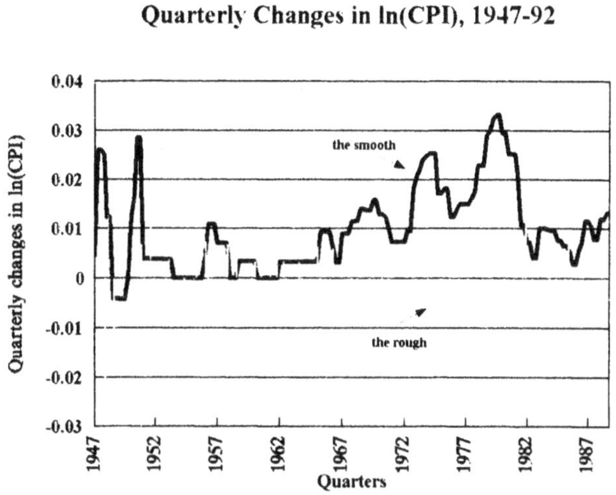

FIGURE 13
Data source: U.S. Dept. of Labor

is my story. By 1982 everyone in the industry, including regulators, was convinced that inflation was dangerous. In an attempt to protect themselves against an inflation which all expected to continue, S&Ls changed, with regulatory blessings, their standard operating procedures. While the changes seemed prudent at the time, they subsequently *forced* some S&Ls into the acquisition of non-traditional assets such as commercial mortgages, land loans, and direct equity investments, assets the holding of which we now know to be correlated with a relatively high propensity to fail (Barth, Bartholomew and Bradley, 1989; Barth, Bartholomew and Labich, 1989; White, 1991).

How inflation caused non-traditional lending

It probably occurred to most S&Ls in 1982 that the inflation they were experiencing had some sort of negative impact on their rates of return. But how could they protect their portfolios against continuing inflation? Figures 15 and 16 suggest one way in which inflation was related to rates of return during the 1970s and early '80s. The mortgage spread, i.e., the

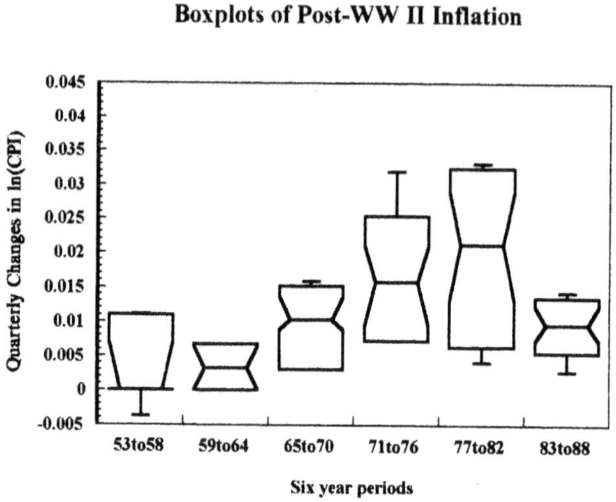

FIGURE 14
Data source: U.S. Dept. of Labor

difference between the average yield on the S&L mortgage portfolio and the average cost of funding it, is positively correlated with the rate of return on net worth, while increases in inflation tend (with a time lag) to reduce mortgage spreads.[14] The relationship between the mortgage spread and the rate of return on net worth is strong (Figure 15). The same cannot be said of the relationship between current inflation changes and later mortgage spread changes (Figure 16). Is the latter relationship causal, is it a spurious correlation, or do we have mere randomness masquerading as a pattern?

The data points labeled A and Z in Figure 16 are the observations that are the most contrary to the estimated inverse relationship between inflation changes and later mortgage spread changes. Are A and Z unique events, or could similar observations occur later?

[14] The average yield on the S&L mortgage portfolio and the average cost of funds for S&Ls are based on numbers found in FHLB semiannual supervisory reports. To calculate the average mortgage yield, the FHLBB takes interest earned and divides by an average mortgage balance which is net of loans in process. To calculate the average cost of funds, the FHLBB takes the total interest costs of savings and borrowings in a six month period and divides by an average balance of savings and borrowings.

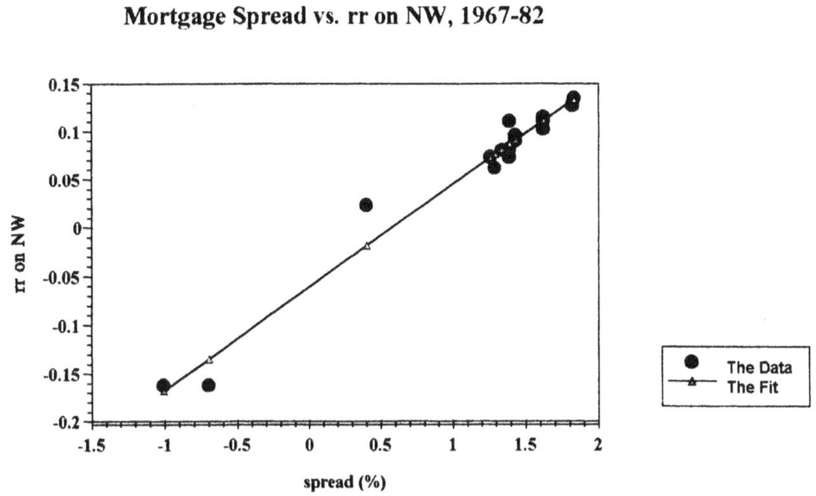

FIGURE 15

Regression line: $\hat{y} = -0.060 + 0.106x$, $R^2 = .97$

Point Z—the observation of the change in the mortgage spread from 1974 to 1975 as related to the change in inflation from 1973 to 1974—shows that it is possible to have a small mortgage spread increase after a large inflation increase. Point A—the observation of the change in mortgage spread from 1980 to 1981 as related to the change in inflation from 1979 to 1980—shows that it is also possible for a very large spread decrease to follow a moderate inflation increase. If such events can both occur with regularity, perhaps there is no real pattern here. Perhaps the S&Ls were mistaken in worrying so much about future inflation.

I think that Z is unique, but not A. Hence the S&Ls were correct to believe, in 1982, that their environment included the inverse relationship estimated in Figure 16.[15] My reasons are as follows. During the 1970s there were two separate episodes of double-digit inflation. In the first episode the trough was 1972 (3.3 percent increase in the CPI) and the peak was 1974 (11 percent); in the second, the trough was 1976 (5.7 percent) and the peak

[15] Looking at the data, the proper fit appears to be nonlinear: the greater the increase in inflation, the greater the negative impact on mortgage spreads.

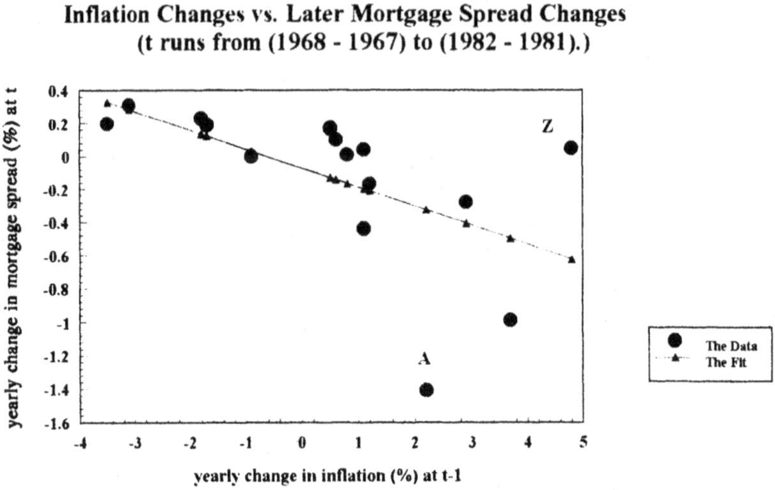

FIGURE 16

Regression line: $\hat{y} = -0.07 - 0.115x$, $R^2 = .32$, $t_x = -2.49$

was 1980 (13.5 percent). Both Z and A therefore occur at inflation peaks. Z, however, came at a time when high inflation was new and unexpected. Furthermore, few institutions (such as money market mutual funds) existed to help small savers avoid inflation. By the time A came, high inflation was old news and everyone had experience in avoiding the costs of inflation.

Evidence of learning from experience can be seen in the numbers. From 1972 to 1974, the annual inflation rate increased by 233 percent, while the percentage increases in the 1-year Treasury bill rate, the average S&L deposit rate, the average S&L cost-of-funding rate, and the average yield on a S&L mortgage portfolio were, respectively, only 90 percent, 11 percent, 13.5 percent, and 6.5 percent.[16] The second time around, from 1976 to 1980, the percentage increases in the 1-year Treasury bill rate (114 percent), the average S&L deposit rate (39 percent), the average S&L cost of funding rate (40 percent), and the average yield on a S&L mortgage portfolio (16.7

[16] Treasury bill rates are from the *Federal Reserve Bulletin*, the average S&L deposit rate from the FHLBB. The latter rate is based on monthly FHLBB supervisory reports and represents interest paid as a per cent of average monthly savings held.

percent), came much closer to matching the percentage increase in the annual inflation rate during that period (137 percent).

In the first episode, expectations of further inflation did not arise. In 1975, both the inflation rate and the 1-year Treasury bill rate fell. So even though the percentage increase in the average S&L deposit rate was dwarfed by the percentage increases in inflation and market interest rates, by 1975 the difference between the 1-year Treasury bill rate and the average S&L deposit rate was only 58 basis points (in favor of the Treasury bill).[17] Since the means to exploit this slender difference were not yet fully developed, the S&Ls escaped disintermediation. The industry's net new deposit inflow from 1974 to 1975 actually increased by more than $24.6 billion (FHLBB data).

In the second episode, expectations of further inflation did arise. While the annual inflation rate decreased in 1981 by 23 percent, the 1-year Treasury bill rate increased by 17 percent. Combined with the slower rise over 1976–80 of the average S&L deposit rate as compared to market rates, this caused the difference between the rates to widen. In 1976, the difference between the average S&L deposit rate and the 1-year Treasury bill rate was 54 basis points in favor of the deposit rate: in 1980, the difference was 355 basis points in favor of the Treasury rate, and in 1981 it was 395 basis points in favor of the Treasury rate. This dramatic difference, when added to expectations of further inflation and the existence of new institutions that cut the cost of inflation-avoidance, brought about massive disintermediation. Even though the average S&L deposit rate increased by 22 percent from 1980 to 1981, the industry's net deposit inflow fell by more than 36 billion dollars. The big increase in deposit costs was not matched by a similar increase in the average yield of the S&L mortgage portfolio (which increased by only 6.1 percent), so the mortgage spread fell precipitously.

The S&Ls were therefore correct in thinking that data points like Z were long gone by 1982. Data points like A were a sign of the future. The industry and its regulators must have agreed that the way to increase the return on net worth, and also to decrease its dispersion, was to invest in such a way that future high inflation could not ravage mortgage spreads.

[17] It helped that in 1972 the difference between the rates was 207 basis points in favor of the average S&L deposit rate.

There are three basic ways S&Ls can protect their spreads from inflation (Downs, 1985, pp. 29–30). First, if they continue to offer fixed-rate mortgages, they must increase the traditional spread over cost so that these long-term debt instruments have a higher net real yield. Second, they can invest more in adjustable-rate mortgages, so that future yields can be adjusted to match future inflation. Third, they can find ways to acquire equity interests in property, hence getting a share of the appreciating value of the property.

Beginning in 1982 the S&L industry changed its standard operating procedures so as to do more of the above inflation hedging. Investment increased in 1-to-4 family mortgages with adjustable rates. According to the 1984 *Savings Institution Sourcebook*, by the end of 1983 more than 60 percent of their new conventional home mortgages had adjustable rates. Also, as shown in Figure 17, after 1982 the spreads on fixed rate mortgages increased significantly.[18] Finally, the boxplots of Figure 18 confirm that S&Ls acquired more equity interests in property during the early 1980s; from 1980 to 1985 there was a clear trend toward non-traditional lending.[19] Unlike single-family owner-occupied homes, the properties associated with non-traditional loans (office buildings, shopping malls, apartment complexes, condominiums and land) offer the S&L an opportunity to gain an equity interest.

Now we begin to see the reason for the increase in non-traditional lending. This has nothing to do with intentional risk-taking due to low net worth; rather it is a prudent reaction to an uncontrollable event—1970s-style inflation—that had already devastated the S&Ls. Indeed, if we examine the alternatives we see that the industry had little choice in the matter.

Consider an unintended consequence of raising the traditional spread on fixed rate mortgages. Mortgage rates were already at historic highs in the early 1980s. In addition, housing prices appreciated rapidly throughout the '70s as it gradually dawned on people that a house, purchased with a

[18] The base used to compute the spread is the secondary-market rate for a 3-month CD. A two-sample z-test on means (μ_1 = mean spread before 1982 and μ_2 = mean spread after 1982) leads to rejection of the null hypothesis ($\mu_1 = \mu_2$), with a z-value of -8.453.

[19] Once again the boxplots are based on aggregated figures gathered across the 12 districts of the FHLB system. For Figure 18, the following types of loans were counted as non-traditional: construction and permanent loans on 5 or more dwelling units, construction and permanent loans on nonresidential buildings, and land loans. (These are FHLBB loan categories.)

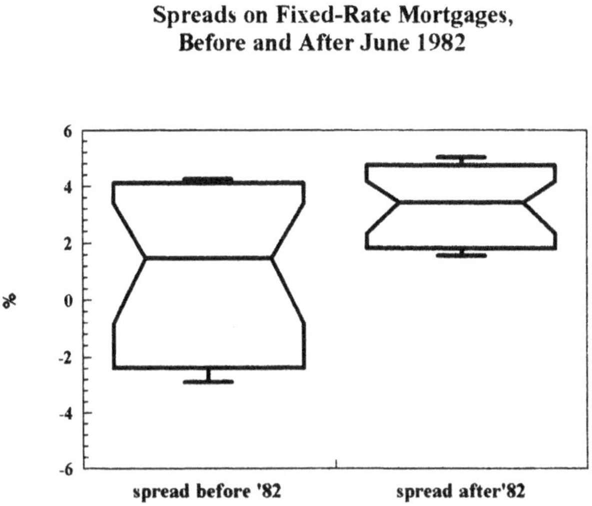

FIGURE 17
(Spread = fixed mortgage rate minus secondary market rate on 3-month CD)
Data sources: Federal Housing Finance Board and *Federal Reserve Bulletin*

fixed rate mortgage, is the perfect asset to own during inflationary times. Since S&Ls generally require a downpayment of as much as 20 percent of the purchase price, and follow a rule of no lending unless the monthly mortgage payment is about 28 percent or less of monthly income, there was talk of a housing affordability crisis in the early '80s (Downs, 1985). The problem of affordability was especially acute for first-time homebuyers. Table 1 gives an admittedly extreme example of the problem.[20]

The effort to promote adjustable-rate mortgages (ARMs) also had unintended consequences. Such a mortgage transfers risk to the borrower. Households, notably risk-averse, will therefore demand a rate concession, especially if they expect high inflation to continue. Figure 19 shows the degree to which ARMs have been discounted relative to fixed rate mortgages. Naturally most S&Ls would have found such discounts undesirable.

[20] For each year from 1976 to 1982, contrast the minimum yearly income needed to qualify for a 30-year mortgage on an average-priced, newly-built, L.A. home with the 1975 minimum yearly income, adjusted for inflation.

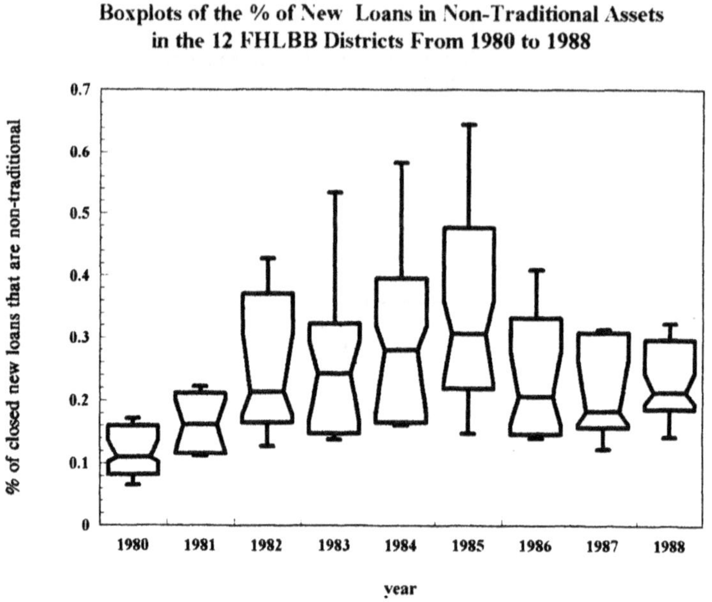

FIGURE 18
Data source: FHLBB

Note that these two factors—borrower affordability problems at high mortgage rates, and the need for substantial rate concessions on ARMs—do *not* slow lending on income and non-residential properties. In these properties occupancy costs are usually a relatively small portion of the tenant's total income (Downs, 1985, p. 112). Not only are builders and developers less risk-averse by nature than households, and thus less likely to demand significant rate concessions on ARMs; in addition they may think that higher payments on an ARM, caused by accelerating inflation, can easily be offset by charging higher rents. In the market for ARMs in the early 1980s, builders and developers would be attractive borrowers, even to the most prudent S&L.

Thus, there are several (real estate) market-oriented reasons why an S&L, during the debacle, would find itself with a portfolio containing a much higher than normal percentage of non-traditional assets. Are these reasons sufficient to generate the kind of increases seen in Figure 18? Probably so. Since 1-to-4 family mortgages were such a large percentage of S&L lending before 1982, even a small percentage decrease in 1-to-4

TABLE 1
HOUSING AFFORDABILITY IN THE
LOS ANGELES/LONG BEACH/ANAHEIM METROPOLITAN AREA
1976–1982

	Purchase price[a]	Contract interest rate (%)[b]	Approx. monthly payment[c]	Min. yearly income[d]	1975 min. yearly Income[e]
1975	$51,400	8.93	$331	$14,185	$14,185
1976	$65,900	8.93	$424	$18,180	$15,485
1977	$72,500	9.04	$466	$20,001	$16,308
1978	$84,900	9.77	$571	$24,476	$17,432
1979	$92,400	10.91	$704	$30,170	$18,757
1980	$110,700	12.89	$979	$41,985	$20,877
1981	$116,200	14.49	$1,138	$48,786	$23,695
1982	$122,300	14.5	$1,198	$51,360	$26,159

Notes: [a]Newly built single-family house. [b]The contract rate on conventional (fixed rate) first mortgage loans. Initial fees and charges not included. [c]Assuming a downpayment of 20 percent of the purchase price and a 30-year mortgage. [d]Assuming the lender requires that the monthly payment not exceed 28 percent of monthly income. [e]Adjusted for inflation using the CPI.

family mortgage lending can cause a large percentage increase in non-traditional lending.[21]

Let me conclude this discussion by presenting the first causal relation in the alternative account. Let us use the following two predicates as primitives.

70sINF(x): x experiences 1970s-style inflation (which means two episodes of double-digit inflation within a decade after more than two decades of negligible inflation).

[21] For example, in 1978 (their last good year before the debacle) S&Ls lent $20,136 million in 1-to-4 family construction loans, $65,585 million in 1-to-4 family purchase loans, and $9,072 million in non-traditional loans. If 5 percent of the 1-to-4 family loans are diverted toward non-traditional loans, non-traditional lending increases by 47 percent. (Data source: FHLBB.)

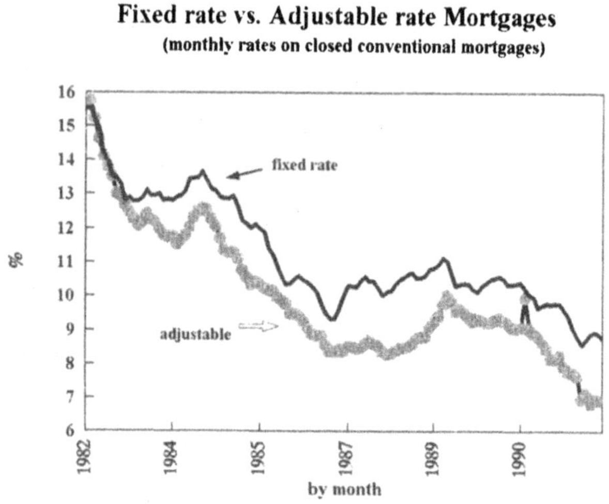

FIGURE 19
Data source: FHLBB

H%NTA(x): From 1982 to 1985, x invests an historically high percentage of its mortgage portfolio in construction and purchase loans for 5 or more family residences, non-residential buildings, and land.

The two predicates are related as cause and effect

$$70\text{sINF}(x) \rightarrow \text{H\%NTA}(x),$$

and the mechanism producing this causal relation is based on these claims:

A1 *At the beginning of the debacle, S&Ls aimed for target mortgage spreads and believed that mortgage spreads were positively correlated with the rate of return on net worth.*

A2 *At the beginning of the debacle, S&Ls believed that inflation changes were negatively correlated with later mortgage spread changes.*

A3 *At the beginning of the debacle, S&Ls wanted to protect their mortgage spreads from inflation that was expected to continue into the 1980s.*

Local growth as a contributing cause

Have I explained too much? Am I guilty of the same offense of which I accused Barth, Kane and White? Thus far it appears that every S&L had the incentive to use non-traditional assets as an inflation hedge, since high inflation was omnipresent. Yet there is a lot of dispersion in the boxplots of Figure 18.

The reason, I think, for this high degree of dispersion is that location is a contributing cause of non-traditional lending. Local growth rates in the U.S. always differ. Some areas are booming, others are stable, others depressed. Now an important symptom of a booming local economy is rapidly rising real estate values, and a large, active, and confident coterie of developers. Ever-increasing real estate values and development mania, when combined with the inflation-fighting steps taken by all S&Ls, *force* the S&Ls in booming areas to greatly increase their non-traditional assets.

To illustrate the kind of forces at work, let us take two localities that differ in growth rates and follow the behavior of S&Ls in the two places over time. The Killeen–Temple, Texas metropolitan area and the Battle Creek, Michigan metropolitan area will be the localities examined, and the time span will be from 1976 to 1984.[22] According to the Census Bureau, in 1970 the Killeen–Temple area had a population of 159,794 while the Battle Creek area had a population of 141,963. In 1980 the respective population figures were 214,656 and 187,338, and in 1990 they were 255,301 and 135,982. Killeen–Temple will therefore serve as our sample of local growth, and Battle Creek as our sample of local stagnation. Table 2 presents data on the fate of S&Ls in the two areas over the period 1976 to 1984.[23]

Let us now try to make sense of the numbers in Table 2. Picture yourself as a 1982 S&L manager in booming Killeen, Texas. New Killeen residents keep coming in the front door depositing their savings.[24] On the one hand you are happy—here is some badly needed liquidity, the disintermediation of 1981 appears over. On the other hand you are nervous—deposit rates are

[22] The end point of 1984 was not freely chosen: the FHLBB stopped publishing SMSA data on S&Ls after this date.

[23] Definitely one, maybe two, of the Killeen–Temple S&Ls are on the failure list found in Barth, Bartholomew and Bradley (1989). None of the Battle Creek S&Ls are on the failure list.

[24] Back in the days before interstate banking, when you moved to another state, you moved your car, couch, cat... and savings deposit.

TABLE 2

S&L Activity in Killeen–Temple (K–T), Texas, and Battle Creek (B.C.), Michigan, 1976–1984

		No. of S&Ls	Assets ($m)[a]	Savings ($m)[b]	RNW ($m)[c]	FIRR[d]	NND ($m)	BM ($m)	1–4 f. const. ($m)[e]	1–4 f. purch. ($m)[f]	Non-trad. loans[g]	Mort. repay. ($m)[h]
1976	K–T	5	230	204	13	0.064	24.0	0	12.0	59	15	n.a.
	B.C.	5	267	239	19	0.079	23.0	0	7.0	34	1	n.a.
1977	K–T	5	277	277	15	0.063	23.0	1	12.0	61	6	n.a.
	B.C.	5	310	310	21	0.076	20.0	0	12	43	1	n.a.
1978	K–T	5	314	269	17	0.063	18.0	1	11.0	68	5	35
	B.C.	5	146	127	9	0.071	6.0	0	5.0	22	3	20
1979[i]	K–T	5	289	253	18	0.071	10.8	0	11.0	35	1	30
	B.C.	4	155	139	10	0.072	4.6	0	4.0	13	0	14
1980	K–T	5	316	284	19	0.067	12.1	0	1.0	19	0	18
	B.C.	4	171	154	10	0.065	6.5	0	2.0	7	1	10
1981	K–T	5	338	305	17	0.056	−2.5	3	2	15	0	19
	B.C.	4	172	155	8	0.052	−9.3	0	2	5	2	7
1982	K–T	5	479	426	20	0.047	91.3	9	8	4	44	34
	B.C.	4	172	155	6	0.039	−10.6	0	0	3	0	9
1983	K–T	5	1028	836	52	0.062	375.0	6	253	54	289	186
	B.C.	4	179	165	6	0.036	0.3	0	1	10	0	17
1984	K–T	5	2311	1675	83	0.050	n.a.	473	21	20	634	309
	B.C.	4	191	175	7	0.040	n.a.	1	2	17	0	15

NOTES TO TABLE 2

[a]Total assets as of December 31. [b]Total insured deposits as of December 31. [c]Total regulatory net worth of S&Ls in the area (see White, 1991, pp. 82–7 for discussion of RNW). [d]Estimate of federal insurance reserve ratio (total insured deposits divided by total regulatory net worth) for S&Ls in the metropolitan area. [e]Total mortgage lending on 1-to-4 family residential construction. [f]Total mortgage lending on 1-to-4 family residential purchases. [g]Includes construction and purchase loans on 5- or more family residences and on non-residential property ($m). [h]Total principal payments and other credits less interest and taxes. [i]The fall in B.C. assets in 1978 is probably due to the failure or merger of the 1st Federal S&L of Battle Creek, a mutual with $171 million in assets at the beginning of 1978. This insititution was not listed in the 1979 *Directory of American S&L Associations.*

very high (in 1982) and there is so much new money coming in. How can you put it to work in such a short time? You want to make loans at a decent spread so that you can gradually accumulate some net worth and please the regulators. You would prefer to stick with what you know best—single family fixed-rate mortgages—but the market is weak. The fixed rates are so high, and housing prices in Killeen seem to increase each day. Fewer and fewer households have the income you consider necessary to meet the monthly mortgage payments. You try to make some adjustable-rate home mortgage loans, but most Killeen households will not accept the risk of a variable rate without a huge discount. You cannot afford such discounts because you have a very expensive deposit inflow, and you need a decent spread to build up profits.

In walks developer Dan who has a plan to put up some apartment buildings and a mall to meet the housing and shopping needs of all the new Killeen residents. You are somewhat skeptical—you know that *past* default rates on loans for income and non-residential properties are high—but Dan reminds you of a few things. First, the population of Killeen–Temple grew by more than 34 percent during the 1970s, yet since 1978 not much has been built other than single family homes. Second, nearby Fort Hood is thriving. And third, we are talking about the future of Big, Bad Texas, God's country! Of course Killeen and Texas are going to do even better in the '80s. You have to admit that Dan has a good case, and besides you can't just let those expensive new deposit dollars sit in the vault. You begin to bargain hard, trying to get as many concessions as possible. Dan responds by saying that you need him more than he needs you. Once again, he is right. No one at the S&L can pull off the kind of development he is planning, and you know that every other S&L and bank in town has your problem—everyone is flush with expensive new deposits. So you make the deal with Dan. It is not too bad, the loan has an adjustable rate and comes with a decent upfront fee; but it is far from perfect. Then again, are you responsible for its imperfections? Did you really have a choice?

Now picture yourself as an S&L manager in Battle Creek, Michigan, in 1982. Battle Creek had solid growth throughout the '70s, but the recent recession has devastated the region. Unemployment is stubbornly high, and local migration to the Sunbelt is becoming worrisome. You have not seen a decent deposit inflow since 1977; in recent years the primary source of funding has been mortgage repayments.[25] In a way that is good because these mortgage repayments seem not to have a price tag, and as a result you do not feel pressure to make riskier loans in order to get higher yields. Though your fixed rates for home mortgages are historically high, there is still a market for them since housing prices in the area are falling. The supply of Battle Creek homes has begun to exceed the demand. In addition, you sell a number of adjustable-rate home mortgages. Thanks to the stagnating local conditions, developers are not crowding out households in the ARM market; in fact you have not seen a developer in Battle Creek for four years. Furthermore, your funding—mortgage repayments—is essentially free. As a result of these two factors, your opportunity costs are so low you are willing to accede to the discounts your customers demand for accepting an ARM. Of course your recent lending is not doing much for your profits, your S&L's net worth is dwindling away. Nevertheless, the regulators are playing it cool, for they understand that you are trying your best to uphold your part of the bargain: no unwarranted risks in return for forbearance. Local circumstances make it easy to keep that promise. Do you really have a choice in Battle Creek?

Hence the second causal relation in the alternative account is as follows. Take the predicate RLG(x)—indicating that x is in an area experiencing

[25] S&Ls relying on mortgage repayments were quite willing, in the early 1980s, to initiate refinancing so as to speed up that sole source of inflow. Tom Tiemann tells me that in 1980 the Ladoga Federal S&L (Crawfordsville, Indiana) offered to cut half a percentage point off the interest rate on his 30-year fixed rate mortgage if he would increase his monthly payment by 50 percent.

rapid local growth from 1982 to 1985—as a primitive. RLG and H%NTA stand in the relation

$$\text{RLG}(x) \rightarrow \text{H\%NTA}(x),$$

and the mechanism producing this causal relation is based on these claims:

A4 *In areas of rapid growth, housing prices tend to be higher.*

A5 *In areas of rapid growth, net deposit inflow tends to be greater.*

A6 *In areas of rapid growth, there tend to be more builders and developers.*

Summary

The challenge for this alternative account is to explain how a general desire on the part of the industry not to engage in imprudent risk-taking led *some* S&Ls to engage in behavior which at the time did not seem like IRT, but which *now* does, given the record of failures. That only some S&Ls did this is especially perplexing given the S&L uniformity "axiom" (see Section 3).

The challenge is met through a focus on non-traditional lending (on land, commercial property, and multi-family residential property). With hindsight, such lending appears dangerous. Yet in the early 1980s it seemed a prudent way of coping with the most pressing issue of the time—the effects of high inflation. For S&Ls located in high-growth areas in particular, there was little alternative to the non-traditional lending strategy. Since most of these future failures had few choices during the debacle, and little of what happened could have been foreseen, most of these debacle failures were essentially struck down by disastrous (real estate) market forces.

References

Barth, James R. 1991. *The Great Savings and Loan Debacle.* AEI Press.

Barth, James R., Philip F. Bartholomew and Michael G. Bradley 1989. "The Determinants of Thrift Resolution Costs." Research Paper no. 89-03, Office of the Chief Economist, Office of Thrift Supervision, November.

Barth, James R., Philip F. Bartholomew and Carol J. Labich 1989. "Moral Hazard and the Thrift Crisis: An Analysis of 1988 Resolutions," in Federal Reserve Bank of Chicago, *Banking System Risk: Charting a New Course.* Chicago: 344–84.

Barth, James R., John J. Feid, Gabriel Riedel and M. Hampton Tunis 1989. "Alternative Federal Deposit Insurance Regimes." Research Paper no. 152, Office of Policy and Economic Research, Federal Home Loan Bank Board, January.

Bodfish, H. M. and A. D. Theobald 1938. *Savings and Loan Principles.* New York, NY: Prentice-Hall.

Bowman, Edward H. 1980. "A Risk-Return Paradox for Strategic Management." *Sloan Management Review* 21: 17–31.

Brewer, Elijah, III 1989. "Full-Blown Crisis, Half-Measure Cure." Federal Reserve Bank of Chicago *Economic Perspectives* 13: 2–16.

Downs, Anthony 1985. *The Revolution in Real Estate Finance.* Washington D.C.: Brookings Institution.

Federal Home Loan Bank Board 1976–1989. *Savings & Home Financing Source Book.* Washington, D.C. (annual).

Glymour, Clark, Richard Scheines, Peter Spirtes and Kevin Kelly 1987. *Discovering Causal Structure: Artificial Intelligence, Philosophy of Science, and Statistical Modeling.* San Diego, CA.: Academic Press.

Jaffee, Dwight M. 1976. "The Asset/Liability Maturity Mix of S&Ls: Problems and Solutions." In *Change in the Savings and Loan Industry: Proceedings of the 2nd Annual Conference.* San Francisco, CA.: Federal Home Loan Bank of San Francisco: 59–88.

______. 1989. "Symposium on Federal Deposit Insurance for S&L Institutions." *The Journal of Economic Perspectives* 3: 3–9.

Kane, Edward J. 1989a. *The S&L Insurance Mess: How Did It Happen?* Washington, D.C.: Urban Institute Press.

______. 1989b. "The High Cost of Incompletely Funding the FSLIC's Shortage of Explicit Capital." *The Journal of Economic Perspectives* 3: 31–47.

Kendall, Leon T. 1962. *The Savings and Loan Business.* Englewood Cliffs, NJ.: Prentice-Hall.

Kormendi, Roger C., Victor L. Bernard, S. Craig Pirrong and Edward Snyder 1989. *Crisis Resolution in the Thrift Industry.* Report of the Mid-America Institute Task Force on the Thrift Crisis.

Mosteller, Frederick and John W. Tukey 1977. *Data Analysis and Regression.* Reading, MA.: Addison-Wesley.

Nicols, Alfred 1972. *Management and Control in the Mutual Savings and Loan Association.* Lexington, MA.: Lexington Books.

Roessner, Gilbert 1976. "Comment on Jaffee." In *Change in the Savings and Loan Industry: Proceedings of the 2nd Annual Conference.* San Francisco, CA.: Federal Home Loan Bank of San Francisco: 103–7.

Samuelson, Paul A. 1945. "The Effects of Interest Rate Increases on the Banking System," *American Economic Review* (March): 16–27.

______. 1969. "An Analytic Evaluation of Interest Rate Ceilings for Savings and Loan Associations and Competitive Institutions." In Irwin Friend (ed.) *Study of the Savings and Loan Industry*, 4 vols. Washington, D.C., Federal Home Loan Bank Board: 1561–90.

Solow, Robert M. 1979. "What We Know and Don't Know About Inflation." *Technology Review* (December/January): 31–46.

Stiglitz, Joseph E. 1993. *Economics.* New York, NY: Norton.

Tukey, John W. 1977. *Exploratory Data Analysis.* Reading, MA.: Addison-Wesley.

White, Lawrence J. 1991. *The S&L Debacle: Public Policy Lessons for Bank and Thrift Regulation.* New York, NY.: Oxford University Press.

7

WHAT ARE THE CONNECTIONS BETWEEN DEPOSIT INSURANCE AND BANK FAILURES?

Allin F. Cottrell, Michael S. Lawlor and John H. Wood

Wake Forest University

Federal insurance of bank deposits was the most important structural change in the banking system to result from the 1933 panic, and, indeed in our view, the structural change most conducive to monetary stability since state bank notes were taxed out of existence immediately after the Civil War.

—Friedman and Schwartz (1963)

Federal deposit insurance currently subsidizes in a largely *hidden* way important categories of deposit-institution risk bearing.... [The resulting] incentive problems create a system of guarantees that over time has grown increasingly costly, unfair, dangerous, and unreliable.

—Edward Kane (1987)

1 Introduction

The purpose of this paper is to examine the historical evidence on commercial bank failures in the United States in order to assess the validity of the widespread belief that deposit insurance has increased bank failures due to the moral hazard that it represents for bank management.[1] It seems

[1] Federal deposit insurance was introduced by the Banking Act of 1933. All Federal Reserve member banks were required to insure their deposits with the Federal Deposit Insurance Corporation. Nonmember banks meeting certain requirements could also obtain insurance. Most did so, and over ninety percent of commercial banks have had FDIC insurance since its inception. Coverage was initially set at $5,000 per account and was raised in steps to $100,000 in 1980. The coverage available to depositors was much greater than these amounts because each depositor could hold unlimited numbers of insured accounts in any bank, in as many banks as they chose. Furthermore, there was a widespread belief, justified by experience, that the government would also reimburse depositors for the

paradoxical that this belief has passed into the conventional wisdom when little more than a decade ago its opposite was generally accepted. In 1980 it was widely believed that the historically low failure rates enjoyed since the Great Depression were due to the introduction of federal deposit insurance in 1934.[2] By the end of the 1980s deposit insurance was considered the major cause of bank failures. Can it be both? The remainder of the introduction describes the essential elements of potentially fruitful approaches to this question followed by an outline of our approach and a preview of our results.

Since the resumption of a high rate of bank failures in the early 1980s (to slightly more than the average rate prevailing between the Civil War and 1920), a great many studies have attempted to demonstrate that failures are caused primarily by the incentive to undertake risk which federal deposit insurance offers to banks. Although the incentive undoubtedly exists, we maintain that its empirical importance has yet to be measured. For all the theory tells us, the impact of deposit insurance on bank behavior might be imperceptible. There are many reasons, some of them connected with long-run personal goals not easily measured, why bankers might resist the temptation to risk failure. Any attempt to determine whether deposit insurance has significantly affected the risk-taking behavior and therefore the failure rate of banks must also consider experiences in the absence of deposit insurance. This is the basis of our attempt to answer the question posed in the title of the paper. For federal deposit insurance, it means a data set beginning well before 1934. We know of no study of bank failures which has made use of such data—and therefore no study which has attempted to estimate the influence of deposit insurance on bank failures—even though reliable data on failures are available from the nineteenth century to the present. The exacerbating influence of deposit insurance on bank failures has simply been assumed.

uninsured portions of their accounts. Until 1989 the insurance premium paid by banks was one twelfth of 1 percent of their total domestic deposits, insured and uninsured, regardless of risk exposure. The law provided for refunds of premiums after the insurance fund reached a certain proportion of deposits, and refunds were slightly more than half of premiums between 1950 and 1983. (See FDIC *Annual Reports*.)

[2] The average annual number of commercial bank failures (and average annual percentage of banks failing) during 1934–81 was 15 (0.10%), compared with 69 (0.72%) during 1864–1920, 639 (2.23%) during 1921–29, 2,547 (12.64%) during 1930–33, and 132 (0.93%) during 1982–90. In only one year between 1871 and 1933 were there as few failures (11 in 1881) as the average number between 1934 and 1981.

Furthermore, deposit insurance cannot meaningfully be considered independently of other New Deal financial legislation, including the creation of the Federal Deposit Insurance Corporation to supervise deposit insurance and prevent bank risk-taking at the insurance fund's expense, the federal credit agencies established or expanded to assume much of the burden of loans to high-risk groups, particularly farmers and low-income home buyers, and programs to bolster bank profits, such as easier access to the Federal Reserve discount window and new restrictions on entry.[3] In particular, the FDIC provided the first systematic supervision of many state-chartered banks. If deposit insurance had been introduced without these accompaniments, we could simply assume with others that it has tended to cause bank failures (whether the tendency has been realized would still remain to be determined). But it is inappropriate to discuss the empirical effects of deposit insurance except as part of the package in which it was delivered, especially when some of the other parts of the package, such as increased bank supervision, were thought by legislators to be implied by deposit insurance. Considered in this light, we are compelled to admit the possibility that the package as a whole might have reduced failures. Throughout this paper, when discussing the effects of deposit insurance we mean the combined effects of insurance and its accompaniments, some integral parts of the insurance package and some introduced about the same time for reasons that might have been unrelated to deposit insurance, although all were addressed to what Congress believed to be the causes of the catastrophic financial failures of the Great Depression.

The paper is organized as follows. In Section 2 we examine data on aggregate U.S. bank failures and their probable causes, including deposit insurance, from 1864 to the end of the 1980s. Two main results emerge. First, it appears that federal deposit insurance has been associated with a lower rate of bank failures, after controlling for other shocks to the banking system. Second, there is a strong link between bank failures and agricultural depressions. The latter observation leads us to examine, in Section 3, a panel of nine Midwestern, agricultural, unit-banking states.

[3] For example, the Farm Credit Act of 1933 made federal credit more accessible to farmers, the Federal Housing Act of 1934 insured private lenders against loss on many low-income and low-down-payment home mortgages, the Banking Acts of 1933 and 1935 restricted access to national bank charters as well as to federal deposit insurance for state banks by imposing conditions related to capital adequacy, earnings prospects, managerial character, and community need (Spong, 1985, p. 21), and the collateral required for loans from the Federal Reserve was liberalized.

Besides comprising observations before and after the adoption of federal deposit insurance, this data set enables us to estimate the common farm-economy effects on bank failures in these states, while also reflecting their differing experiences with deposit insurance, four of the states having had state deposit insurance between 1909 and 1929. The results confirm that the structure of the banking system changed after 1933 in such a way that banks, especially state banks, became less prone to failure. On the other hand, the *state* insurance systems were associated with increased failure rates.

Some alternative explanations of our results are canvassed in Section 4, but it will be helpful at the outset to explain how the data presented in Sections 2 and 3 may fit into a larger picture of the causation of bank failures. Instead of the typical partial equilibrium deposit-insurance/moral-hazard explanation of bank failure, with regulatory restraints and other aspects of the environment held constant, consider the more general mechanism in Figure 1. Banks may fail for a variety of reasons. In the absence of deposit insurance, failures result from the risks offered by the economic environment and bankers' responses to those risks. These failures may lead to runs, and hence to more failures through liquidity crises. Now introduce deposit insurance. The FDIC system was created to prevent runs while preserving the structure of the banking system (Golembe, 1961). This intervention altered the potential for failure in several ways. In particular, it reduced the likelihood of runs but increased banks' incentives to take risks. However, the latter effect was at least partially offset by increased supervision of banks and somewhat less opportunity for risky investments. So the introduction of federal deposit insurance—or rather the federal deposit insurance *system*—might, despite moral hazard, have reduced failures. This account is consistent with our observation that state insurance systems, which were not accompanied by the same regulatory restraints and other structural changes as federal insurance, were associated with increased failure rates.

Some observers have argued that federal deposit insurance reduced failures before 1980 because banks were tightly regulated, but increased failures after the deregulation of the early 1980s. This argument is more appropriate for savings and loan associations, which are beyond the scope of this paper, than for banks. The latter received no significant new investment powers and were empowered to compete for deposits more freely through variable interest rates instead of being restricted to more costly

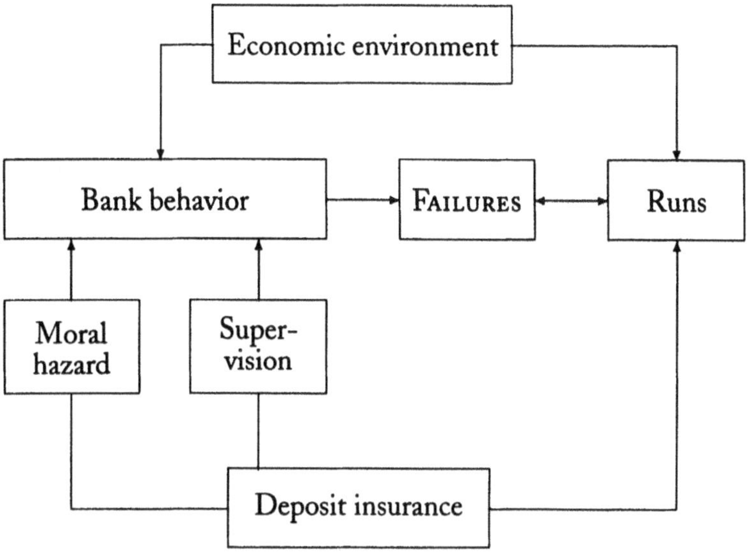

FIGURE 1: THE CAUSATION OF BANK FAILURES

forms of nonprice competition.[4] In any case, we find no evidence that structural changes in the 1980s contributed to bank failures. We find that the changes of the 1930s tended to reduce failures throughout the entire subsequent period, including the 1980s. Indeed, in view of the economic events of the latter decade, in particular the collapse of oil prices and the most severe agricultural depression in American history, we have to ask not why there were so *many* failures in the 1980s, but why there were so few.

[4] *The Financial Institutions Regulatory and Interest Rate Control Act of 1978* sought to prevent undue concentrations of bank ownership and management, although *The Garn–St Germain Depository Institutions Act of 1982* increased lending limits to individual borrowers. *The Depository Institutions Deregulation and Monetary Control Act of 1980* drastically reduced reserve requirements and phased out interest ceilings (lending as well as borrowing). The latter action was primarily a legalization of already common practices, such as NOW accounts and Automatic Transfer Services, under pressure from the courts. (See *US Court of Appeals for the District of Columbia* Circuit, Sept. term, 1978, nos. 78–1337, 78–1849, 78–2206; and Wood and Wood, 1985, pp. 61–3.)

2 Federal deposit insurance and bank failures, 1864–1989

The annual record of commercial bank failures is displayed in Figure 2. The depression years of 1930–33, and the panics of 1931 and 1933 in particular, dominate the figure. Outside the Great Depression, when all sectors suffered, every episode of high failures included a disproportionate number in agricultural areas. These episodes—1892–97, 1921–29, 1982–89—were also characterized by agricultural depression. The maps in Figures 3 and 4 illustrate this point. The bank failures of the 1920s were highly concentrated in farm states, particularly the North Central and Southeastern regions. The 1931 panic, on the other hand, was primarily an urban phenomenon.

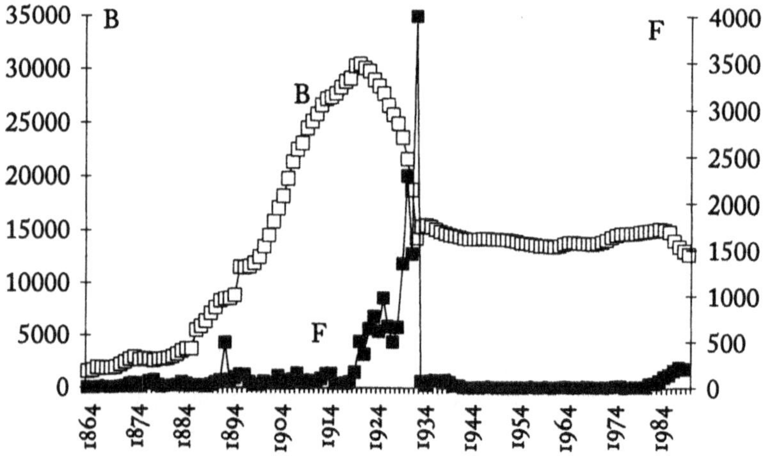

Figure 2: Number of Commercial Banks (B) and Bank Failures (F) in the U.S., Annual, 1864–1989

Sources of data used in figures and tables given in Data Appendix

Figures 5–7 compare the failure rates of state and national banks with the price of wheat and farm values (the latter available only since 1910) during three agricultural depressions. Table 1 (page 172) lists failure rates for the United States and the North Central states (all unit-bank states), and Table 2 (p. 173) lists prices and nominal and real farm values immediately

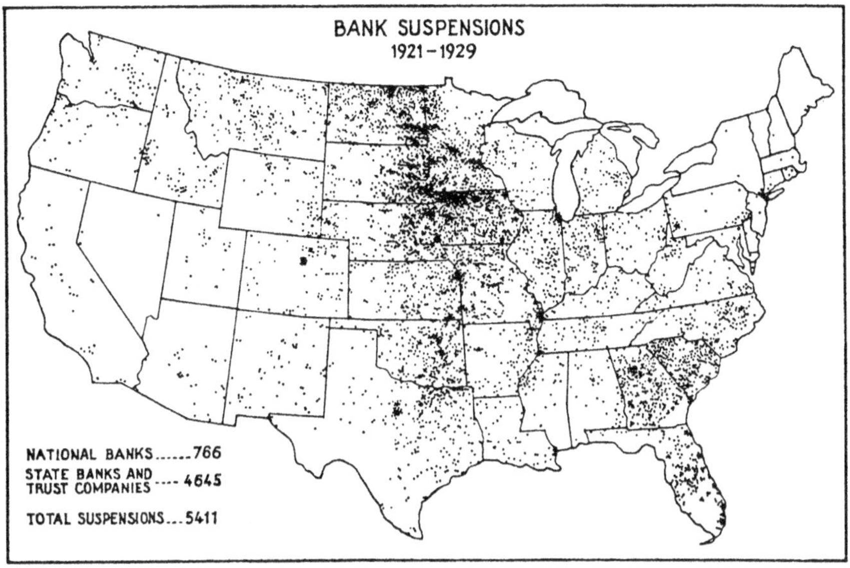

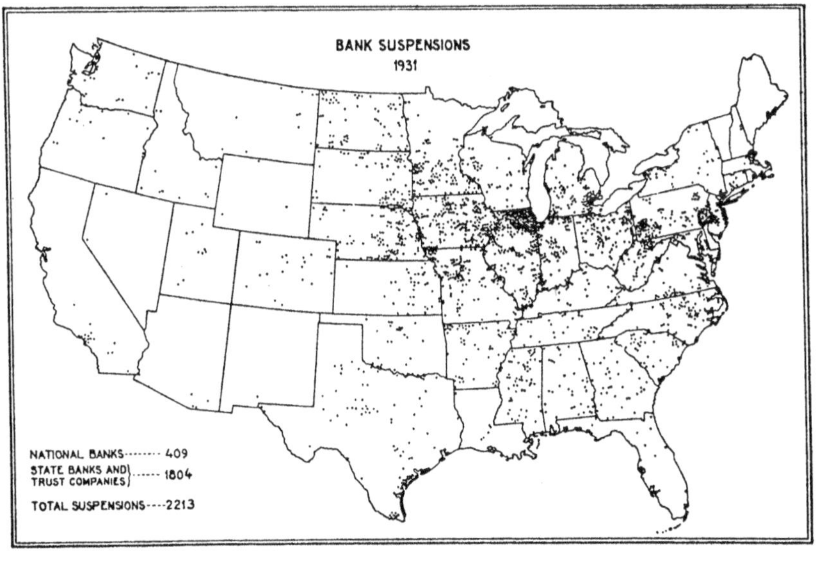

FIGURE 4

Source: Federal Reserve Committee on Branch, Group and Chain Banking, 1932

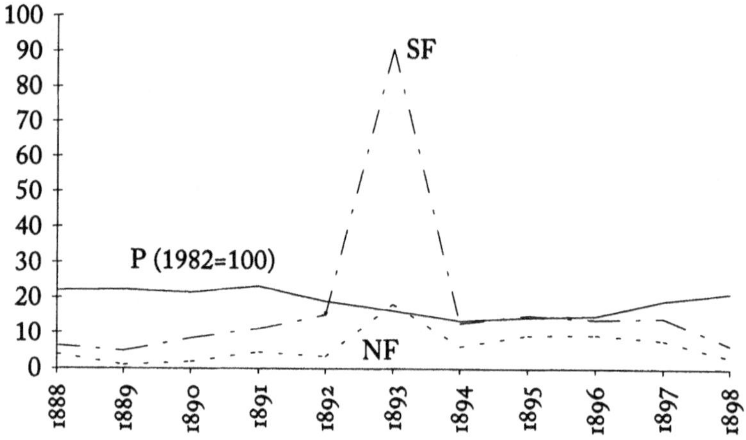

FIGURE 5: WHEAT PRICE (P) AND TEN TIMES THE PERCENTAGES OF STATE AND NATIONAL BANK FAILURES, SF AND NF, 1888–98

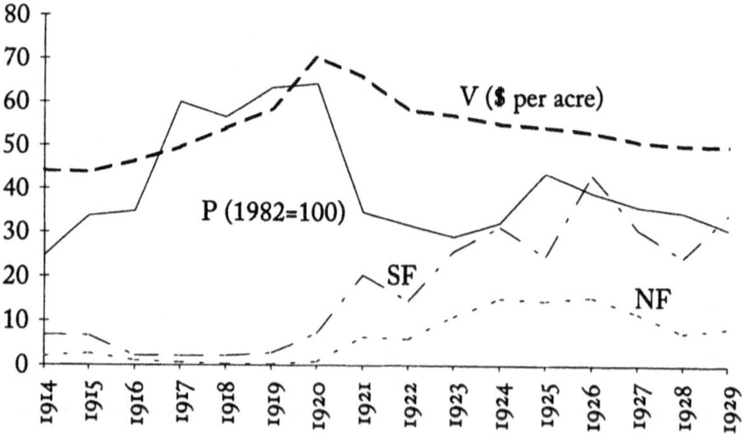

FIGURE 6: AVERAGE FARM VALUE (V), WHEAT PRICE (P), AND TEN TIMES THE PERCENTAGES OF STATE AND NATIONAL BANK FAILURES, SF AND NF, 1914–29

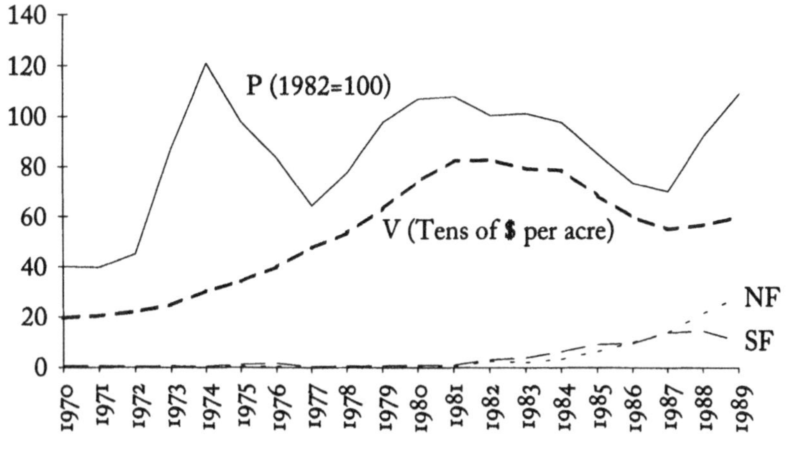

FIGURE 7: AVERAGE FARM VALUE (V), WHEAT PRICE (P), AND TEN TIMES THE PERCENTAGES OF STATE AND NATIONAL BANK FAILURES, SF AND NF, 1970–89

preceding and during each period. Together, these indicate the large role of the agricultural sector in the history of U.S. bank failures. In addition, Table 2 shows that the agricultural depression of the 1980s was worse than that of the 1920s: farm values fell 34 percent between 1982 and 1987, compared with 29 percent between 1920 and 1929. The difference in real terms was even greater, 47 percent compared with 19 percent between the peak and trough years.

Considering the worse state of agriculture (and remembering that agricultural banks are the prime source of failures) and the lower rate of growth of the economy in general in the 1980s than the 1920s (at annual rates, real GNP rose about 6 and 4 percent, respectively, during 1921–29 and 1982–89), it is surprising that failure rates were not higher in the more recent period. Can deposit insurance be an explanation? Table 3 (page 174) presents the results of regressing bank failure rates on rates of change of wheat prices (PWD, which performed somewhat better than other agricultural prices), real GNP (YD), a dummy variable (FDIC) corresponding to the existence of federal deposit insurance, and a dummy variable (HOLI) to control for the extreme spike of bank failures associated with the 1933

TABLE 1
THREE PERIODS OF HIGH FAILURE RATES FOR NATIONAL (N) AND STATE (S) BANKS
(AVERAGE ANNUAL PERCENTAGE FAILURE RATES IN PARENTHESES)

	1892–97				1921–29				1982–89			
	No. banks		Failures		No. banks		Failures		No. banks		Failures	
	N	S	N	S	N	S	N	S	N	S	N	S
US	3759	4520	200(0.9)	844(3.1)	8150	22,306	766(1.0)	4946(2.5)	4579	10,384	386(1.1)	653(0.8)
ND	34	71	8(3.9)	5(1.2)	180	675	62(3.8)	365(6.0)	40	140	0(0.0)	5(0.4)
SD	40	119	7(2.9)	12(1.7)	134	566	51(4.2)	345(6.8)	34	120	1(0.4)	6(0.6)
NE	137	525	17(2.1)	76(2.4)	186	1025	28(1.7)	338(3.7)	121	350	2(0.2)	31(1.1)
KS	143	444	14(1.6)	63(2.4)	267	1112	11(0.5)	209(2.1)	151	471	7(0.6)	50(1.3)
S_1	354	1159	46(2.2)	156(2.2)	767	3378	152(2.2)	1257(4.1)	346	1081	10(0.4)	92(1.1)
MN	72	173	3(0.7)	47(4.5)	341	1187	57(1.9)	362(3.4)	202	561	6(0.4)	29(0.6)
IA	162	438	7(0.7)	46(1.8)	354	1555	92(2.9)	437(3.1)	100	549	10(1.3)	30(0.7)
MO	81	522	4(0.8)	61(1.9)	131	1541	7(0.6)	288(2.1)	118	621	2(0.2)	26(0.5)
WI	77	219	2(0.4)	42(3.2)	153	838	8(0.6)	70(0.9)	127	503	0(0.0)	0(0.0)
IL	212	257	6(0.5)	52(3.4)	494	1403	16(0.4)	116(0.9)	404	895	7(0.2)	16(0.2)
S_2	604	1609	22(0.6)	248(2.6)	1473	6524	180(1.4)	1273(2.2)	951	3129	25(0.3)	101(0.2)
S_3	958	2768	68(1.1)	404(2.4)	2240	9902	332(1.6)	2530(2.8)	1257	4210	35(0.3)	193(0.4)

Definitions: "No. banks" is the number of commercial banks in the initial year; "Failures" is the number of failures during the entire period. S_1, S_2, and S_3 are sums for states with periods of state deposit insurance, without state deposit insurance, and all North Central unit banking states, respectively. Sources of the data are given in the Data Appendix.

TABLE 2
PRICES, OUTPUT, AND FARM VALUES DURING THREE PERIODS OF NUMEROUS BANK FAILURES

	PA	PW	PY	FV	FV/PY
1888	12.0	22.0	7.3		
1890	13.7	21.5	7.2		
1895	10.0	14.4	6.4		
1898	11.5	21.3	6.5		
1914	17.9	24.5	8.9	44.1	498
1920	38.0	64.1	19.1	70.3	369
1922	23.7	31.7	14.4	58.1	403
1929	26.4	34.8	14.6	50.0	342
1970	46	40	42	196	467
1976	79	83	63	397	629
1981	105	108	94	819	871
1986	93	73	114	595	523
1989	111	109	126	597	473

Definitions: Agricultural (PA) and wheat (PW) prices, and GNP deflator (PY), all on a 1982 base, and the average value per acre of farm land and buildings (FV).

Bank Holiday.[5] In this basic model the significant negative coefficient on FDIC indicates that failures have been less frequent in the presence of deposit insurance, after accounting for other economic variables associated with bank failures.

Table 4 (page 178) extends the basic model by including two more dummy variables. RUNS equals 1 for 1930–33, years of large U.S. bank runs, and zero otherwise. The 80s dummy is designed to test the hypothesis that deregulation in the banking industry in the 1980s was a factor in the recent increase in bank failures (80s equals 1 after 1980 when Congress

[5] The first three columns use data as far back as we have (1865 for levels, 1866 for first differences, 1871 with 5 lags); columns 4–6 begin with the increase in the reliability of the data on numbers and failures of state banks (and when data by states are available); and columns 7–9 are for the period when land value data are available, making the period comparable to that of a more precise model presented in Section 3.

TABLE 3
REGRESSIONS OF ANNUAL FAILURE RATES (R) OF ALL COMMERCIAL BANKS (B), STATE BANKS (S), AND NATIONAL BANKS (N)

	1871–1990			1893–1990			1912–1990		
	BR	SR	NR	BR	SR	NR	BR	SR	NR
CNST	.0167	.0265	.0622	.0201	.0230	.0545	.0626	.0712	.0495
	(4.73)	(5.29)	(1.98)	(4.41)	(4.73)	(2.39)	(4.37)	(4.42)	(3.67)
PWD	−.0149	−.0263	−.0036	−.0143	−.0192	−.0036	−.0118	−.0149	−.0047
	(2.88)	(2.82)	(1.49)	(2.47)	(2.42)	(1.27)	(2.59)	(2.81)	(1.50)
PWD(1)	−.0150	−.0128	−.0056	−.0178	−.0234	−.0059	−.0100	−.0120	−.0059
	(2.69)	(1.30)	(2.08)	(2.91)	(2.85)	(1.91)	(2.01)	(2.06)	(1.73)
PWD(2)	−.0109	−.0159	−.0047	−.0109	−.0135	−.0044	−.0095	−.0116	−.0052
	(1.99)	(1.66)	(1.79)	(1.81)	(1.67)	(1.45)	(1.95)	(2.03)	(1.56)
PWD(3)	−.0122	−.0168	−.0061	−.0139	−.0177	−.0069	−.0102	−.0117	−.0064
	(2.25)	(1.77)	(2.35)	(2.30)	(2.20)	(2.26)	(2.14)	(2.12)	(2.00)
PWD(4)	−.0107	−.0197	−.0058	−.0097	−.0120	−.0059	−.0092	−.0105	−.0066
	(2.00)	(2.08)	(2.30)	(1.60)	(1.47)	(1.95)	(1.92)	(1.87)	(2.02)
PWD(5)	−.0103	−.0087	−.0066	−.0133	−.0156	−.0074	−.0138	−.0159	−.0086
	(2.04)	(0.96)	(2.86)	(2.29)	(1.96)	(2.65)	(3.13)	(3.10)	(2.86)

YD	−.0279	−.0463	−.0035	−.0249	−.0366	−.0029	−.0164	−.0211	−.0062
	(1.88)	(1.69)	(0.54)	(1.53)	(1.61)	(0.39)	(1.21)	(1.33)	(0.67)
FDIC	−.0131	−.0209	−.0413	−.0162	−.0175	−.0413	−.0590	−.0684	−.0404
	(2.63)	(2.92)	(5.72)	(2.79)	(2.78)	(5.17)	(5.14)	(5.16)	(4.91)
HOLI	.2376	.2596	.1817	.2352	.2576	.1817	.2131	.2296	.1825
	(28.5)	(17.1)	(36.5)	(26.3)	(20.9)	(33.0)	(26.3)	(24.4)	(32.2)
ρ	.6670	.5777	.9860	.6631	.5698	.9760	.9203	.9157	.9483
	(8. 41)	(7.07)	(46.3)	(7.19)	(5.77)	(35.5)	(21.1)	(20.3)	(25.8)
$\bar{R}^2$	.8978	.7947	.9542	.9062	.8688	.9551	.9556	.9525	.9636
DW	2.03	1.94	2.30	1.81	1.79	2.15	2.01	1.97	2.08
Q	19.99	28.50	11.57	12.09	12.97	8.23	14.18	15.24	8.80

Definitions: PWD(i) = rate of change of wheat price, lagged i years. YD = rate of change of real GNP. FDIC = 1 during 1934–90, 0 otherwise. HOLI = 1 in 1933, 0 otherwise. DW = Durbin–Watson statistic. Q = Ljung–Box autocorrelation statistic. All regressions use AR1 routine to correct for serially correlated errors; ρ is the Cochrane–Orcutt first-order autocorrelation coefficient. Absolute values of t-statistics in parentheses.

passed the Depository Institutions Deregulation and Monetary Control Act). The addition of these dummies reduces serial correlation (leaving less variance to be explained by the Cochrane–Orcutt ρ) and improves the fit. However the latter dummy reduces the significance of national income, YD, completely eliminating its impact, although the first lag, YD(1), remains significant in some of the regressions.

The estimates in these tables underline the role of agricultural factors in U.S. bank failures. While the wheat-price variable, PWD, is significant in every equation, YD sometimes is not, especially once the Great Depression effects are controlled for by HOLI and RUNS (which always exhibit significant positive coefficients).

In every case the coefficient on the FDIC dummy variable is negative and significant. But note that the absolute value of the FDIC coefficient is much greater for state banks than for national banks in the better-fitting expanded model of Table 4. National banks also almost always display a significantly smaller absolute value of the coefficients on the other explanatory variables. This differential supports the view that the regulatory environments in which state and national banks operated differed from each other in every time-period considered (with state banks being more prone to failure), and that national banks were less affected than were state banks, in terms of their probability of failure, by the introduction of the FDIC.

To assess the suggestion made by Friedman and Schwartz (1963) that the introduction of FDIC insurance changed the "structure" of the banking system, we conduct a Chow test for structural change on the extended (Table 4) model before and after 1934. Columns 1–4 of Table 5 report the results of an unrestricted version of the extended model which allows the slope terms to differ between the subperiods by interacting FDIC with the explanatory variables. It can be seen that for some lags of both YD and PWD individually, there is a significant change in slope. All the significant changes indicate that for both national and state banks the introduction of deposit insurance reduced background, or otherwise unexplained, failures (FDIC), with the effect on state banks (−0.0200) being approximately twice as large as on national banks (−0.0099). Further, the changes in the coefficients on YD and PWD after 1933 indicate that banks became less sensitive to declines in the agricultural sector and the national economy.[6]

[6] The post-FDIC slope coefficients are found by adding the overall coefficient and the interaction term. Thus for example, the PWD(5) coefficient for state banks is −0.0287 for the period before deposit insurance and .0007 (= −0.0287 + 0.0294) for the period

Finally, the F-statistics reported in Table 5 indicate a strong rejection of the hypothesis that the parameters of the U.S. bank failure process remained unchanged after the introduction of FDIC insurance, consistent with Friedman and Schwartz's view.

Finally we consider the bank failures of the 1980s. Notice in Tables 4 and 5 that the coefficient on the dummy for this period (80s) is positive, but not robust in significance. It has become a regulators' (and journalists') cliché that the increase in failures in the 1980s was due to reduced regulatory restrictions on the activities of banks, but the following evidence contradicts this interpretation.

(1) A large proportion of the failures of the 1980s occurred in Texas following the decline of the oil industry after 1982.[7] In the last two columns of Table 5 we re-estimate the extended model excluding Texas banks. This eliminates the significance of the 80s dummy.

(2) In the aggregate (see Figure 8), the ratio of bank real estate loans to total bank loans (which, as we argue below, is important for failure rates of farm-state banks) rose rapidly from 1973 to 1980, remained approximately constant until 1985 and then began to rise again. 1980 was evidently not the turning point in real-estate lending by banks.

(3) Regarding competition for deposits, which had been increasing for some time before 1980, the Depository Institutions Deregulation and Monetary Control Act merely validated existing evasions.[8] Furthermore, that legislation actually kept official deposit rates further behind market rates during the "phase in" period of the early 1980s than had been the case prior to 1980.

It would appear that at the aggregate national level, the bank failures of the 1980s are largely explained by the spectacular oil and real-estate crashes in Texas and by agricultural depression in Midwestern farm states—in combination with actions initiated by the banks in the 1970s. As is often

after the institution of deposit insurance. This example is representative: in all cases the sum of the coefficient on the independent variable and the coefficient on the corresponding interaction term is close to zero (and not significantly different from zero, as assessed via *t*-tests).

[7] Texas accounted for 59 percent of national bank failures and 21 percent of state bank failures between 1982 and 1989.

[8] See the reference at the end of footnote 4.

TABLE 4
REGRESSIONS OF ANNUAL FAILURE RATES (R) OF ALL COMMERCIAL BANKS (B), STATE BANKS (S), AND NATIONAL BANKS (N)

	1871–1990			1893–1990			1912–1990		
	BR	SR	NR	BR	SR	NR	BR	SR	NR
CNST	.0113	.0223	.0050	.0122	.0151	.0065	.0171	.0208	.0094
	(7.63)	(5.25)	(4.34)	(6.99)	(6.67)	(4.54)	(6.48)	(6.62)	(3.77)
PWD	−.0095	−.0195	−.0030	−.0085	−.0117	−.0033	−.0075	−.0095	−.0030
	(2.05)	(2.08)	(1.20)	(1.65)	(1.65)	(1.12)	(1.78)	(1.95)	(0.90)
PWD(1)	−.0079	−.0054	−.0054	−.0105	−.0138	−.0062	−.0091	−.0107	−.0062
	(1.71)	(0.55)	(2.06)	(2.10)	(2.00)	(2.09)	(2.16)	(2.21)	(1.89)
PWD(2)	−.0052	−.0094	−.0042	−.0053	−.0054	−.0043	−.0060	−.0070	−.0040
	(1.21)	(1.02)	(1.67)	(1.10)	(0.82)	(1.51)	(1.50)	(1.52)	(1.25)
PWD(3)	−.0088	−.0129	−.0054	−.0107	−.0128	−.0068	−.0100	−.0113	−.0066
	(2.04)	(1.43)	(2.20)	(2.25)	(1.94)	(2.42)	(2.53)	(2.51)	(2.14)
PWD(4)	−.0044	−.0132	−.0035	−.0031	−.0033	−.0039	−.0026	−.0024	−.0034
	(1.00)	(1.43)	(1.39)	(0.63)	(0.48)	(1.35)	(0.64)	(0.51)	(1.05)
PWD(5)	−.0082	−.0056	−.0060	−.0112	−.0127	−.0072	−.0142	−.0166	−.0086
	(1.89)	(0.64)	(2.53)	(2.29)	(1.89)	(2.56)	(3.57)	(3.65)	(2.79)

YD(1)	−.0160 (1.15)	−.0189 (0.70)	−.0127 (1.73)	−.0143 (0.96)	−.0149 (0.73)	−.0129 (1.55)	−.0247 (1.92)	−.0286 (1.94)	−.0186 (1.89)
FDIC	−.0081 (3.76)	−.0181 (2.88)	−.0030 (1.74)	−.0089 (3.98)	−.0112 (3.86)	−.0044 (2.32)	−.0132 (4.31)	−.0162 (4.43)	−.0068 (2.37)
HOLI	.2077 (23.0)	.2292 (13.3)	.1858 (40.2)	.2057 (21.5)	.2192 (16.5)	.1852 (36.2)	.2079 (30.2)	.2223 (28.4)	.1848 (35.6)
RUNS	.0571 (9.46)	.0530 (3.78)	.0275 (7.27)	.0575 (9.37)	.0705 (8.62)	.0269 (6.55)	.0485 (8.69)	.0585 (9.04)	.0240 (5.29)
80s	.0047 (1.34)	.0020 (0.21)	.0074 (2.85)	.0047 (1.39)	.0031 (0.71)	.0073 (2.77)	.0033 (0.97)	.0014 (0.34)	.0064 (2.09)
ρ	.2745 (2.87)	.5016 (5.88)	.5069 (5.65)	.2069 (1.87)	.1557 (1.40)	.4628 (4.45)	.4529 (3.94)	.4755 (4.13)	.5534 (4.95)
$\bar{R}^2$	.9280	.8099	.9612	.9373	.9094	.9628	.9700	.9691	.9686
DW	2.14	2.00	2.21	1.70	1.53	2.02	2.41	2.47	2.14
Q	24.12	26.35	14.49	32.21	28.15	12.44	24.58	30.42	13.57

Definitions: RUNS = 1 in 1930–33, 0 otherwise. 80s = 1 in 1980–89, 0 otherwise. YD(i) = rate of change of real GNP, lagged i years. Other variables are defined below Table 3.

TABLE 5
TEST FOR STRUCTURAL CHANGE IN FAILURE RATES OF STATE (SR) AND NATIONAL (NR) BANKS (1912–90)

	Estimates with slope dummies to test for structural change in 1934				Excluding Texas (omitting slope dummies)	
	SR		NR		SRXTX	NRXTX
		×FDIC		×FDIC		
CNST	.0214 (8.92)		.0107 (4.11)		.0209 (6.67)	.0076 (6.16)
PWD	−.0176 (2.04)	.0117 (1.09)	−.0039 (0.68)	.0021 (0.29)	−.0096 (1.97)	−.0034 (1.19)
PWD(1)	−.0241 (3.40)	.0226 (2.43)	−.0152 (3.00)	.0164 (2.51)	−.0106 (2.19)	−.0069 (2.51)
PWD(2)	−.0102 (1.63)	.0065 (0.74)	−.0053 (1.18)	.0023 (0.36)	−.0073 (1.59)	−.0035 (1.34)
PWD(3)	−.0172 (2.84)	.0171 (1.94)	−.0107 (2.52)	.0106 (1.69)	−.0114 (2.50)	−.0058 (2.27)
PWD(4)	−.0099 (1.41)	.0103 (1.11)	−.0052 (1.05)	.0032 (0.49)	−.0022 (0.46)	−.0026 (0.95)
PWD(5)	−.0287 (4.57)	.0294 (3.34)	−.0147 (3.54)	.0160 (2.67)	−.0167 (3.64)	−.0091 (3.44)
YD(1)	−.0551 (2.00)	.0569 (1.74)	−.0511 (2.93)	.0521 (2.51)	−.0285 (1.92)	−.0157 (1.83)
FDIC	−.0200 (6.68)		−.0099 (3.16)		−.0163 (4.49)	−.0055 (3.90)
HOLI	.2204 (22.2)		.1811 (28.9)		2343 .(29.7)	.1971 (40.4)
RUNS	.0546 (8.58)		.0196 (4.07)		.0606 (9.34)	.0299 (9.24)
80s	.0055 (1.70)		.0084 (2.64)		.0003 (0.06)	.0025 (1.50)
ρ	.3372 (2.56)		.6072 (5.36)		.4692 (4.03)	.2123 (1.79)
$F_{8,59}$ (p-value)	6.60 (.000004)		3.26 (.0038)			
$\bar{R}^2$	.9741		.9737		.9711	.9798
DW	2.31		1.99		2.48	2.13

Definitions: SRXTX, NRXTX = State and national bank failures excluding Texas.

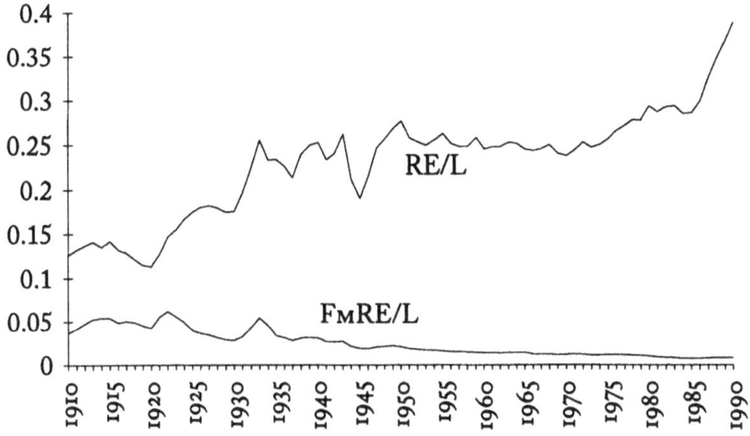

FIGURE 8: REAL ESTATE LOANS (RE/L) AND FARM MORTGAGE LOANS (FMRE/L) BY COMMERCIAL BANKS AS PROPORTIONS OF TOTAL BANK LOANS

the case, deregulation, like regulation, is best explained as effect rather than cause.

3 BANK FAILURES IN NINE FARM STATES, 1892–1990

> [I]ndebtedness is neither good nor evil in itself. Such a judgement can rest only on a comparison of the interest charges with the gain through increased productivity or increased selling price. . . . The most critical situation arises when debts are incurred in a period of rising prices, and must be carried, the interest charges met, and the principal paid off or the debt renewed, in a period of falling prices. This latter condition . . . is unfortunately . . . very likely to arise.
>
> —Clara Eliot (1927)

The association between agricultural depression and bank failures invites investigation into the specifics of farm-bank failures. Of particular interest is the banking experience of the states in the North Central region of the United States—those states between Oklahoma and Arkansas and the Canadian border. Between 1892 and the present, North Dakota,

South Dakota, Kansas, Missouri, Minnesota, Nebraska, Iowa, Wisconsin and Illinois provide an interesting record of the performance of unit banking systems in largely agricultural economies under a variety of economic conditions and regulatory circumstances.[9] While their economies and banking structures display a high degree of uniformity, four of the states—North Dakota, South Dakota, Kansas and Nebraska—had state deposit insurance schemes between 1909 and 1929. The pooled sample therefore provides a natural experiment in both economic forces associated with bank failures, and the possible influence on bank failure rates exerted by deposit insurance. Regulatory histories and descriptive statistics for the nine states are presented in Table 6.

TABLE 6
DESCRIPTIVE STATISTICS ON FARM-STATE PANEL DATA SET

	Period of State Insurance	Branches per bank		State bank failure rate		National bank failure rate	
		1920	1990	Mean	Max. (year)	Mean	Max. (year)
ND	1917–28	0.0	1.1	.019	.267 (1933)	.012	.149 (1933)
SD	1915–26	0.0	1.4	.019	.281 (1926)	.011	.141 (1931)
NE	1909–28	0.002	0.7	.017	.656 (1933)	.008	.193 (1933)
KS	1909–28	0.0	0.8	.008	.095 (1933)	.004	.106 (1933)
MN	–	0.0	1.0	.012	.206 (1933)	.005	.132 (1933)
IA	–	0.0	1.0	.019	.958 (1933)	.015	.720 (1933)
MO	–	0.0	1.7	.012	.430 (1933)	.005	.156 (1933)
WI	–	0.009	1.8	.016	1.04 (1933)*	.006	.452 (1933)
IL	–	0.0	1.1	.012	.225 (1933)	.008	.457 (1933)
US	–	0.04	4.0	.013	.311 (1933)	.007	.225 (1933)
CA	–	1.69	10.1	.006	.180 (1933)	.007	.163 (1933)

*Failure rates may exceed 1 because they are ratios of annual failures to numbers of banks on June 30.

[9] The rationale for choosing these states can be appreciated by reference to the map in Figure 3. We wished to examine those states in the middle of the country where agricultural bank failures have been most significant. From this general category we excluded states that did not have a strong history of unit banking and those—like Oklahoma and Texas—where the impact of other industries (oil in particular) diluted the uniformity of the sample. For evidence of the continuing importance of this sample in relation to the national bank failure rate, and the extent to which these states are still largely agricultural, see Melichar (1986).

Of particular importance in understanding farm-state bank failures is the use of bank credit to purchase farm real estate. In the previous section we used the price of wheat as an index of the swings in the fortunes of farm economies. Since the value of land is the discounted present value of expected returns to farming, land prices are dependent on current and expected commodity prices. It is through the impact of changing farm prices on the value of farm land pledged as collateral on farm real estate loans that the fortunes of the banking system are tied to the agricultural economy. And, as noted in the epigraph to this section, farm credit is especially vulnerable when acquired during a boom.

During the post-World War II era, as in the 1920s, farm values have followed farm income. Both trended gently upward until the mid-1970s, when poor crops in the Soviet Union and elsewhere caused high demands for U.S. output and sharp increases in agricultural prices and U.S. farm income. The increased income was projected into the future in the form of high farm values (see Table 2 and Figure 7).[10] Those who borrowed to buy farms in the 1970s, in anticipation of continued high or even rising farm incomes, were squeezed by falling incomes and farm values and rising interest rates in the 1980s, like an earlier generation in the 1920s. The trajectories of agricultural prices and farm values during the three most severe agricultural depressions (excepting 1929–33) of the last hundred years are shown in Table 2 and Figures 5–7.

For continuity with the regressions of the previous section, we begin our statistical analysis of the farm-state panel by assessing the explanatory power of the price-of-wheat model in this context. In Table 7 (page 184) the price of wheat and real GNP are significantly inversely related to bank failures—although the RUNS dummy reduces the significance of the latter, as in the aggregate results. The 80s dummy is insignificant in the panel data. The FDIC coefficient is again robustly negative. The interesting difference from the aggregate data concerns the dummy for the state insurance systems (STINS), which is positive and significant in three of the regressions reported. (The Comptroller of the Currency prevented national banks from participating in the state insurance systems.) Is there reason to suspect that the state insurance schemes—unlike the FDIC system—caused failures?

[10] See Melichar (1984, 1986, 1987) and Falk (1991) for discussions of the rise and fall of farm incomes and land values.

TABLE 7
REGRESSIONS OF THE BASIC PRICE OF WHEAT MODEL
USING A PANEL OF DATA FROM NINE STATES*

	1892–1989				1913–1989			
	SR		NR		SR		NR	
CNST	.0239	.0106	.0145	.0092	.0350	.0164	.0190	.0127
	(8.67)	(3.55)	(9.76)	(5.58)	(8.13)	(3.41)	(9.14)	(5.48)
PWD	.0418	−.0148	−.0178	−.0056	−.0409	−.0171	−.0180	−.0070
	(4.62)	(1.63)	(3.32)	(1.02)	(3.85)	(1.59)	(2.91)	(1.10)
PWD(1)	.0266	−.0113	−.0155	−.0085	−.0248	−.0114	−.0142	−.0079
	(2.87)	(1.26)	(2.82)	(1.57)	(2.26)	(1.06)	(2.22)	(1.24)
PWD(2)	−.0287	−.0110	−.0138	−.0058	−.0259	−.0096	−.0135	−.0060
	(3.17)	(1.24)	(2.57)	(1.08)	(2.44)	(0.92)	(2.19)	(0.92)
PWD(3)	−.0282	−.0177	−.0167	−.0118	−.0230	−.0165	−.0310	−.0099
	(3.16)	(2.06)	(3.16)	(2.27)	(2.22)	(1.64)	(2.17)	(1.66)
PWD(4)	−.0226	−.0015	−.0146	−.0084	−.0224	−.0014	−.0141	−.0046
	(2.47)	(0.17)	(2.69)	(0.93)	(2.10)	(0.14)	(2.26)	(0.74)
PWD(5)	−.0360	−.0263	−.0226	−.0181	−.0367	−.0272	−.0225	−.0180
	(4.04)	(3.05)	(4.27)	(3.46)	(3.52)	(2.66)	(3.69)	(2.96)

YD	−.1224	−.0059	−.0649	−.0122	−.1150	−.0023	−.0642	−.0125
	(4.73)	(0.21)	(4.23)	(0.73)	(3.74)	(0.10)	(3.59)	(0.63)
FDIC	−.0122	−.0061	−.0087	−.0067	−.0328	−.0120	−.0133	−.0102
	(3.65)	(1.80)	(4.25)	(3.51)	(4.75)	(2.32)	(5.36)	(4.00)
HOLI	.4073	.3300	.2496	.2148	.3989	.3320	.2465	.2160
	(25.8)	(19.2)	(26.7)	(20.7)	(22.7)	(17.4)	(24.2)	(19.0)
STINS	.0163	.0235			.0079	.0209		
	(2.68)	(4.02)			(1.03)	(2.74)		
RUNS		.0980		.0437		.0922		.0400
		(9.23)		(6.84)		(7.46)		(5.50)
80s		.0060		.0006		.0005		.0009
		(0.12)		(0.21)		(0.10)		(0.27)
$\bar{R}^2$	.5524	.5930	.5633	.5859	.5620	.5948	.5798	.5974
DW	1.58	1.71	1.46	1.51	1.62	1.73	1.51	1.56

*OLS estimation. Although the DWs indicate serial correlation, correction by an AR1 procedure yielded no changes in significance or orders of magnitude. Time periods reported are for the dependent variables, reduced to allow for lags. The periods chosen reflect data availability on state failures (from 1892) and state land values (from 1913).

It should be noted that all of these state insurance systems were in place by the beginning of the farm depression that began in 1920, following the collapse of European demand. North Dakota and South Dakota started their systems near the start of the downturn. Kansas and Nebraska, on the other hand, had ten years to get their systems up and running before their baptism in fire. Can our panel data can give us any indication of the impact on bank failures of the state insurance systems, as distinct from the unfortunate times or local circumstances in which they had to operate? This question is addressed by the estimates in Table 8, where the failure rates for both state banks and national banks are regressed (separately) on three dummy variables. STINS equals 1 for all observations (states and years) in which state deposit insurance schemes were actually in operation; STATES equals 1 for all observations on states that had state deposit insurance at some time during the sample period, regardless of whether such insurance was in force or not; and PERIOD equals 1 for all observations during the average period of existence of the state insurance schemes, i.e. 1913–28.[11] (All the dummies are set equal to zero when not equal to 1.)

TABLE 8
TESTING FOR EFFECTS OF STATE INSURANCE ON BANK FAILURE RATES USING PANEL DATA, 1892–1929

	CONSTANT	STINS	PERIOD	STATES	R^2
State banks	.0077 (2.82)	.0201 (3.55)	.0054 (1.43)	−.0005 (0.14)	.0880
National banks	.0083 (1.66)	.0002 (0.06)	.0036 (1.33)	.0086 (2.90)	.0399

For definitions of variables see text; *t*-statistics in parentheses.

So far as the state banks are concerned, it appears that even when the STATE and PERIOD effects are controlled for, the failure rate was significantly higher (on average 2 per cent higher) when state insurance schemes were in place. As regards the national banks (which were not

[11] Thus STINS is close to being the product of STATES and PERIOD, but is not exactly so, since the actual periods during which state insurance was in force differed across the states.

eligible for participation in the state insurance schemes), on the other hand, the STATES effect is significant (an elevation of the average failure rate by somewhat less than 1 per cent) while STINS is not. This suggests that while the 'insurance states' were relatively failure-prone in general, as reflected in the national bank figures, nonetheless the finding that their insurance schemes were associated with especially high state bank failure rates does not appear to be spurious.

Our discussion has concentrated on the role of farm real estate debt in predicting high rates of bank failure during periods of rapid declines in farm values. The use of state panel data allows us to take into account the particular conditions of each state, while increasing the power of tests on the common elements such as deposit insurance. To this end we constructed a variable named BURDEN, as follows:

$$\text{BURDEN} = \frac{\text{FVO} \times \text{RE}}{\text{FY}}$$

where FVO denotes the negative percentage changes in farm values by state, RE denotes the levels of real estate debt, also by state, and FY is a measure of nominal farm income at the national level.[12] BURDEN is designed to capture the phenomenon of a decline in farm values relative to the outstanding farm real estate debt held by commercial banks, perhaps the key factor triggering farm-state bank failures. The deflation by FY relates the series to current farm prices. Figure 9 displays BURDEN against the rate of state bank failures for each of our nine states. The degree to which movement in this variable mirrors the bank failure rate is striking.

Table 9 (p. 190) reports regression results for various models using the BURDEN variable. BURDEN is powerful and robust in explaining farm bank failures, indicating the key role of farm real estate dynamics. Again we see a significant negative correlation between FDIC insurance and both state and national bank failures. But notice that inclusion of the RUNS dummy robs FDIC of significance in the regressions for state bank failures. One aspect of the ability of the FDIC to reduce bank failures is its success in eliminating the contagious spread of bank runs. Controlling for RUNS in the presence of the FDIC dummy amounts, in effect, to accounting for the influence of bank runs twice. Also the fact that this occurred only in the case of the state banks in the panel suggests the possibility that state banks

[12] Sources and descriptions of the data are given in the Data Appendix on p. 198.

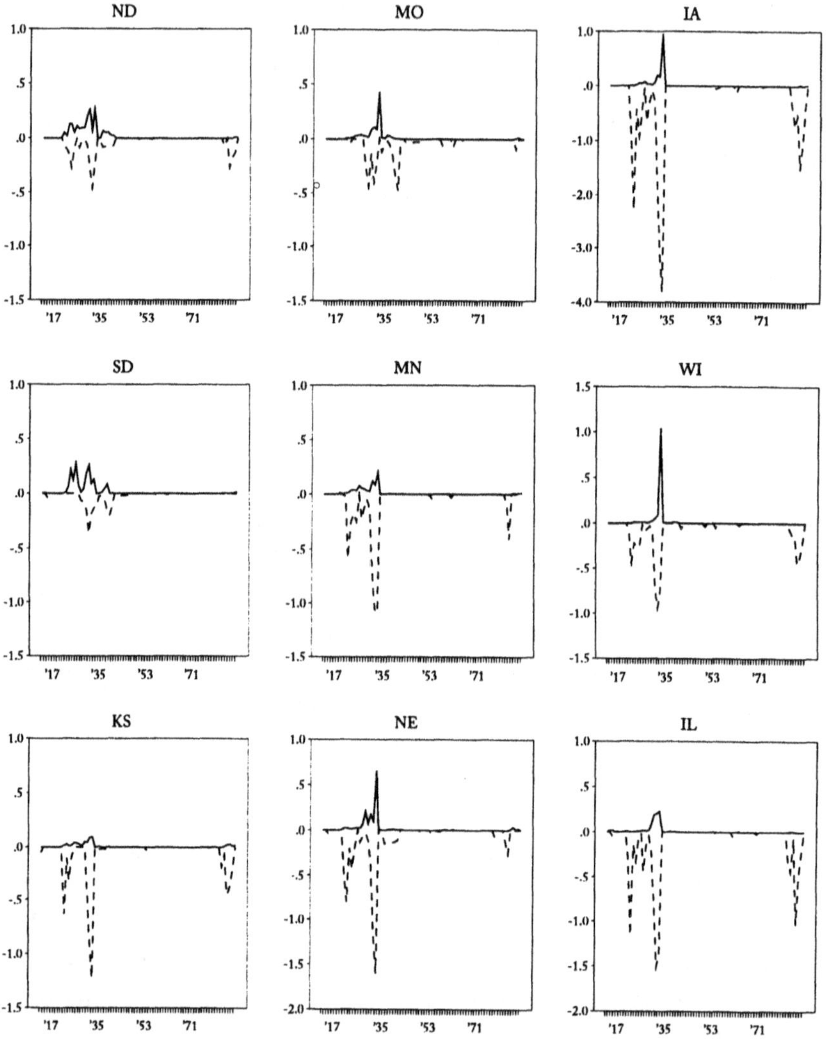

FIGURE 9: BURDEN-OF-DEBT (≤ 0) AND BANK FAILURE RATES (≥ 0) IN NINE FARM STATES

may have been more prone than national banks to run-induced failures. State insurance, though at times only marginally significant, continues to have a positive relationship with bank failures. YD is not robust for the BURDEN models in the panel data set, losing its significance when the runs of the 1930s are controlled for by RUNS. This is consistent with the largely agricultural character of these states. The 80s dummy is insignificant in the farm-state panel, consistent with our earlier findings.

Finally, we would like to know if the same significant structural shift that we observed in the aggregate bank failure relationship is detectable in the farm-state panel. Table 10 (p. 192) reports regression results and F-tests similar to those of Table 5: the null hypothesis is no change in the intercept nor slope parameters after the introduction of FDIC insurance. The coefficients on the interaction terms BURDFDIC and YDFDIC (particularly the former) indicate that both state and national farm banks have become less sensitive, in terms of their propensity to fail, to declines in the national and farm economies since 1934. The F-tests indicate a strong rejection of the hypothesis that no structural change took place, for both state and national banks. As with the aggregate data, the farm-state panel provides no support for the claim that the federal deposit insurance system is to blame for the bank failures of the last ten years.

4 Conclusions

> The framers of the legislation creating the FDIC realized that the power to grant or withhold deposit insurance would give the new agency considerable influence on bank operations. Thus, they used the FDIC as a lever to upgrade overall standards of the banking industry. The FDIC was empowered to prescribe certain minimum operative requirements which a bank had to meet and maintain in order to qualify for insurance. This power, of course, was also necessary to limit potential losses. In order to make sure its requirements were being met, the FDIC hired a staff of bank examiners.
>
> —American Institute of Banking (1966)

Many commentators have laid the blame for recent bank failures on federal deposit insurance. Taking a longer historical perspective on bank failures, we find no evidence to support this view. Failures are largely explained by systemic events such as the Great Depression and recurrent

TABLE 9A
REGRESSIONS OF PANELLED STATE FAILURE RATES FOR STATE BANKS USING BURDEN-OF-DEBT MODELS, 1913–89

		CNST	BUR-DEN	YD	FDIC	RUNS	HOLI	STINS	80s	$\bar{R}^2$ DW
1	SR	.0214	−6.77	−.0611	−.0189		.3464	.0107		.5953
		(4.85)	(9.99)	(2.13)	(3.87)		(20.6)	(1.44)		1.62
2	SR	.0071	−5.23	−.0256	−.0074	.0822	.2980	.0235		.6232
		(1.50)	(7.64)	(0.86)	(1.50)	(7.50)	(17.1)	(3.20)		1.75
3	SR	.0211	−6.90	−.0628	−.0175		.3453	.0109	−.0063	.5925
		(4.77)	(10.0)	(2.19)	(3.49)		(20.5)	(1.47)	(1.12)	1.63
4	SR	.0070	−5.29	.0243	−.0068	.0817	.2977	.0235	−.0028	.6228
		(1.51)	(7.62)	(0.81)	(1.36)	(7.44)	(17.1)	(3.21)	(0.53)	1.75
5	SR	.0209	−6.97		−.0208		.3460	.0090		.5902
		(4.74)	(10.3)		(4.34)		(20.5)	(1.22)		1.60
6	SR	.0079	−5.22		−.0072	.0786	.3002	.0235		.6233
		(1.73)	(7.64)		(1.46)	(7.79)	(17.4)	(3.21)		1.75
7	SR	.0078	−5.30		−.0066	.0782	.2999	.0235	−.0032	.6263
		(1.71)	(7.63)		(1.31)	(7.74)	(17.4)	(3.21)	(0.60)	1.75

TABLE 9B
REGRESSIONS OF PANELLED STATE FAILURE RATES FOR NATIONAL BANKS USING BURDEN-OF-DEBT MODELS, 1913–89

		CNST	BUR-DEN	YD	FDIC	RUNS	HOLI	STINS	80s	$\bar{R}^2$ DW
1	NR	.0085	−5.37	−.0193	−.0087		.2045			.6625
		(4.32)	(14.7)	(1.25)	(3.87)		(22.4)			1.59
2	NR	.0054	−4.85	.0088	−.0065	.0252	.1887			.6708
		(2.63)	(12.7)	(0.53)	(2.87)	(4.25)	(19.4)			1.63
3	NR	.0084	−5.45	−.0205	−.0079		.2035		−.0044	.6630
		(4.24)	(14.8)	(1.32)	(3.36)		(22.3)		(1.46)	1.59
4	NR	.0054	−4.92	−.0073	−.0059	.0246	.1880		−.0030	.6709
		(2.61)	(12.7)	(0.43)	(2.53)	(4.13)	(19.4)		(1.11)	1.63
5	NR	.0082	−5.44		−.0091		.2040			.6632
		(4.19)	(15.1)		(4.12)		(22.4)			1.57
6	NR	.0057	−4.88		−.0065	.0240	.1894			.6628
		(2.85)	(12.7)		(2.85)	(4.40)	(19.7)			1.58
7	NR	.0056	−4.92		−.0058	−.0360	.1890		−.0034	.6934
		(2.80)	(12.7)		(2.50)	(4.32)	(19.7)		(1.14)	1.61

TABLE 10
CHOW TEST FOR STRUCTURAL CHANGE
CONCIDENT WITH THE INTRODUCTION OF THE FDIC
(SAMPLE PERIOD 1913–89)

	SR1	SR2	NR1	NR2
CONSTANT	.0038 (0.78)	.0195 (4.42)	.0037 (1.66)	.0073 (3.69)
BURDEN	−6.16 (8.15)	−7.52 (10.1)	−5.70 (13.7)	−6.11 (15.2)
BURDFDIC	5.26 (2.82)	6.32 (3,55)	4.74 (4.61)	4.94 (5.15)
YD	.092 (1.51)	−.166 (3.47)	.033 (0.99)	−.041 (1.63)
YDFDIC	−.087 (1.12)	.170 (2.86)	−.032 (0.84)	.041 (1.31)
FDIC	−.002 (0.43)	−.018 (3.49)	−.358 (1.34)	−.007 (2.87)
HOLI	.287 (15.9)	.337 (20.1)	.182 (18.3)	.196 (21.7)
RUNS	.087 (6.52)		.024 (3.36)	
STINS	.024 (3.28)	.015 (2.06)		
80s	.003 (0.46)		.002 (0.58)	
$F_{3,676}$	3.83	12.77	9.55	15.17
p-value	.0096	3×10^{-8}	3×10^{-6}	4×10^{-8}
$\bar{R}^2$	.627	.604	.680	.675
DW	1.75	1.68	1.64	1.62

The F-test is on the hypothesis that the true coefficients on BURDFDIC, YDFDIC, and FDIC are all zero.

farm real-estate booms and busts (as well as the analogous oil cycles in the case of Texas).

An exploration of two questions raised by our study may permit a fuller and more realistic appraisal of federal deposit insurance. First, why were there not *more* bank failures in the 1980s? Figures 6 and 7 and Table 2 indicate that the land bust that began in 1980 was comparable in severity to the crash of the 1920s, yet bank failure rates never approached those of the earlier era. Second, what differentiates the state bank insurance systems, which we find to be associated with higher bank failures, from the FDIC system?

Many factors suggest themselves as part of the explanation for the relatively mild bank failure rate of the 1980s. The difference between the 1920s and the 1980s is especially pronounced in our sample of Midwestern farm states, where banks failed at a rate greater than the national average during the 1920s (2.6 percent compared with 2.1 percent) but less than the national average during the 1980s (0.5 compared with 0.9 percent; see Table 1). The obvious explanation is the smaller role of bank loans to farmers in the latter period, partly because of the relative decline of the farm sector but more importantly because of the growth of federal farm credit. The decline of farm mortgage loans as a proportion of total commercial bank loans nationwide is shown in Figure 8. Unlike the farm credit boom leading up to the bust of the 1920s, which was financed primarily by banks, the 1970s boom was financed primarily by federal agencies.

It may be tempting to conclude that bank failures were less in the more recent period because most of the risky loans had been picked up by the federal government. But that would be inconsistent with the moral hazard explanation of bank failures, which asserts that deposit insurance induces banks to seek risky investments wherever they may be found. In view of the continued importance of real estate loans in general (see Figure 8), it is not likely that the search costs of finding risky loans have increased. And in light of the information displayed in Figures 2 and 9, it appears that bankers' aversion to risk has changed little since the nineteenth century—nor, particularly for small banks in one-industry areas, has their vulnerability to economic catastrophes.

Compare banks and loan defaults with home owners and hurricanes. The costs of building hurricane-proof houses (or investing only in short-term federal securities) are prohibitive. Falling houses, like failing banks, are rare events that usually occur in bunches—as in Figure 9. Subsidized home insurance, whether against hurricane, fire, flood, or earthquake, reduces the incentive to erect protections against those risks. But they are low-probability events with little effect on home owners' behavior—except for the frantic digging of fire-breaks or laying of sandbags when the threat is imminent. The caution of home owners might be increased if a monopolistic insurer with the powers to cancel insurance and seize property (like the FDIC) conducted regular inspections. This analogy is supported by the experience of Texas, where most oil loans remained with banks and failure rates were similar in the 1920s and 1980s. In both areas—Texas and the farm states to the north—banks responded to the credit demands emanating from the local economy, and they were affected similarly to the bulk of their borrowers in about the same degree in the 1980s as the 1920s, with evidence of somewhat more caution in their lending in the later period.

Our evidence on the state deposit insurance systems supports this account of the effects of the federal insurance system. What was different about the state deposit insurance systems, and why were they associated with higher bank failure rates?[13] To account for this result along the lines of our discussion of the "success" of the FDIC system, it is sufficient to note the degree to which the state systems differed in their ability to protect the payment system from run-induced disruption, while avoiding the inducement to excessive risk-taking by banks. There is evidence that these state systems were often structured to limit the effectiveness of supervision by state authorities and other banks in the system.[14] In addition, most of the early-twentieth-century experiments (including all those in our sample) had upper limits on the premiums (usually 2 percent of insured deposits) that banks were liable to pay in the event of high failure rates (FDIC, 1958, pp. 53–4). Thus, from the moral hazard viewpoint, these banks were not only provided an incentive to risk taking (all banks paid the same premium rate), but banks may also have been discouraged from surveillance of each other's behavior since the maximum cost to them was fixed. In almost every

[13] A fuller analysis would look at each system individually. Kansas had fewer failures during its deposit insurance era than in some surrounding states without such legislation. The Kansas system was unique in the voluntary nature of participation in the insurance fund. This meant that rather than winding up the fund when failures depleted accumulated premiums—the common experience of the other states in the 1920s—Kansas saw a mass exodus from its system after a 1926 court decision rendered participating banks not liable for further costs of past and future failure if they exited. Most banks did so.

[14] See Robb (1921), the 1956 FDIC *Annual Report*, and Calomiris (1989).

case (except Texas) the crisis of the 1920s led to suspension of the insurance fund after the maximum premium had been levied for a few years and was felt to be a burden by the banks. State systems, then, may have provided a greater opportunity to abuse deposit insurance than the FDIC system.

In addition to relatively lax supervision under the state systems, the relatively weak fiscal backing of these systems is also relevant. Though it appears not to have been fully understood by all depositors at the time,[15] the state authorities did not financially back these state insurance funds. All payments to depositors of failed institutions came from premiums assessed on the banks. If we attribute part of the FDIC's success in reducing bank failures to its capacity to settle the claims of all depositors of failed institutions *immediately*, and so to eliminate all threats to the payment system—a capacity that ultimately rests on federal fiscal backing—it is clear that no state system could hope to provide the same service. Even though many of the state systems eventually paid out a high proportion of losses to depositors, this took years in many cases.[16] In the crisis of the 1920s, the resources of the state insurance funds, in the form of accumulated premiums, did not permit them to step in and stop runs as the FDIC has been able to do.

This is not to deny that there may be less costly ways than the FDIC for dealing with bank failures consequent upon the kind of shocks recently experienced in the farm belt and the oil patch. But the FDIC has yet to be shown to increase the rate at which banks fail.

References

American Institute of Banking 1966. *Principles of Bank Operation.*

Balke, Nathan S. and Robert J. Gordon 1989. "The Estimation of Prewar Gross National Product: Methodology and New Evidence." *Journal of Political Economy* (February): 38–92.

Berry, Thomas S. 1988. "Production and Population since 1789." Bostwick Paper No. 6. Richmond, VA: Bostwick Press.

[15] See Grant and Crum (1978, p. 86) for evidence that this confusion may have been fostered by the banks themselves. The same phenomenon appears to have figured in the runs on some state S&L deposit insurance system in the 1980s, such as those in Maryland, Rhode Island and Ohio.

[16] The payout records for the state systems are available in the 1956 *Annual Report* of the Comptroller of the Currency.

Calomiris, Charles W. 1989. "Deposit Insurance: Lessons from the Record." Federal Reserve Bank of Chicago *Economic Perspectives* (May/June): 10–30.

Comptroller of the Currency *Annual Reports*.

Eliot, Clara 1927. *The Farmer's Campaign for Credit*. New York: D. Appleton and Company.

Falk, Barry 1991. "Formally Testing the Present Value Model of Farmland Prices." *American Journal of Agricultural Economics* (February): 1–10.

Federal Deposit Insurance Corporation *Annual Reports*.

Federal Reserve Committee on Branch, Group, and Chain Banking 1932. *225 Bank Suspensions: Case Histories from Examiners' Reports*. Federal Reserve Board.

Friedman, Milton and Anna J. Schwartz 1963. *A Monetary History of the United States, 1867–1960*. Princeton, NJ: Princeton University Press.

Golembe, Carter 1961. "The Deposit Insurance Legislation of 1933: An Examination of its Antecedents and its Purposes." *Political Science Quarterly* No. 2: 181–200.

Grant, Joseph M. and Lawrence Crum 1978. *The Development of State-Chartered Banking in Texas*. Austin: University of Texas at Austin.

Kane, Edward J. 1987. "No Room for Weak Links in the Chain of Deposit-Insurance Reform." *Journal of Financial Services Research* (September): 77–111.

Kaufman, George G. 1985. "Implications of Large Bank Problems and Insolvencies for the Banking System and Economic Policy." *Issues in Bank Regulation* (Winter): 35–42.

Melichar, Emanuel 1984. "A Financial Perspective on Agriculture." *Federal Reserve Bulletin* (January): 1–13.

______. 1986. "Agricultural Banks under Stress." *Federal Reserve Bulletin* (July): 437–48.

______. 1987. "Turning the Corner on Troubled Farm Debt." *Federal Reserve Bulletin* (July): 523–36.

Robb, Thomas B. 1921. *The Guaranty of Bank Deposits*. New York: Houghton Mifflin.

Spong, Kenneth 1990. *Banking Regulation: Its Purposes, Implementation, and Effects*, 3rd ed. Federal Reserve Bank of Kansas City.

Wood, John H. and Norma L. Wood 1985. *Financial Markets.* San Diego, CA: Harcourt Brace Jovanovich.

Data Appendix

Key to sources:

HS, BS, SCB, SA: U.S. Dept. of Commerce, *Historical Statistics of the U.S., Business Statistics, Survey of Current Business, Statistical Abstract of the U.S.*

AS, AgR, EI: U.S. Dept. of Agriculture, *Agricultural Statistics, Agricultural Resources, Economic Indicators of the Farm Sector.*

FRB *ASD*: Federal Reserve Board, *Annual Statistical Digests.*

AR: Annual Reports.

Definitions and sources of variables:

Numbers of state and national banks (June 30) and annual failures by state: 1892–95, Comptroller of Currency *AR*; 1896–1955, FRB *All-Bank Statistics*; 1956–69, FDIC *AR*; 1970–89, FRB, *ASD 1970–79, 1980–89*; 1990, FDIC *Statistics on Banking*. Aggregate U.S. data are from *HS*.

Agricultural prices (PA, PW): *HS*; *BS 1961–88*; *SCB*; *AS*.

Real GNP (Y) and the GNP deflator (PY): 1860–68, Berry (1988); 1869–1929, Balke and Gordon (1989); 1929–90, *Economic Reports of the President*.

U.S. farm value per acre (FV): 1910–70, *HS* and *SA*; 1970–89, *SA*; 1990, *AgR*.

Farm values per acre by state (FVO): 1912–43, USDA *Farm Real Estate Situation*; 1944–88, *AS*; 1989–90, *AgR*.

Farm real estate debt by state, Jan 1 (RE): 1930–49, *AS*; 1950–60, *Farm Real Estate Historical Series, 1950–85*; 1961–90, *Farm Sector Balance Sheet, 1960–89*; 1990, *State Financial Summary, 1990* (all USDA). 1910–29, data not available by state, but regional data were used to link this period with state data beginning 1930.

Gross U.S. farm income (FY): 1910–66, *HS*; 1967–82, *AS*; 1983–90, *EI*.

8

BANK FAILURES AS POISSON VARIATES: A REAPPRAISAL

Nurhan Davutyan

Michigan Technological University

1 Introduction

This paper uses a model developed in Davutyan (1989) to appraise alternative possible causes of bank failures from 1947 to 1991, with emphasis on the possibility of structural shifts in these causal relationships as a consequence of deregulation, particularly the Depository Institutions Deregulation and Monetary Control Act (DIDMCA) of 1980. Various factors that may bear upon bank failure are discussed in Section 2, and their effects are estimated in Section 3. Because of the discrete nature of the data, which makes Normal or Gaussian estimation inappropriate, estimates by two additional methods are reported: Poisson and a compound Poisson approach called NegBin. Tests for structural change are reported in Sections 4 and 5 and the principal findings are summarized in Section 6.

2 The model

The dependent variable is FAIL, the annual number of commercial bank failures in the United States as reported by the Federal Deposit Insurance Corporation. The explanatory variables are as follows:

(1) PROFIT is the ratio of total (including overseas) profits to the US Gross National Product. This variable measures the total pool of profits to be distributed between the financial and nonfinancial sectors.[1] Common sense and historical experience suggest an inverse relationship between FAIL and PROFIT.

[1] According to the *Economic Report of the President*, the nonfinancial sector consists of manufacturing, transportation and public utilities, wholesale and retail trade and "other."

(2) BANKPRO is the share of domestic banking profits in total profits. Thus the numerator does not include that portion of overseas profits which is attributable to banking.[2] To that extent, this variable is a downward-biased measure of the share accruing to banks. Again, one would expect an inverse relationship between FAIL and BANKPRO. One might argue that PROFIT and BANKPRO should not be separately meaningful explanatory variables on the grounds that what really counts is their product, namely the ratio of banking profits to GNP; but a likelihood ratio test, not reported here for brevity, established that PROFIT and BANKPRO made independent explanatory contributions.

(3) SHAREFIN is the ratio of the profits of "domestic financial institutions" (referred to as "Other" in the *Economic Report of the President*) to "total domestic financial sector" profits. The latter consists of the former plus the Federal Reserve System.[3] One should expect an inverse relationship between FAIL and SHAREFIN.

(4) BORROW, in constant 1982 dollars, is the outstanding borrowing by depository institutions from the Federal Reserve System in December of each year. Since this borrowing is a last bulwark against bankruptcy, one should expect FAIL to fall as BORROW increases, *ceteris paribus*.

(5) SIZE is the ratio of deposits in failed banks to the number of such banks during a year. It is a measure of the size of the "typical" failed bank.[4] It is included because there is strong evidence that the monetary authorities are less likely to declare a large bank bankrupt.

Before proceeding further, some remarks about the explanatory variables are warranted. First, the so-called LBOs (leveraged buy-outs) and

[2] For 1947, the first year in my data set, the ratio of overseas profits to total (domestic plus overseas) profits is 3.8 percent. This ratio has been rising over time, reflecting the growing internationalization of the American economy. For 1991, the last year in the data set, overseas profits accounted for 19.6 percent of total profits.

[3] Table B-86 of the 1993 *Economic Report of the President* divides the domestic financial industry into Federal Reserve Banks and Other. Thus, "Other" consists of the following sectors: depository institutions; nondepository credit institutions; security and commodity brokers; insurance carriers; regulated investment companies; small business investment companies; and real estate investment trusts.

[4] The following figures give some idea of the size of the "average" failed bank. The value of SIZE, measured in 1982 dollars, was at its minimum (roughly $3 million) in 1954. The maximum value for SIZE ($730 million) occurs in 1974, reflecting the failure of Franklin National. The largest value of SIZE for the 1980s ($407 million) occurs in 1981.

takeovers of the 1980s have attracted a great deal of media attention. Indeed, there has been a perception that those developments and the highly publicized bank failures of the last ten to fifteen years are somehow related (see, for instance, Osterberg, 1993). To the extent that such a relationship exists, it will tend to mask the inverse association between FAIL and BANKPRO posited above. At least in the short run, LBOs, takeovers, and the like reflect a distributional squabble between the financial and the nonfinancial sectors. The essence of these so-called financial innovations is the replacement of equity with debt in the nonfinancial sector, and the interest payments which the debt entails will tend to boost the profitability of the bank or banks which finance the particular LBO or takeover. Thus LBO activity may raise the relative aggregate profits of the banking sector, while at the same time—due to increased risk exposure for particular banks, perhaps—contributing to bank failures.

Second, the tax treatment of central bank profits (seigniorage) has been a perennial issue. Recently this issue has resurfaced under the guise of whether the FDIC will apply the "payout" or the "purchase and assumption" method to failed banks. Unlike the former, the latter has no tax dimension.[5] Moreover, DIDMCA mandated that the services of the Federal Reserve System be available to all depository institutions and not just member banks. According to Kohn (1993, p. 179) the former numbered 44,000 whereas the latter consisted of 5,500 institutions. Since one major service the Fed provides is to operate a payments system, i.e., check clearing and Fedwire, this particular provision of DIDMCA puts the Fed into competition with the large correspondent banks in the check-clearing business.[6] I try to measure the importance of the above mentioned considerations by including SHAREFIN—the ratio of "private financial sector" profits to total domestic financial sector profits—among the explanatory variables. To the extent that bankruptcy is caused by a lack of profits, I expect a negative SHAREFIN coefficient.

[5] See Barro (1982) and Mayer *et al.* (1993, pp. 188–9) for discussions of seigniorage in the U.S. context, and Kohn (1993, p. 437) for the tax implications of the payout and purchase and assumption methods.

[6] The other major service provided by the Fed to the private banks is the discount window facility. That issue is discussed in sections 2 and 5.

3 Econometric issues

FAIL was regressed against the set of explanatory variables using three different approaches: Normal, Poisson and Negative Binomial (or NegBin). In every case the estimation was done by the method of Maximum Likelihood. In the Normal approach, the natural logarithm of FAIL was the left-hand-side variable. In all three approaches the natural logarithms of the explanatory variables were used. As a result, the estimated coefficients are to be interpreted as elasticities and thus are comparable across the approaches. For example, focusing on Table 1 (the restricted regressions) we can see that as BANKPRO goes up 1 percent, the number of bank failures goes down 2.51 percent in the Normal approach, 2.01 percent according to Poisson, and 2.81 percent according to NegBin. These estimates are not far apart. Some remarks about the relative merits of the three approaches to estimation may, however, be helpful.

The assumption that the dependent variable is generated by a Normal or Gaussian process is the traditional, benchmark approach. FAIL, however, can take only integer values and cannot be negative, which clearly violates the assumptions of a Gaussian distribution. These particular difficulties may be overcome by assuming a Poisson process. However, the Poisson approach suffers from a crucial and restrictive characteristic of the Poisson process, namely the independence assumption, which implies the equality of the mean and the variance.[7] In our case, the possibility of "contagion" effects in the bank failure process means that the probability of a given bank's failing in any given year may not be independent of whether other banks happen to fail in that year. If bank failures during a period are not independent of each other—or equivalently, the underlying process is not characterized by mean–variance identity—and one still uses the Poisson regression, the resulting standard error estimates become downward-biased and the *t*-statistics will be biased upward. Note, however, that the coefficient estimates themselves maintain their desirable properties. In the econometric literature this issue is referred to as the "overdispersion problem."[8] In my data sample, FAIL had a mean of 34.1 and a variance of 3488.3. Of course, an underlying process characterized by mean–variance equality can generate a sample with a sample variance

[7] I am grateful to Allin Cottrell for this point.

[8] See Greene (1993, p. 678). The discussions in Cameron and Trivedi (1986, 1990) and Gourieroux (1989, pp. 297–305) are also relevant.

a hundred times greater than the sample mean. Therefore I performed some tests (not reported for brevity) designed to detect "overdispersion." There was some marginal evidence that it was present. Thus, I also tried the Negative Binomial or NegBin formulation.

The NegBin formulation is a variant of the Poisson approach, and models the underlying data-generating process as compound Poisson. It still posits that FAIL is generated by a Poisson process, but it removes the mean–variance identity restriction by introducing an auxiliary error term. This error term can be motivated by invoking either omitted exogenous variables or intrinsic randomness—see Cameron and Trivedi (1986, p. 32). In addition, if one posits that this auxiliary error term follows a gamma distribution, then FAIL will have a negative binomial distribution. The posited relationship between the mean and the variance of the resulting negative binomial distribution will depend on how the gamma is parameterized. The option provided in the LIMDEP package (Greene, 1991) follows the particular parameterization which Cameron and Trivedi (1986, p. 33) call Negbin II. It posits the following relationship between the mean and the variance of FAIL:

$$\mathrm{Var(FAIL)} = \mathrm{E(FAIL)} \times [1 + \alpha \mathrm{E(FAIL)}], \tag{1}$$

where α is a parameter which will be estimated.[9] Thus, Negbin II makes the variance/mean ratio linear in the mean. Other parameterizations will lead to other relationships between the variance and the mean. The interested reader is referred to the sources cited above.

On balance, of the three formulations—Normal, Poisson and compound Poisson or Negbin—there is a presumption that the last is the most appropriate.

4 Structural change

This section presents some test results to help answer the question, Did structural change occur in 1980, the year of DIDMCA? It should be stated at the outset that the test merely establishes the existence of a break during a given year. It does not establish the cause of the break, if there is one. Thus, if the existence of a break in, say, 1980 is established we can identify

[9] For future reference, note that a zero value for α implies mean–variance equality and thus mutual independence of bank failures.

DIDMCA as the cause only to the extent that we view that particular piece of legislation as the "dominant" banking event of the time.

The basic model is as follows:

$$\text{FAIL} = \beta_1 + \beta_2\text{PROFIT} + \beta_3\text{BANKPRO} + \beta_4\text{SHAREFIN}$$
$$+\beta_5\text{BORROW} + \beta_6\text{SIZE} + \epsilon, \qquad (2)$$

where the time subscript is omitted for brevity. Depending on how ϵ is modeled, one of the three formulations—Normal, Poisson, NegBin—will apply. As mentioned previously, all coefficients can be interpreted as elasticities. It should also be noted that, at least for some of them, a behavioral interpretation is possible. For instance, the coefficient on SIZE partly reflects the behavior of the monetary authorities. The coefficients β_3 for BANKPRO and β_4 for SHAREFIN reflect the interplay of competitive forces, legislative processes, and regulatory behavior.

The test procedure for structural change during 1980 (i.e., the first period is 1947–1980, the second 1981–1991) is as follows:

H_0 (Null hypothesis): each pre-1981 β_i equals the corresponding post-1980 β_i, $i = 1, \ldots, 6$.

H_1 (Alternative hypothesis): at least one of the above-mentioned equalities does not hold.

To perform the test we define six dummy variables. The intercept dummy is DALFA, zero for each year before 1981 and one for each year after 1980. Slope dummies are obtained by multiplying each of the five independent variables in equation (2) by DALFA. All of the resulting dummy variables are labeled with a "D" prefix. For instance, DPROFIT is zero before 1981 and is equal to PROFIT after 1980.[10] Thus, an additional equation is defined:

$$\text{FAIL} = \beta_1 + \beta_2\text{PROFIT} + \beta_3\text{BANKPRO} + \beta_4\text{SHAREFIN}$$
$$+\beta_5\text{BORROW} + \beta_6\text{SIZE} + \beta_7\text{DALFA} + \beta_8\text{DPROFIT}$$
$$+\beta_9\text{DBANKPRO} + \beta_{10}\text{DSHAREFIN}+$$
$$\beta_{11}\text{DBORROW} + \beta_{12}\text{DSIZE} + \epsilon. \qquad (3)$$

[10] For a discussion of this method, see Maddala (1992, pp. 318–20).

Equation (3) is the unrestricted equation which allows for different behavior in the post-1980 period. Note that β_7 to β_{12} measure change in behavior during the second period. For instance, greater effectiveness of the discount window tool would be reflected in a negative and significant value for β_{11}, the coefficient on DBORROW. Similarly, a greater ability on the part of large banks to survive in the post-1980 period would show up as a significantly negative DSIZE coefficient.[11] Equation (2) is the restricted specification: by excluding the six dummies, six equality restrictions across 1980 are imposed.

I will use the Likelihood Ratio (LR) test, which is a general large sample test based on the Maximum Likelihood (ML) method.[12] The test consists of looking at the ratio of the restricted likelihood to the unrestricted likelihood. This ratio is necessarily less than one because the denominator will always be larger, i.e., the unrestricted maximum will always exceed the restricted maximum. However, if the restrictions are valid—in our case, if the coefficients across the two periods are equal, as specified by the null hypothesis—the ratio will be close to one. Otherwise, i.e., when H_0 is false, the ratio will be significantly less than one. Since the estimation procedure maximizes log likelihood rather than likelihood (as a matter of computational expediency) "close to one" is translated into a "small" LR test-statistic value, and "significantly less than one" gets translated into a "large" LR test-statistic value.

Table 1 displays the results of testing for structural change in 1980. In each case the LR test statistic is computed as two times the difference between the log likelihood for the unrestricted regression and the log likelihood for the restricted regression. Under the null hypothesis, this statistic is distributed as Chi-square with six degrees of freedom. The relevant values are: 49.94 for the Normal formulation, 518.04 for the Poisson and 57.76 for the NegBin. Thus the null hypothesis is decisively

[11] This greater ability to avoid bankruptcy on the part of large banks could be accounted for in at least two ways. First, larger banks have a greater ability to diversify than smaller banks. Second, the greater risk of financial "contagion" in case of bankruptcy can make the monetary authorities unwilling to declare a large bank bankrupt. In the next section I will explicitly test the "too big to fail doctrine" enunciated in September 1984—see Kohn (1993, p. 458).

[12] See Maddala (1992, pp. 118–23) for a lucid account of this test. There are two other tests based on the ML method, namely the Wald and Lagrange Multiplier tests. But since the results of the Likelihood Ratio tests are strong enough to leave no room for doubt, performing the other tests is unnecessary.

TABLE 1
REGRESSIONS OF FAIL ON VARIOUS EXPLANATORY VARIABLES

	Restricted			Unrestricted		
	Normal	Poisson	NegBin	Normal	Poisson	NegBin
Constant	7.75 (4.79)	9.30 (18.28)	7.87 (3.35)	11.30 (3.04)	10.41 (3.74)	10.66 (2.20)
PROFIT	−6.86 (−7.66)	−7.11 (−35.53)	−7.34 (−6.68)	−0.31 (−0.22)	0.05 (0.04)	0.04 (0.02)
BANKPRO	−2.51 (−3.46)	−2.01 (−9.28)	−2.81 (−3.55)	−0.46 (−0.67)	−0.20 (−0.34)	−0.20 (−0.18)
SHAREFIN	3.38 (3.47)	2.98 (10.75)	3.88 (3.18)	−1.88 (−1.15)	−1.96 (−1.41)	−2.01 (−0.77)
BORROW	−0.26 (−1.97)	−0.37 (−9.63)	−0.28 (−1.85)	−0.15 (−1.65)	−0.22 (−3.14)	−0.21 (−2.07)
SIZE	−0.15 (−1.34)	−0.09 (−2.82)	−0.07 (−0.51)	−0.10 (−1.30)	−0.09 (−1.33)	−0.09 (−0.98)
DALFA				−1.71 (−0.29)	−5.00 (−1.68)	−2.35 (−0.33)
DPROFIT				6.49 (1.76)	4.72 (3.45)	5.97 (1.57)
DBANKPRO				7.12 (3.15)	4.32 (5.75)	6.26 (2.14)
DSHAREFIN				−5.77 (−1.90)	−2.60 (−1.73)	−4.90 (−1.16)
DBORROW				0.76 (1.85)	0.59 (5.89)	0.73 (1.54)
DSIZE				−0.47 (−1.79)	−0.29 (−3.45)	−0.44 (−1.84)
α			0.39 (2.90)			0.05 (1.03)
Log Likelihood	−48.14	−415.34	−158.18	−23.16	−156.32	−129.29

Note: *t*-statistics in parentheses.

rejected on all approaches. (For reference, $\chi^2(6, .999) = 22.458$.) Thus, I conclude that 1980 was indeed a year of structural change in American banking.

I also tested for structural change in 1989, the year of enactment of the Financial Institutions Reform, Recovery and Enforcement Act (FIRREA). In this case, since the second, post-1989, period is too short, the LR test cannot be applied. The only available test I know of is what Maddala (1992, pp. 174–7) calls the predictive Chow test. The numbers are not reported for brevity: the conclusion was that the FIRREA did not make a detectable difference to the parameters of the bank failure equation.

5 Single causes

I will attempt to summarize the picture that emerges from Table 1 in terms of what may be dubbed "single causes." The focus will be on the unrestricted regressions (the last three columns of the table) since the null hypothesis has been rejected. Before proceeding any further, a notational clarification is in order. Let C^{i} and C^{ii} denote the first- and second-period coefficients for any variable. The first six coefficient estimates are the C^{i}s for the respective variables. The coefficients for the six dummies, however, represent not C^{ii} but rather the increment $(C^{ii} - C^{i})$.

Effectiveness of the Fed's discount window

The DIDMC Act of 1980 made the services of the Fed, including that of lender of last resort, available to all depository institutions, not just member banks. The coefficients of BORROW may indicate whether this widened eligibility had any impact on the bank failure process. The respective values are, working from the last NegBin column, $C^{i} = -0.21$ and $C^{ii} = 0.53$. Note that a negative value indicates effectiveness of the discount window tool. Thus, the conclusion has to be that during the post-1980 period the discount window has been ineffective in terms of reducing the number of bankruptcies. However, the evidence on which this conclusion rests is weak: the t-statistic for DBORROW (NegBin, last column of Table 1) is only 1.54. Hoping that a more parsimonious specification might be illuminating, I regressed FAIL against the five main explanatory variables and DBORROW, omitting all the other dummy variables. Column (i) of Table 2 displays the relevant results. As can be seen, in this specification the coefficient on BORROW is statistically insignificant (t-value,

−0.55). Neither is the incremental coefficient on DBORROW significantly different from zero (t-value, −1.13). Thus a balanced assessment of the discount window policy followed by the Fed would have to be that it has been ineffective in terms of reducing the number of bank failures.

TABLE 2
TESTING FOR STRUCTURAL CHANGE:
PARSIMONIOUS SPECIFICATIONS

	(i)	(ii)	(iii)	(iv)
Constant	7.04 (2.80)	6.94 (2.67)	4.75 (2.08)	5.98 (3.41)
PROFIT	−7.38 (−6.43)	−1.00 (−0.55)	−1.30 (−0.75)	−3.91 (−3.14)
BANKPRO	−3.15 (−4.00)	−0.30 (−0.28)	−0.12 (−0.12)	−1.74 (−2.34)
SHAREFIN	4.23 (3.27)	−0.62 (−0.35)	−0.04 (−0.02)	1.98 (1.73)
BORROW	−0.14 (−0.55)	−0.12 (−1.29)	−0.17 (−1.64)	−0.21 (1.77)
SIZE	−0.08 (−0.58)	−0.14 (−1.40)	−0.11 (−1.02)	−0.015 (−0.15)
DBORROW	−0.41 (−1.13)			
DBANKPRO		1.21 (4.69)		
DSHAREFIN			0.63 (4.52)	
DSIZE84				−0.64 (−4.78)
α	0.37 (2.74)	0.14 (2.34)	0.16 (2.68)	0.22 (2.54)
Log Likelihood	−156.71	−140.69	−142.46	−147.31

Notes: t-statistics in parentheses; NegBin formulation used throughout.

"Too big to fail"

Returning to the last column of Table 1, we see that the coefficient of DSIZE is negative (−0.44) and significant, albeit marginally (*t*-value, −1.84). Also, C^{i} for SIZE is −0.09, whereas C^{ii} is −0.53, much larger in absolute value. This suggests that in the post-1980 period small banks failed more often—the authorities were, perhaps, less reluctant to let smaller banks fail. Of course, when it comes to analyzing the attitude of the regulatory authorities toward bank size, the crucial year is 1984. In September of that year, the Comptroller of the Currency (regulator of the national banks) declared in testimony to Congress that the eleven largest banks would not be allowed to fail. I regressed FAIL against the original set of explanatory variables plus DSIZE84 (zero from 1947 to 1984 and equal to SIZE for the years after 1984). The results are presented in column (iv) of Table 2. The coefficient for DSIZE84 is −0.64 with a *t*-value of −4.78. Thus, one has to conclude that in the post-1984 period larger banks have failed less often than smaller banks.

Deregulation and banking profitability

The evidence in Table 1 pertaining to deregulation and banking profitability can be summarized as follows.[13] The C^{i} for BANKPRO is −0.20 and C^{ii} is 6.06 (the incremental change for the second period being 6.26 with a *t*-value of 2.14). Thus, for the years after 1980, there appears to have been a *positive* association between the share of banking profits in total profits and the number of bank failures. To examine this counterintuitive result further, I regressed FAIL against the main explanatory variables plus DBANKPRO (again omitting all other dummies). From column (ii) of Table 2 we see that the DBANKPRO coefficient is 1.21 with a *t*-value of 4.69. While the estimated effect is smaller here, the puzzling positive association between FAIL and BANKPRO, for the later period, still stands. It would appear that a shift has occurred in the relationship between the relative profitability of the banking sector and the number of bank failures, possibly reflecting a change in concentration in this sector.[14]

[13] It should be stressed in this context that 1980 has to be viewed not merely as the year of the enactment of DIDMCA, but also the year in which deregulation in general began.

[14] Recall also the discussion on page 201, which suggested that the LBO and takeover activity of the 1980s might mask the expected inverse relationship between FAIL and BANKPRO.

Private versus public financial sector

The explanatory variable SHAREFIN was included to address the "private versus public" issue. The picture that emerges from Table 1 pertaining to this issue can be summarized as follows. In the unrestricted regressions, the coefficient on SHAREFIN is consistently negative, as expected: as the share of private financial sector profits in the pool of total (i.e., private plus public) financial-sector profits goes up, the number of bank failures goes down. The parameter estimates for DSHAREFIN (equal to zero for 1947–1980, and equal to SHAREFIN for 1981–1991) are also negative, indicating a strengthening of this relationship for the years after 1980. The evidence on these matters is, however, weak. In the preferred NegBin specification, the *t*-values for SHAREFIN and DSHAREFIN are −0.77 and −1.16 respectively. Thus, following the advice offered by Maddala (1992, p. 319), I regressed FAIL against the five main explanatory variables plus DSHAREFIN. The results are displayed in column (iii) of Table 2. In this specification, it appears that there was a positive association between SHAREFIN and the number of bank failures after 1980, a puzzling finding akin to that of the previous subsection. The difference between the estimates shown in the last column of Table 1 and column (iii) of Table 2, however, casts some doubt on the robustness of this result.

"Contagion"

Ever since the Great Depression, "contagion," which can be defined as one bank's failure making another one's failure more likely, has been a recurrent theme in the money and banking literature. In the present study, the statistical evidence on this point is mixed. Recall that the parameter α, in the NegBin formulation as shown in equation (1), is the key to assessing whether or not bank failures are independently distributed. If $\alpha = 0$, then Var(FAIL) = E(FAIL), implying mutual independence of bank failures. As can be seen, the α estimate for the most general regression (Table 1, last column) is 0.05 with a *t*-value of 1.03. On this basis, the null hypothesis of mean–variance equality and independence cannot be rejected. On the other hand, the α estimates obtained from the more parsimonious specifications of Table 2 are all significantly different from zero, indicating some degree of interdependence. In this author's opinion more disaggregated data would be needed to settle this point.

6 Summary of results

The 1980s were years of structural change in American banking, although the FIRREA of 1989 exerted no additional discernible impact. Of the explanatory variables included, the Federal Reserve discount window had no effect on bank failures during the 1980s, and failures were relatively less common among large banks during this period than earlier, but the various aggregate profit variable were *positively* related to failures during the 1980s. This suggests the desirability of further research into the relationships between bank failures and the distribution of profits, possibly arising from changes in bank concentration.

References

Barro, R. 1982. "Measuring the Fed's Revenue from Money Creation." *Economics Letters* 10: 327–32.

Cameron, C. and P. Trivedi 1986. "Econometric Models Based on Count Data: Comparisons and Applications of Some Estimators and Tests." *Journal of Applied Econometrics* 1: 29–53.

______. 1990. "Regression Based Tests for Overdispersion in the Poisson Model." *Journal of Econometrics* 46: 347–64.

Davutyan, N. 1989. "Bank Failures as Poisson Variates." *Economics Letters* 29: 333–8.

Gourieroux, C. 1989. *Économétrie des Variables Qualitatives*. Second Edition, Paris: Economica.

Greene, W. 1991. *LIMDEP Version 6.0, User's Manual and Reference Guide*. New York: Econometric Software.

______. 1993. *Econometric Analysis*. Second Edition, New York: MacMillan.

Kohn, M. 1993. *Money, Banking and Financial Markets*. Second Edition, Fort Worth, TX: Dryden Press.

Maddala, G. 1992. *Introduction to Econometrics*. Second Edition, New York: MacMillan.

Mayer, T., J. Duesenberry and R. Aliber 1993. *Money, Banking and the Economy*. Fifth Edition, New York: Norton.

Osterberg, W. 1993. "Bank Exposure to Highly Leveraged Transactions." *Economic Commentary*, Federal Reserve Bank of Cleveland, January.

9

A TRIGGERING MECHANISM OF ECONOMYWIDE BANK RUNS

Sangkyun Park

Federal Reserve Bank of New York

1 Introduction

Bank failures differ from other business failures in that failures of some banks can result in systemwide bank runs that can paralyze the entire economy. This unique feature of the banking business has attracted considerable attention in the 1980s when banking problems re-emerged. Although the financial structure of banks improved in the early 1990s, the possibility of banking instability remains as an important concern in formulating banking policies.

The literature of recent years on bank runs can be broadly classified into two groups, one focusing on the liquidity of banks and the other highlighting the importance of information on banks' solvency. According to the studies emphasizing liquidity—e.g., Diamond and Dybvig (1983), Waldo (1985), and Postlewaite and Vives (1987)—the demand-deposit contract and banks' investment in illiquid assets make banks vulnerable to runs. A bank has to liquidate illiquid assets at a loss if withdrawals exceed its holdings of liquid assets. In this situation, the possibility of excessive withdrawals can create an expectations bubble. If a depositor expects that others will withdraw, he/she will withdraw to avoid the loss from liquidation. This expectation about others' behavior induces depositors to run collectively on a bank and forces the bank into liquidation. The bubble theories usually assume that the expectation of depositors can be altered

The views expressed are my own and do not necessarily reflect those of the Federal Reserve Bank of New York or the Federal Reserve System. I would like to thank Axel Leijonhufvud, Guido Tabellini, Kenneth Sokoloff, John McCall, and Michael Brennan for helpful comments and suggestions.

by anything, i.e., "sunspots." Hence, they are vague about the mechanism that triggers bank runs.

Some other studies have taken an information-theoretic approach, seeing incomplete information about the solvency of banks as the main problem, e.g., Gorton (1985), Chari and Jagannathan (1988), and Jacklin and Bhattacharya (1988). In these models, depositors extract a signal about the soundness of banks from some inaccurate indicators and mistakenly run on solvent banks. Those indicators, they suggest, can be some unknown macroeconomic variables or behavior of better informed depositors. These studies, which leave the nature of the information unanswered, do not satisfactorily identify the underlying causes of bank runs.

Park (1991) focuses on the contagion of bank failures from insolvent banks to solvent ones and more specifically recognizes the nature of the information problem. The study shows that the government or banks stopped U.S. banking panics mainly by providing financial information on banks and argues that the lack of bank-specific information was responsible for runs on solvent banks.

Depositors run on solvent banks as well as insolvent ones when they lose confidence in the banking system as a whole. Historically, runs on solvent banks were preceded by failures of insolvent ones. Then the main question is why failures of insolvent banks cause the loss of public confidence in sound banks. This paper presents an analytical model showing the main triggering mechanism of economywide bank runs. In the model, solvent banks suffer runs when depositors cannot separate solvent banks from insolvent banks. Thus, economywide bank runs are triggered by a lack of bank-specific information that prevents rational depositors from distinguishing between sound and impaired banks.

Since bank assets are information-intensive, appraising the creditworthiness of banks involves unusual difficulties. For example, the evaluation of the quality of loans requires information on borrowers and sophisticated knowledge of accounting. Due to the difficulty of evaluating the financial condition of individual banks, bank-specific information is not readily available to the public. Depositors, who lack bank-specific information, infer the soundness of a particular bank from the condition of the banking system as a whole. A high ratio of bank failures signals an adverse condition within the banking system. Thus, when depositors observe a high failure ratio, they conjecture that their banks may also be unsound and withdraw deposits. These developments explain banking panics in U.S.

history, characterized by the phenomenon of general bank runs following a large number of bank failures.

Gorton (1988) examines various hypotheses about banking panics using U.S. data and argues that bank failures are insignificant in explaining financial crises. The ground on which he rejects the "failure hypothesis" does not appear to be firm. It is very difficult econometrically to identify variables affecting perceived risk. Apart from methodology, data problems seem serious. For instance, the study uses data on national banks. In the national banking era of the U.S., national banks in general were better regulated and hence safer.[1] State banks and trust companies, thus, played the major role in financial crises.[2] In particular, most banking panics in U.S. history involved failures of large trust companies, Messrs Kenyon, Cox & Co. in 1873, Grant & Ward in 1884, National Cordage Company in 1893, and Knickerbocker Trust Company in 1907 for example (see Appendix). Data on national bank failures, hence, can be misleading. Gorton finds that the liabilities of failed businesses significantly affect the perceived risk of depositors. This result is plausible and does not contradict the failure hypothesis. Depositors may take the condition of other sectors into their consideration in assessing the condition of the banking sector. An adverse state of other sectors of the economy, however, does not appear to be a sufficient condition. Historically, contagion of bank failures from insolvent banks to solvent ones was an essential step leading to a banking panic, which may be defined as runs on solvent banks as well as insolvent ones (see Appendix).

The rest of this paper is organized as follows. Section 2 discusses the pattern of banking panics in U.S. history to support the relevance of bank-specific information. Section 3 models an economy in which individuals rationally maximize utility using a Bayesian inference rule and shows how failures of insolvent banks trigger economywide bank runs. Section 4 summarizes the article's findings.

[1] "The Comptroller desires to call attention to the fact that only eleven national banks failed in the United States during the year ending November 1, 1884, although more than one hundred banks and bankers other than national failed during the same period" (Comptroller of the Currency, 1884, p. 36).

[2] Before the enactment of the Banking Act of 1933, trust companies typically had trust department and banking department whose function was similar to that of commercial banks (American Institute of Banking, 1924, p. 233).

2 Stylized Facts

It is difficult to generalize causes of financial panics in our history. A single panic may involve several causes, and the causes may vary across panics. Nevertheless, we can still find some common features in the history of banking panics. The analysis of such stylized facts offers a fair amount of insight into banking panics in general.

Banking panics in U.S. history are particularly interesting, since the U.S. had a more competitive banking structure than other countries and experienced recurrent banking panics before the enactment of the Banking Act of 1933. Banking panics in U.S. history involved some typical stages: occurrence of an unfavorable economic event, a large number of bank failures, runs on relatively unsound banks, and spread of runs to sound banks (see Appendix). In general, banking panics were preceded by economic events that might undermine the financial structure of a large number of banks. For example, the panic of 1837 was preceded by the failure of cotton businesses. Since cotton was one of the most important products at that time, the financial involvement of banks in cotton production was rather a common practice.[3] In 1857 and 1873, decreased profitability and stock prices of railroad businesses impaired the financial condition of banks that had made heavy advances to railroad companies. Such unfavorable economic events resulted in insolvency of banks that had taken excessive risk by holding risky portfolios. As some risky banks failed, bank runs started on other risky banks. The problem became serious when those failures undermined public confidence in banks in general. Depositors, when they became suspicious about the soundness of the banking system as a whole, withdrew deposits compelling solvent banks as well as insolvent ones to liquidate their assets and call in loans. The liquidation of assets further decreased the price of securities and resulted in severe monetary stringency. These results aggravated the financial difficulties of banks. This process was self-reinforcing due to the rising price of liquidity.

A notable fact is that bank runs, in general, started on insolvent banks first and then spread to solvent ones. This pattern allows us to infer that the primary concern of depositors is the solvency of banks. If depositors were simply concerned about liquidity, they would not necessarily run

[3] Nicholas Biddle, former president of the Second Bank of the United States and one of leading bankers in the nation, attempted to corner the cotton market and issued currency against the crop (Sobel, 1968, p. 70).

on insolvent banks first. Thus, banking panics were triggered by fear of insolvency. Another important point is that banking panics were preceded by an unfavorable economic event. In other words, banking panics occurred when the average financial condition ofbanks seemed unfavorable. Thomas Kane, who served in the Bureau of the Currency for thirty-six years, is also emphatic on this point:

> Every panic that has occurred during the existence of the national banking system has found its precipitating cause in some bank or business failure occurring at a time when conditions throughout the country were favorable to disturbance. The same disturbance happening at another period would probably not have extended beyond the city in which it occurred. (Kane, 1923, p. 75)

This fact suggests that depositors had rational grounds when they became suspicious of the condition of banks. In sum, banking panics were triggered by depositors' fear of insolvency, and the fear had a rational ground. Bank runs, hence, are rational behavior.

The rationality, however, does not justify banking panics that disturb the entire banking system. Even in periods of severe financial strain, most banks were in fundamentally sound conditions. For example, even in 1933, the bank examination conducted after the nation-wide suspension found that approximately seventy five percent of banks was fundamentally solvent.[4] The fact of sound majority underscores the seriousness of bank failure contagion. The main problem is the dissemination of bank runs from insolvent banks to sound ones. Therefore, it is a worthwhile approach to focus on the link connecting "ailing" banks and "healthy" ones.

Depositors are rational and mainly concerned about the solvency of banks. Yet depositors run on sound banks when they observe failures of insolvent ones. This seemingly inconsistent behavior can be explained by incomplete information. Depositors run on solvent banks because they do not know if their banks are solvent. To be more specific, the problem is that depositors cannot distinguish sound banks in operation from previously failed banks. Based on these analyses, this study highlights the contagion of bank failures as the major problem, and recognizes the scarcity of bank-specific information as its cause.

[4] After the examination, the banking authorities licensed 12,817 banks to reopen without requiring a reorganization of financial structure, while they reorganized or liquidated 4,215 banks (Upham and Lamke, 1934, pp. 46, 47).

3 The model

This section studies a simple economy in which no bank-specific information is available. Information about the financial structure of individual banks is assumed costly. In this hypothetical world, neither depositors nor banks have economic incentives to bear this cost. Thus, individuals maximize utility without the financial information specific to each bank. This economy of no information is, of course, a simplified version of incomplete information.

The economy

The structure of the economy resembles that of Diamond and Dybvig (1983). This model, however, extends the time horizon to infinity and develops an overlapping generation structure in order to focus on the dissemination of bank runs rather than runs on a single bank.[5] The structure is described by an infinite sequence of generations lasting two periods each. A new generation comes into existence at the beginning of every period so that two generations (old and young) coexist at any given time.

Each generation is composed of the same number of *ex ante* identical individuals. Individuals who are endowed with goods consume only in the last period of their lives (A1).[6] While most people are destined to live two periods (type 2 individuals), some people die early at the end of the first period of their lives (type 1 individuals). Hence, type 1 individuals consume in the first period, and type 2 individuals consume in the second period of their lives. At the outset of their lives, individuals are identical with an independent probability of q ($0 < q < 1$) of early death (A2). They are informed of their types sometime during the first period of their lives.

There exists one homogeneous good which can be either costlessly stored or invested in long-term production. Self-storage is characterized by zero rate of return and perfect liquidity (A3). In contrast, production yields a positive expected return but is illiquid and risky. Production may fail in any given period with probability p. This probability is assumed to be inde-

[5] The word generation should not be literally interpreted. One generation here is a short decision-making period. This model adopts the overlapping generation structure to avoid unnecessary complications arising from changes in the endowment of individuals each period.

[6] A stands for assumption, C for condition, and E for equation.

pendent across production projects (A4). The outcome of the investment in production becomes known at the beginning of each period. A portion of the initial investment is recovered from a failed or liquidated project.

The role of banks in this economy is to pool the liquidity risk of individuals stemming from the need for early consumption and to intermediate between generations. The costs of making a pooling arrangement and undertaking inter-generational transactions among individuals are assumed to be prohibitive, i.e., greater than the maximum gain from production. On the other hand, banks have a superior exchange technology that enables them to intermediate at no cost.

Deposit contract and intermediation

Utilizing the superior exchange technology, banks offer a demand deposit contract that allows individuals to take advantage of production technology and to minimize the potential utility loss arising from early death. This contract may be explained by the insurance aspect of demand deposits suggested by Bryant (1980) and Diamond and Dybvig (1983).

In order to focus on individuals' maximizing behavior and its role in generating bank runs, this model adopts a partial equilibrium approach that does not explicitly consider the maximization of banks. The terms of the deposit contract are taken as given by both banks and depositors. Every bank offers the same deposit contract, and hence the amount of deposits is exogenously determined for individual banks. Each bank keeps a portion of deposited goods in its storage and invests the rest in production. Since the maximization of banks is not explicitly considered, the capital of banks is ignored (assumed to be 0) for simplicity. The return from the investment is used for the payment of interest and dividends. If the investment of a bank fails, the bank distributes the goods recovered from the liquidated production to depositors. The success of a bank's investment guarantees the solvency of the bank. Provided that a bank remains solvent, it pays $1+r$ ($0 < r < 1$) units per unit deposited for a full period. Type 1 depositors, who withdraw prematurely, are repaid the principal.[7] The deposit contract is summarized in Table 1.

[7] Net return of zero has been chosen for analytical convenience. Qualitative results of this model would not change as long as the return is smaller than $1+r$ and greater than the amount that makes perfectly safe deposits equally attractive to self-storage.

TABLE 1
THE DEPOSIT CONTRACT

	No Bank Failure		Bank Failure	
Time	Type 1	Type 2	Type 1	Type 2
1	−1	1	−1	−1
	1	0	1	0
2	0	$1+r$	0	S

Note: $S<1$ is the *pro rata* share of the liquidation value of a failed bank.

Banks do not need to liquidate their investments to repay matured deposits if the young generation chooses deposits over self-storage. It is assumed that deposits by the young generation occur simultaneously with withdrawals by the old generation. However, banks are forced into liquidation if the asset selection of the young generation becomes self-storage (bank runs). Provided that bank runs do not occur, banks use the proceeds from investment and the goods deposited by the young to pay off matured deposits (principal plus interest). Withdrawals by type 1 depositors are met by the reserves of banks (stored goods). At the beginning of the following period, banks replenish the reserves with goods deposited by the young generation. The profits (proceeds from investment minus interest payment) are distributed to the shareholders of banks. Hence, survived banks start each period with the same amounts of investment and reserves.

This model, which focuses on the solvency problem of banks, does not consider the possibility that a bank fails due to stochastic withdrawals that occur during the first period of each generation (withdrawals by type 1 depositors). The law of large numbers enables banks fairly well to predict the amount of the stochastic withdrawals. The liquidity problem of banks is pronounced when depositors run on banks. There is a trivial chance that purely stochastic withdrawals force a bank into liquidation.

The banking sector

The banking sector consists of N banks having the same amount of deposits (A5). For analytical convenience, it is assumed that the economy starts each period with the same number of banks, N. Banks that failed in the previous period are replaced by an equal number of new banks at the beginning of each period.

Each bank independently undertakes an investment project. Investment projects are subject to random shocks that increase the probability of failure. Once an investment is affected by a shock, the probability that the investment fails in a given period increases permanently from p_A to p_B. In other words, random shocks impair the financial structure of banks. The vulnerability of banks' investments to a shock depends on the nature of the shock and the portfolio decision of banks. For example, a decline of a major industry is likely to impair the financial structure of a large number of banks. Similarly, if banks in general aggressively expanded loans during an economic boom, an economic slump following the boom may produce a large number of risky banks. Assuming that individuals can observe shocks, they may partly infer the proportion of risky investments from the occurrence of shocks. In order for the inference to be complete, however, it has to be complemented by a judgment about the portfolios of banks.

Based on the state of investments, banks are classified into two types: type A and type B. Type A banks are safe and have a low probability of failure (p_A); type B banks are risky and have a relatively high probability of failure (p_B). Given this structure of the banking sector and assumption A4 (the independent probability of the failure of investment), the number of bank failures in a given period is binomially distributed for each type:

$$n_A \sim b(N_A, p_A) \quad \text{and} \quad n_B \sim b(N_B, p_B)$$

where N_i denotes the total number of type i banks, and n_i denotes the number of the failures of type i banks. These distributions are independent of each other, since every bank, regardless of its type, has an independent probability of failure. Naturally, the expected number of bank failures increases with the proportion of type B banks. Hence, a large number of bank failures signals a high proportion of risky banks.

Maximization of individuals

Individuals begin their lives with an endowment of one unit of the good each, which is the only resource in their lives. By assumption A1, everybody is concerned only about consumption in the last period of his/her life. Hence, type 1 individuals consume in the first period, and type 2 postpone their consumption until the second period. For analytical convenience, individuals are assumed to be risk neutral and have state independent utility function. In other words, the utility function does not depend on the outcome of the individuals' type. Thus, at the outset of their lives (at the beginning of period t), individuals (of the tth generation) maximize the expected amount of consumption by choosing between self-storage and deposits.

The expected amount of consumption is 1 when depositors choose self-storage (by A3). From deposits, the expected amount is:

$$E_t(C) = q + (1 - q)[(1 - p_t)(1 + r) + p_t S] \tag{E1}$$

where p_t denotes the probability that a bank fails at the beginning of the next period,[8] r denotes the interest rate on matured deposits, and S denotes the *pro rata* share of the liquidation value of a failed bank. A type 1 depositor (q) withdraws 1 unit before his/her bank fails. A type 2 depositor ($1 - q$) receives $1 + r$ units if the bank remains solvent ($1 - p_t$), and S if the bank fails (p_t) at the beginning of period $t + 1$.

Individuals hold deposits if $E(C) > 1$, but they will rely on self-storage if $E(C) \leq 1$. Using E1,

$$E_t(C) > 1 \quad \text{if} \quad p_t < \frac{r}{1 + r - S} = p^* \tag{C1}$$

This is the condition that individuals choose deposits over self-storage. The optimal asset holding of individuals shifts from deposits to self-storage when p_t becomes greater than p^*. Then bank runs occur. When a generation is interpreted as a short decision-making period by the same individuals, the decision of not making deposits is equivalent to withdrawals.

Estimation of the expected return from deposits

Depositors lacking bank-specific information infer the failure probability of a particular bank from the condition of the banking system as a whole. In this model, the measure of the condition of the banking system is the proportion of risky banks (type B). Depositors do not know the riskiness of a particular bank, but they understand that there are safe banks with a low probability of failure (p_A) and risky banks with a high probability of failure (p_B). In other words, depositors are intelligent enough to understand

[8] Subscript t represents the period in which the estimation is made.

that the failure probability is higher for banks with an impaired financial structure. The problem is that they cannot identify the banks with an impaired financial structure. The banking system is sound if only a small portion of banks is risky.

At the beginning of each period, the young generation estimates the proportion of risky banks (θ) and chooses between deposits and self-storage based on the estimated θ. Individuals estimate the distribution of θ using a Bayesian inference rule and use the mean value of the distribution as the estimate of θ. For analytical convenience, a very simple conjugate prior is assumed. Depositors believe that θ is either θ_1 or θ_2 ($\theta_1 < \theta_2$), and revise the probability that θ equals θ_i ($i = 1, 2$) each period. Since the decision rule of depositors is to use the mean value of the distribution, an assumption of a more complicated distribution would not result in qualitative differences.

Algebraically, the estimate of θ at time t is given by:

$$\theta_t = x_t\,\theta_1 + (1 - x_t)\theta_2 = \theta_2 + (\theta_1 - \theta_2)x_t \tag{E2}$$

$$\frac{\partial \theta_t}{\partial x_t} = \theta_1 - \theta_2 < 0 \tag{C2}$$

where x_t is the estimated probability that $\theta = \theta_1$ at time t.

By the Bayesian inference rule:

$$x_t = \frac{L(n_t \mid \theta_1)x_{t-1}}{L(n_t \mid \theta_1)x_{t-1} + L(n_t \mid \theta_2)(1 - x_{t-1})} \tag{E3}$$

where n_t denotes the number of bank failures at time t; $L(n \mid \theta_i)$ denotes the likelihood of observing n given $\theta = \theta_i$; and x_{t-1} denotes the estimate of x on the basis of information available at time $t - 1$. This last variable represents the prior belief of generation t. Communications with the previous generation inform each generation of x that was estimated by the previous generation (x_{t-1}). At the beginning of period t, the tth generation revises x_t using the current information, n_t.

Given $\theta_1 < \theta_2$,

$$\Delta\frac{L(n \mid \theta_1)}{L(n \mid \theta_2)}/\Delta n < 0 \tag{E4}$$

That is, the ratio of $L(n \mid \theta_1)$ to $L(n \mid \theta_2)$ monotonically decreases as n increases. Hence, for any given x_{t-1}, we have

$$\frac{\partial x_t}{\partial n} < 0 \tag{C3}$$

Based on the estimated value of θ, individuals calculate the probability of bank failures. The probability estimated at the beginning of period t is given by:

$$p_t = (1 - \theta_t)p_A + \theta_t p_B = p_A + (p_B - p_A)\theta_t \tag{E4}$$

$$\frac{\partial p_t}{\partial \theta_t} = p_B - p_A > 0 \tag{C4}$$

where p_t is the estimated probability that any specific bank fails at the beginning of period $t + 1$, and θ_t is the estimated value of θ at time t.

Banks are of identical size (by A5) and cannot be distinguished by depositors. Thus for a depositor, the probability of his/her bank being type B is θ. Accordingly, the probability of the failure of any particular bank is the weighted average of p_A and p_B where the weights are the proportions of each type of banks, $(1 - \theta)$ and θ.

Substituting E4 into E1,

$$\begin{aligned} E_t(C) &= 1 + (1 - q)r - (1 - q)p_A(1 + r - S) \\ &\quad -(1 - q)(p_B - p_A)(1 + r - S)\theta_t && \text{(E5)} \\ \frac{\partial E_t(C)}{\partial \theta_t} &= -(1 - q)(p_B - p_A)(1 + r - S) < 0 && \text{(C5)} \end{aligned}$$

Combining C2, C3, and C5,

$$\frac{\partial E_t(C)}{\partial n_t} = \underbrace{\frac{\partial E_t(C)}{\partial \theta_t}}_{-}\underbrace{\frac{\partial \theta_t}{\partial x_t}}_{-}\underbrace{\frac{\partial x_t}{\partial n_t}}_{-} < 0$$

Hence the estimation procedure leads to a low expected return from deposits when the number of failures is large. A large number of bank failures makes it less likely that the proportion of risky banks is small (by C3). Thus, depositors conjecture that there are more risky banks (by C2), and perceive a high probability of their banks being risky (by C4). As a result, every bank is perceived riskier by depositors. Then the expected return from deposits becomes low (by C5).

Bank runs

Bank runs occur when the optimal asset of individuals shifts from deposits to currency holdings, i.e., when the expected return from deposits falls below that from self-storage. From E5, we can derive the condition that individuals hold deposit ($E_t(C) > 1$) with respect to θ_t:

$$\theta_t < \frac{r - p_A(1 + r - S)}{(p_A - p_B)(1 + r - S)} = \theta^* \qquad \text{(C6)}$$

Let $\theta_1 < \theta^* < \theta_2$. Then, if the true value of θ is known, the individual's optimal decision is to hold deposits if $\theta_t = \theta_1$, and select self-storage if $\theta_t = \theta_2$.

In this economy, θ_t has to be estimated. θ_t is the mean value of the posterior distribution of θ. Thus, θ_t is determined by x_t, which summarizes the posterior distribution of θ.

To illustrate bank runs, let us start from a situation in which everybody holds deposits and estimates a high probability that θ equals θ_1, i.e., $x_t = 1 - \epsilon$ where ϵ is a very small number. Now suppose that a shock (e.g., a decline in the price of collateral or an interest shock) has increased the proportion of risky banks from θ_1 to θ_2. A natural consequence of this change is that depositors observe a large number of failures in succession. The Bayesian inference rule described above makes θ converge to its true value: x_t converges to 0, and hence θ_t converges to θ_2. When θ falls below θ^*, the optimal asset of depositors becomes self-storage instead of deposits. Every depositor then runs on his/her bank, forcing solvent banks as well as insolvent ones into liquidation.

In this model, bank runs result from individuals' inability to distinguish between type A and type B banks. If bank-specific information were available, depositors would not infer the soundness of individual banks from the condition of the banking system as a whole. Because of the lack of bank-specific information every bank is treated equally by depositors, and safe banks end up sharing the problem of risky ones that have a weaker financial structure.

Consistency of the model with the pattern of panics

In this model, whether or not bank runs occur in a given period depends on the prior belief of depositors and the number of failures in the current period. Given that depositors update their belief each period, the prior embodies bank failures that occurred in previous periods. In addition, it is reasonable to assume that the prior also depends on the general economic condition. In other words, depositors believe that there are more risky banks when the economic condition is unfavorable. The incorporation of this assumption to the model would make bank runs more probable when the economic condition was unfavorable. Then the maximizing behavior of depositors in the model is consistent with the historical pattern: Banking panics in general were preceded by an unfavorable economic event and a large number of bank failures.

By relaxing the assumption of no bank-specific information, the model can also explain the phenomenon of bank runs spreading from insolvent to solvent banks. We can allow some bank-specific information by modifying E4 as follows:

$$p_{ti} = [1 - (\theta_t - a_i)]p_A + (\theta_t - a_i)p_B = p_A + (p_B - p_A)(\theta_t - a_i),$$

$$\theta_t - 1 \leq a_i \leq \theta_t.$$

For a given θ_t, p_{ti} (the estimated probability that bank i fails at the beginning of period $t+1$) is a decreasing function of a_i. A positive value of a_i means that bank i is perceived to be relatively safe (safer than the average) by its depositors, while a negative value of a_i indicates the opposite. If depositors of bank i are certain that their bank is risky, $a_i = \theta_t - 1$ and hence $p_{ti} = p_B$. On the other hand, a_i and p_{ti} respectively become θ_t and p_A when depositors of bank i have no doubt about the soundness of the bank. As long as the bank specific information is incomplete ($\theta_t - 1 < a_i < \theta_t$), θ_t continues to signal the riskiness of a particular bank. Assuming the incomplete information is correct on average, runs should start on insolvent banks first and then spread to solvent ones.

4 Conclusion

The major cause of banking panics is the lack of information on the financial structure of individual banks. The pattern of banking panics in our history supports the importance of bank-specific information. Historically, banking panics involved some typical stages: occurrence of an unfavorable economic event, a large number of bank failures, runs on relatively unsound banks, and spread of runs to sound banks. These developments are fairly well explained by the model in which depositors maximize utility with incomplete information on the financial structure of individual banks. For depositors lacking bank-specific information, it is rational to run on sound banks as well as insolvent ones when they observe a large number of bank failures.

This analysis implies that the particular danger of bank failures relative to other business failures stems primarily from the difficulty of evaluating the soundness of banks. The possibility of facing a liquidity problem is rather secondary. Given this analysis, the availability of information on banks' solvency can substantially reduce the risk of economywide bank runs.

References

American Institute of Banking 1924. *Standard Banking*. (New York, NY).

Bryant, John 1980. "A Model of Reserves, Bank Runs, and Deposit Insurance." *Journal of Banking and Finance* 4: 335–44.

Chari, V.V. and Ravi Jagannathan 1988. "Banking Panics, Information, and Rational Expectations Equilibrium." *Journal of Finance* 43: 749–61.

Collman, Charles A. 1931. *Our Mysterious Panics, 1830–1930*. New York: William Morrow and Co.

Commercial and Financial Chronicle: Hunt's Merchants' Magazine 17, 1873. New York: William B. Dona and Co.

Comptroller of the Currency 1873, 1884, 1907. *Annual Report*. Washington, D.C.: U.S. Government Printing Office.

Diamond, Douglas W. and Philip H. Dybvig 1983. "Bank Runs, Deposit Insurance, and Liquidity." *Journal of Political Economy* 91: 401–19.

Gorton, Gary 1985. "Bank Suspension of Convertibility." *Journal of Monetary Economics* 15: 177–93.

______. 1988. "Banking Panics and Business Cycles." *Oxford Economic Papers* 40: 751–81.

Jacklin, Charles J. and Sudipto Bhattacharya 1988. "Distinguishing Panics and Information-based Bank Runs: Welfare and Policy Implications." *Journal of Political Economy* 96: 568–92.

Kane, Thomas P. 1923. *The Romance and Tragedy of Banking*. New York: The Bankers Publishing Co.

Kennedy, Susan E. 1973. *The Banking Crisis of 1933*. Lexington, KY: University Press of Kentucky.

Lightner, Otto C. 1922. *The History of Business Depressions*. New York: Northeastern Press.

Park, Sangkyun 1991. "Bank Failure Contagion in Historical Perspective." *Journal of Monetary Economics* 28: 271–86.

Postlewaite, Andrew and Xavier Vives 1987. "Bank Runs as an Equilibrium Phenomenon." *Journal of Political Economy* 95: 485–91.

Sobel, Robert 1968. *Panics on Wall Street: A History of American Financial Disasters*. New York: Macmillan Company.

Sprague, O. M. W. 1910. *History of Crisis under the National Banking System*. Washington, D.C.: U.S. Government Printing Office.

Upham, Cyril B. and Edwin Lamke 1934. *Closed and Distressed Banks*. Washington, D.C.: Brookings Institutions.

Waldo, Douglas G. 1985. "Bank Runs, the Deposit-Currency Ratio and the Interest Rate." *Journal of Monetary Economics* 15: 269–77.

APPENDIX
Banking Panics in the United States

1837

Economic environment: Land and cotton boom in the 1830s.
Proximate Cause: Collapse of the cotton business.
Major events:

Mar. 14	Bankruptcy of cotton houses in New Orleans.
May 10	New York banks suspended specie payments.

Sources: Lightner (1922, pp. 126, 127) and Collman (1931, pp. 59–65).

1857

Economic environment: Railroad boom; speculation in the stock market in the 1850s.
Proximate Cause: Stock market crash caused by failures of railroad companies.
Major events:

Aug. 20	Failure of the Ohio Life Insurance & Trust Company which had made imprudent advances to Western Railroads. The stock of Western Railroads was substantially overvalued, and the failure became a major disturbance in the stock market.
September	Runs on the Metropolitan Bank and the Bank of Commerce.
Oct. 15	Banks in New York City suspended specie payments.

Sources: Sobel (1968, pp. 99–106) and Collman (1931, pp. 83–8).

1873

Economic environment: Railroad boom; four years of rapid economic growth.
Proximate Cause: Excessive loan expansion to railroad companies and decline of the railroad business.
Major events:

Sep. 8	Suspension of the New York Warehouse and Security Company which was financially involved with the Missouri, Kansas, and Texas Railroad.
Sep. 13	Failure of Messrs Kenyon, Cox & Co. that endorsed Canada Southern Railway paper.
Sep. 18	Major bank runs started.
Sep. 20	Closing of New York Stock Exchange.
Sep. 24	Suspension of currency payments by New York banks.

Sources: Commercial and Financial Chronicle (1873, p.382), Comptroller of the Currency (1873, pp. 26–31), and Sprague (1910, pp. 153–80).

1884

Economic environment: Moderate economic downturn; decline of the general price level.
Proximate Cause: Disclosure of fraud and embezzlement.
Major events:

May 6	Failure of the Marine National Bank that was financially connected with an insolvent brokerage firm, Grant & Ward.
May 8	Failure of Grant & Ward, which committed a major fraud.
May 13	Disclosure of an embezzlement by the president of the Second National Bank.
May 14	Runs on New York banks. Authorization of Clearing house loan certificates.

Sources: Comptroller of the Currency (1884, pp. 33, 34).

1893

Economic environment: Monetary disturbance caused by Sherman Silver Purchase Act and international gold flows.
Proximate Cause: Stock market collapse in May.
Major events:

Feb. 26	Failure of the Philadelphia and Reading Railroad.
May 4	Failure of the National Cordage Company (Trust Company) which caused the stock market collapse.
July	Numerous bank failures throughout the nation. Reserve outflows from New York banks.
Aug. 5	Suspension of payment by New York banks.

Sources: Sprague (1910, pp. 153–80) and Sobel (1968, pp. 251–5).

1907

Economic environment: Steady rise in the price level and economic boom in 1900s.
Proximate Cause: Failure of an attempt to corner copper stocks.
Major events:

Oct. 17	Runs on the Mercantile National Bank that attempted to corner the stock of the United Copper Company.
Oct. 21	Runs on Knickerbocker Trust Company that was financially involved with the Mercantile National Bank. Major bank runs started.
Oct. 22	Suspension of Knickerbocker Trust Company.
Oct. 23	Major runs on trust companies.

Sources: Comptroller of the Currency (1907, p. 70) and Sprague (pp. 246–60).

1933

Economic environment: Economic depression following the speculative boom of the 1920s.
Proximate Cause: Stock market crash in 1929.
Major events:

Dec. 11, 1930	Failure of the Bank of United States in New York City.
1930–1933	Large number of bank failures and sustained deposit outflows.
Oct. 31, 1932	Statewide bank suspension in Nevada.
Feb. 14, 1933	Statewide bank suspension in Michigan.
Mar. 6, 1933	Nationwide bank suspension.

Sources: Upham and Lamke (1934, pp. 6–16) and Kennedy (1973).

10

HERD BEHAVIOR OR ANIMAL SPIRITS: A POSSIBLE EXPLANATION OF CREDIT CRUNCHES AND BUBBLES

Thomas S. Mondschean and Rowena A. Pecchenino

DePaul University, Michigan State University

1 Introduction

Casual observation of bank behavior would suggest that banks often act in tandem, expanding and contracting lending in concert. Sometimes banks' actions are consistent with aggregate economic activity and attract little notice. At other times, bank lending practices receive greater scrutiny because either economic conditions do not appear to warrant expansion or contraction or their behavior appears, at least ex post, to contradict sound banking practices. Two recent examples of rapidly increasing aggregate lending were the expansion of loans to less developed countries (LDCs) in the 1970s and loans to finance real estate expansion in the United States during the mid-1980s. Examples of credit crunches are the real estate credit crunch of 1989–1992 as well as those in 1966 and 1969.

This pattern of bank lending where a bank participates in or withdraws from loan markets because other banks are doing so has been described in other contexts as "herd behavior." To explain herd behavior in investment, Scharfstein and Stein (1990) show that a rational manager's optimal response to labor market incentives is to do what other managers are doing. Using a different model, Banerjee (1992) shows that it can be optimal for agents to abandon their own signals and follow others even when they are not really sure that the other person is right. Both authors point out that this behavior can lead to outcomes that are inefficient in an ex ante welfare sense. Their models formalize Keynes's (1936) observation that a manager who stands out from the crowd gets a reputation for being rash, while one whose actions mirror the crowd gets a reputation for prudence. If one follows the crowd and the crowd is wrong, one does not appear to have misjudged the situation; rather, an unforeseen and unforeseeable shock changed the expected outcome for the worse. If the crowd is right, one basks in shared glory. Thus, wide swings in lending could be rooted in labor market incentives.

These models, while not explicitly models of banking, could provide an explanation for expansions or contractions of particular types of lending: individual banks expand or contract lending because everyone else is doing so. The literature on credit crunches provides an alternative explanation for portfolio contractions. For example, Bernanke and Lown (1991) define a credit crunch as a significant reduction in bank lending or a leftward shift in the credit supply curve given unchanged market conditions, while Owens and Schreft (1992), Friedman (1991), and Green and Oh (1991) specify a credit crunch as a period of sharply increased nonprice credit rationing. However, the reason why banks that differ in size, risk preference, location, etc., should all independently choose to contract credit simultaneously is left unexplored, or is attributed to business cycle phenomena. Further, only crunches are examined, implicitly suggesting that either simultaneous expansions of credit lead to a reduction in nonprice credit rationing, or that credit booms and crunches are driven by different phenomena and so must be explained with different models.

In this paper, we develop a model of a competitive banking market in which credit booms and crunches are jointly explained. Bank managers are assumed to differ in their preferences towards risk. Bank risk is known to the market and risk neutral depositors distribute their funds so that they earn an expected return equal to the risk-free rate. The banks, taking into account the behavior of their rivals as well as the cost of changing portfolio risk, optimally choose size and risk exposure given their expectations of aggregate lending.

Comparative static analysis of our model indicates that banks expand their lending and increase portfolio risk if they expect aggregate lending to increase. Thus, if all banks simultaneously believe that aggregate lending will increase, their expectations will be self-fulfilling: animal spirits will be at work. Equivalently, if each bank expects all other banks to increase their lending so that aggregate lending increases, then they will increase their lending as well (herd behavior). Because of the endogenous increase in risk, bank failure rates should rise as a result of a lending boom and fall as a consequence of a credit crunch. Further, we find that macroeconomic phenomena, such as a falling risk-free rate of return in response, for example, to expansionary monetary policy, will lead to a credit expansion holding expectations of aggregate lending constant. If, in addition, expectations are affected, so that the decline in the risk-free rate leads bankers to expect an increase in aggregate lending, then a multiplier type effect could result. Thus, herd behavior by banks may both induce and magnify cyclical fluctuations.

The paper is divided into five sections. Section two presents the basic model, and section three contains comparative static results. Section four examines the model's efficacy by comparing the results of the model with recent examples of credit crunches and bubbles. Section five concludes.

2 A MODEL OF BANK LOAN HERDING BEHAVIOR

The model is based on one developed in Pecchenino (1992). There are two classes of agents: banks and depositors. There are N banks, $i = 1, \ldots, N$, where banks differ by the risk preference of their management. Bank type is common knowledge. All agents know the portfolio of assets available to banks and the portfolio return distributions. The gross risk-free rate of return on lending is represented by $r\alpha(L)$, where L measures aggregate loanable funds, and $r > 0$ is a shift parameter. Thus, an increase in L represents a shift in the aggregate supply of loanable funds to the market, which will, in general, lead to a decrease in all interest rates, so that $\alpha' < 0$. Depositors are risk neutral.

There is one cause of bank failure in the model: portfolio risk. Portfolio risk, indexed by σ, is chosen optimally by banks given their preferences toward risk and depositor behavior. Let $\pi(\sigma)$ be the probability that a bank holding a portfolio of risk σ fails, where $\pi(\sigma) \in [0,1]$ for all σ. Assume that the probability of bank failure is increasing quasiconvex in bank risk: $\pi_\sigma > 0$ and $\pi_{\sigma\sigma} \geq 0$. This assumption follows the basic portfolio theory outlined in Sharpe (1970). In Sharpe's framework, expected returns increase with risk at a decreasing rate, so the probability of insufficient cash flows increases at an nondecreasing rate. The $\pi(\sigma)$ function is common knowledge.

Given the common knowledge of bank risk preferences, risk neutral depositors allocate their funds among banks to equalize expected returns across banks. That is, the expected return per dollar deposited, d, in a bank with portfolio risk σ and with value $\hat{A}$ per dollar of deposits if insolvent, is

$$[1 - \pi(\sigma)]d + \pi(\sigma)\hat{A} = r\alpha(L) \tag{1}$$

where $r\alpha(L)$ is the gross risk-free rate of return, defined above. Thus,

$$d(\sigma, L; r) = \frac{r\alpha(L) - \pi(\sigma)\hat{A}}{[1 - \pi(\sigma)]} \tag{2}$$

where, if $\alpha(L) > \hat{A}$, then $d_\sigma > 0$, $d_L < 0$, $d_{\sigma\sigma} > 0$, $d_{\sigma L} < 0$, and $d_r > 0$. Without loss of generality, assume $\hat{A} = 0$.

Following the empirical findings of Keeton and Morris (1987) that banks' managements differ in their preferences towards risk, the N banks, $N \geq 2$, are differentiated by their risk preference. Assume banks can be ranked by their risk preference parameters, γ_i, where $\gamma_i < \gamma_j$, $i < j$, $\gamma_i \geq 1$ for all i. Thus, a type j bank has greater preference for risk than a type i bank, $j > i$. This preference for risk can be represented by an internal bank discount placed on portfolio risk. That is, a bank with risk preference γ that invests in a portfolio of risk σ evaluates its probability of failure at only $\pi(\sigma)/\gamma$. This lower evaluation of risk may arise from restrictive covenants on loans, inside information, etc.

Assume banks are small relative to the market so that they take the effects of their lending on market returns to be infinitesimal. Assume, however, that portfolio returns, adjusted for risk, are declining in aggregate lending, also measured by L. Further, assume that deposit costs increase with bank size relative to the market. Thus, if banks need to raise funds outside their normal deposit base, it is more costly.

Conditional on solvency, the market value of the assets of a portfolio of risk σ per dollar of deposits is $A(\sigma, L; \theta^A)$, with $A_\sigma > 0$, $A_{\sigma\sigma} \leq 0$, $A_L < 0$, $A_{\sigma L} = 0$, and where θ^A is a shift parameter that represents multiplicative shocks to the asset value function. The market value of the bank's l deposits (loanable funds) is

$$D(\sigma, L, l; r, \theta^D)l = [d(\sigma, L; r) + c(l)]l\theta^D$$

where $c' > 0$, $c'' > 0$, and θ^D is a shift parameter that represents multiplicative shocks to the deposit value function. Thus, $D_\sigma > 0$, $D_{\sigma\sigma} > 0$, $D_l > 0$, $D_{ll} > 0$, $D_{\sigma l} < 0$, $D_L < 0$, $D_{\sigma L} = 0$, $D_{lL} = 0$, $D_r > 0$, $D_{\sigma r} > 0$, and $D_{lr} = 0$. If the market value of a bank's assets falls below the value of its liabilities, it is immediately closed (by statute). Since a bank's assets are assumed to be worthless in the event of failure, both bank depositors and stockholders absorb the loss.

Suppose that banks must make their lending decisions prior to knowing the level of aggregate lending. Let $\hat{L}$ denote the expectation of aggregate lending on the part of a representative bank of type i. Given this expectation, the type i bank chooses σ, its portfolio risk, and its portfolio size, l, to maximize its expected profits:

$$\max_{\sigma, l} \quad [1 - \frac{\pi(\sigma)}{\gamma_i}][A(\sigma, \hat{L}; \theta^A) - D(\sigma, \hat{L}, l; r, \theta^D)]l. \tag{3}$$

The first-order conditions are

$$-\frac{\pi'}{\gamma_i}[A(\cdot) - D(\cdot)] + (1 - \frac{\pi}{\gamma_i})[A_\sigma - D_\sigma] = 0, \tag{4}$$

$$\text{and} \quad [A(\cdot) - D(\cdot)] - D_l l = 0. \tag{5}$$

The second-order conditions are satisfied, since the relevant determinant

$$\Delta = \begin{vmatrix} -\frac{\pi''}{\gamma_i}(A-D) - \frac{2\pi'}{\gamma_i}(A_\sigma - D_\sigma) + \lambda(A_{\sigma\sigma} - D_{\sigma\sigma}) & \frac{\pi'}{\gamma_i}D_l \\ (A_\sigma - D_\sigma) & -2D_l - D_{ll}\,l \end{vmatrix}$$

is positive ($\lambda \equiv 1 - \frac{\pi}{\gamma_i}$).

3 Comparative static results

To derive the effects of changes in exogenous variables on the bank's lending and portfolio risk decision, totally differentiate the first-order conditions:

$$\begin{bmatrix} -\frac{\pi''}{\gamma_i}(A-D) - \frac{2\pi'}{\gamma_i}(A_\sigma - D_\sigma) + \lambda(A_{\sigma\sigma} - D_{\sigma\sigma}) & \frac{\pi'}{\gamma_i}D_l \\ (A_\sigma - D_\sigma) & -2D_l - D_{ll}l \end{bmatrix} \begin{bmatrix} d\sigma \\ dl \end{bmatrix}$$

$$= \begin{bmatrix} \frac{\pi'}{\gamma_i}(A_{\hat{L}} - D_{\hat{L}}) + \lambda D_{\sigma\hat{L}} \\ -(A_{\hat{L}} - D_{\hat{L}}) \end{bmatrix} d\hat{L} + \begin{bmatrix} \frac{\pi'}{\gamma_i^2}(A-D) - \frac{\pi}{\gamma_i^2}(A_\sigma - D_\sigma) \\ 0 \end{bmatrix} d\gamma_i +$$

$$\begin{bmatrix} -\frac{\pi'}{\gamma_i}D_r + \lambda D_{\sigma r} \\ \\ D_r \end{bmatrix} dr + \begin{bmatrix} \frac{\pi'}{\gamma_i}A + \lambda A_\sigma \\ \\ A \end{bmatrix} d\theta^A + \begin{bmatrix} -\frac{\pi'}{\gamma_i}D + \lambda D_\sigma \\ \\ D + D_l l \end{bmatrix} d\theta^D$$

Evaluating these derivatives yields the following results.

Proposition 1: Following the Herd (or A Case of Animal Spirits). If $A_{\hat{L}} - D_{\hat{L}} > 0$ and the manager of a type *i* bank believes that all other banks are going to expand their lending so that $\hat{L}$ rises, then he will expand his lending also: $dl/d\hat{L} > 0$.

Proposition 2: The Lemming Problem. If a manager of a type *i* bank believes that all other banks are going to increase their lending so that $\hat{L}$ rises, then he will increase portfolio risk: $d\sigma/d\hat{L} > 0$.

The condition that the net marginal return to lending, $A_{\hat{L}} - D_{\hat{L}}$, is positive is sufficient but not necessary for proposition 1 to hold. This result suggests that a credit crunch, given Bernanke and Lown's (1991) definition, will occur if all banks simultaneously get a case of the jitters. Moreover, as proposition 2 suggests, Owens' and Schreft's (1992) definition may also be satisfied because banks choose to reduce the riskiness of their portfolios, perhaps by nonprice means. Since the expectations of lower aggregate lending that lead to these credit-crunch-like phenomena are not linked in any way to the fundamental behavior of the economy, such crunches are not those described by Eckstein and Sinai (1986), Wojnilower (1980), or Green and Oh (1991). Expectations of lower aggregate lending could, however, lead to an economic downturn and thus, ex post, appear consistent with their definition as well.

Propositions 1 and 2 suggest further that lending expansions linked to optimistic expectations rather than economic fundamentals can also result in increases in bank failure rates. This appears consistent with increases in bank failure rates during the 1980s as a result of the real estate lending boom, and with decreases in bank failure rates in the early 1990s as a result of the credit crunch.

Proposition 3: If a bank's asset (deposit) value function sustains a positive shock increasing the market value of all assets (deposits), then the bank will increase (decrease) its lending, and will take on more or less risk.

Over the course of the business cycle, economic fundamentals underlying the value of a bank's assets and the cost of its liabilities change. These changes cause a bank to adjust its portfolio size upward when the value of its assets rises relative to the cost of its liabilities, and vice versa. However, it may or may not choose to increase its portfolio risk. This suggests that economic shocks which do not change the expected level of aggregate lending have no discernible effect on bank risk. However, economic shocks that raise both the market value of bank assets and expected aggregate lending would lead to increased portfolio risk if the conditions for Proposition 1 are satisfied.

Proposition 4: If a bank management's preference toward risk increases, it increases both the riskiness and the size of its portfolio: $d\sigma/d\gamma_i > 0$ and $dl/d\gamma_i > 0$.

This result suggests that a change in regulation that encourages bank risk-taking will lead individual banks to increase their lending also. This effect could be intensified if the change in regulations also leads to a change in expectations concerning aggregate lending. For example, the rapid growth in risky loans by savings and loan associations as a result of a relaxation of regulatory standards in the 1980s would be consistent with this result. Conversely, recent regulatory changes—risk-based deposit insurance premiums and tougher capital adequacy standards—that impose higher regulatory costs on poorly capitalized banks may have resulted in a lower preference for risk on the part of bank management. Our model implies that such behavior would lead to retrenchment by individual banks, and if it changed expectations concerning aggregate lending, a multiplier effect could ensue.

Proposition 5: If the risk-free rate of return rises for all levels of aggregate lending, then banks will reduce the size and riskiness of their portfolios: $dl/dr < 0$ and $d\sigma/dr < 0$.

This result can be interpreted as a crowding out argument. If the government drives up the risk-free rate of return, it also drives up banks' costs. In response, banks both shrink, and reduce the riskiness of, their portfolios. If banks use their response to forecast other banks' responses, then they may also expect aggregate lending to fall in response to the increase in the risk-free rate. This could lead to a sort of multiplier effect on bank loan supply and a magnification of the cyclical response.

4 Macroeconomic evidence

Several researchers have analyzed in detail examples of credit crunches and bubbles over the past thirty years. The purpose of this section is to draw on that literature to illustrate how consistent the results of our model are with recent banking history. To summarize from the previous section, our model predicts that:

(1) An increase in expected aggregate lending leads individual banks to increase both lending and portfolio risk. This implies that herd behavior leads to higher (lower) expected bank failure rates in the aftermath of credit bubbles (crunches).
(2) A positive (negative) shift of the asset (deposit) market value function leads individual banks to increase lending.
(3) An increase in managerial risk preference results in increases in both lending and portfolio risk.
(4) An increase in a bank's cost of funds (greater market discipline) will result in a decrease in lending.
(5) An increase in the risk-free rate of interest lowers lending and risk for individual banks. If banks expect aggregate lending to decline as well, lending and risk fall even further.

Credit crunches in the 1960s and 1970s

Wojnilower (1980) presents a detailed history of U. S. experiences with credit crunches in the 1960s and 1970s. During this period Regulation Q was in effect, so when money market interest rates rose above the ceiling rates disintermediation forced banks to curtail lending. While large commercial banks were able to ease the problem of disintermediation by using negotiable CDs, Eurodollar deposits, and repurchase agreements to raise funds at market rates, other depositories such as savings and loan associations and smaller banks experienced deposit outflows. Under such circumstances, these institutions would curtail new lending until market rates fall below the ceiling rates and disintermediation eased.

These events are consistent with our model, because these credit crunches were precipitated by an increase in the risk-free rate of interest due to both rising inflation and a tightening of monetary policy. The existence of deposit rate ceilings intensified the credit crunch by reducing bank liquidity, but this is also consistent with the model because individual banks would expect a decrease in aggregate lending and curtail their own lending even more.

The third world debt expansion of the 1970s

According to World Bank figures quoted in the *Economist* (1993), external debt of less developed countries (LDCs) rose from approximately $100 billion to over $650 billion between 1972 and 1981. The causes for such an increase in indebtedness are well-known. The OPEC oil price shock of 1973–1974 increased revenues of oil exporters, who placed a large part of the proceeds with the international banks. At the same time, short-term U. S. interest rates fell below the rate of inflation. After the 1974–1975 recession, banks competed aggressively to "recycle" oil revenues back to oil-importing countries. Lending terms to LDCs eased considerably between 1975 and 1979. According to Federal Reserve Board calculations reported in Darity and Horn (1988), the average interest rate spread (over LIBOR) for Eurocurrency credits to non-OPEC LDCs fell from 165 basis points in 1976 to 76 basis points in 1979. During the same period, the average maturity rose from 5.44 years to 10.11 years. Darity and Horn also report that more favorable credit terms were granted to the largest LDC debtor nations—Argentina, Brazil, Chile, Mexico, Poland, South Korea, and Venezuela. This "credit bubble" was eventually burst by a combination of a second oil price shock in 1978, the adoption of restrictive monetary policy in the U.S., which raised interest costs to LDC debtors, and a sharp reduction in commodity prices (reducing LDC export revenue) due to the worldwide recession in 1981–82.

Again, our model is consistent with the basic facts of the LDC debt expansion. The risk-free interest rate (and therefore the banks' cost of funds) fell below the rate of inflation in the mid-1970s, giving banks incentives to increase both lending and portfolio risk. The expected net marginal return to lending was high enough to allow banks to lower non-price credit terms and still expect to make money from these loans. Further, the rapid growth of loan demand during this period provided an additional incentive to lend more at terms increasingly favorable to borrowers. Even though loan demand was expanding rapidly, loan supply was rising even faster, since equilibrium credit terms were becoming more favorable to borrowers. This is strong evidence that herd behavior was present during this period.

Commercial real estate lending in the 1980s

From the fourth quarter of 1982 to the third quarter of 1990, real GDP grew by 30.4 percent. Over the same period, total loans secured by real estate rose by 104.7 percent in 1987 dollars. Commercial real estate loans outstanding rose by 143.7 percent after adjusting for inflation. Most of the increase occurred between 1982 and 1987, when real commercial real estate lending rose by 109 percent. In a recent survey, Fergus and Goodman (1993) attribute this rapid growth to several factors. First, the federal tax laws enacted in 1981 that permitted accelerated depreciation made real estate a more attractive investment. Second, the economic recovery following the 1981–82 recession led to an increased demand for industrial, retail, and office space. Third, the Garn–St Germain Act of 1982 granted savings and loan associations permission to make commercial real estate loans and also relaxed capital adequacy standards, enabling poorly capitalized S&Ls to make additional loans. Greater competition from S&Ls led to an easing in credit terms offered to borrowers. Fourth, declining market interest rates during this period increased the expected profitability of real estate lending. Fifth, problems with LDC loans and greater competition for business loans from the commercial paper market made real estate lending an increasingly important line of business.

The factors that led to the real estate lending boom of the mid-1980's are again consistent with our model. First, the less restrictive regulatory environment that banks and S&Ls faced after 1982 induced banks to increase both lending and portfolio risk because it would increase managerial risk preference. Several studies, such as Barth (1991), Brewer and Mondschean (1994), and Kane (1989), have shown that S&Ls increased their risk exposure as a result of easier regulatory standards and capital forbearance. Second, the entry into these markets by S&Ls increased the expected amount of aggregate loanable funds available for commercial real estate lending. This would, of course, increase the incentive for individual banks to lend more. Our model also predicts that a lower risk-free rate would increase both lending and portfolio risk, and from 1982 to 1987, the federal funds rate fell from 12.26 percent to 6.66 percent. Since all of these factors tend to increase both lending and risk-taking by individual banks, the explosive growth in real estate lending by banks and S&Ls should not have been surprising.

After the Tax Reform Act of 1986 was passed, eliminating the accelerated depreciation rules enacted in the 1981 Act, the real estate lending boom ended. These changes in the law combined with less than expected demand for commercial space due to corporate downsizing and other factors made commercial lending less attractive. A third factor leading to what is now referred to as the "real estate credit crunch" was the resolution of the S&L crisis. The resolution of hundreds of insolvent thrifts by federal regulators reduced the number of S&Ls that could make new loans. Moreover, in two bills—the Financial Institutions Reform, Recovery, and Enforcement Act (FIRREA) of 1989 and the FDIC Improvement Act (FDICIA) of 1991—Congress significantly tightened regulation of poorly capitalized banks and S&Ls. These bills required the FDIC to charge higher deposit insurance premiums and to restrict the business activities of poorly capitalized institutions. The institution of risk-based capital requirements also affected commercial real estate lending, making such lending less attractive relative to investing in government securities. In short, the restrictions FIRREA and FDICIA have imposed on poorly capitalized depository institutions reduced the moral hazard incentives of deposit insurance that was a contributing factor to the excessive risk-taking by many S&Ls during the 1980s. As a result of all these factors, commercial real estate loans became much harder to obtain and credit terms became more stringent. This behavior is broadly consistent with our model because lower expected aggregate lending and a decline in managerial risk preference due to tightening regulatory oversight would induce banks to reduce both lending and portfolio risk.

5 Conclusions

This paper attempts to provide an explanation of bank lending behavior that would be consistent with both credit bubbles and credit crunches. We argue that the literature on herd behavior—the notion that banks tend to act like other banks—provides insights into why bubbles and crunches occur. We develop a model in which banks will find it optimal to increase size and portfolio risk if they expect aggregate lending to increase. We find the results of the model are broadly consistent with recent macroeconomic history in the United States.

As against our characterization of excessive increases or decreases in lending as a case of herd behavior, others may contend that individual banks are simply reacting to aggregate shocks. We do not deny that aggregate shocks are important: it is clear that events shocks such as changes in monetary, tax, or regulatory policy can affect bank lending. Our view, however, is that herd behavior can magnify the effects of these shocks and potentially increase cyclical fluctuations. Additional empirical work is needed to separate out the effects of aggregate shocks from herd behavior. Although it will be difficult to use cross-sectional regression analysis to test for herd behavior, we believe that an empirical method that can test for herd behavior would be helpful in gaining a better understanding of cyclical fluctuations in bank lending.

References

Banerjee, Abhijit V. 1992. "A Simple Model of Herd Behavior." *Quarterly Journal of Economics* 107 (August): 797–818.

Barth, James R. 1991. *The Great Savings and Loan Debacle*. Washington, D.C.: AEI Press.

Bernanke, Ben S. and Cara S. Lown 1991. "The Credit Crunch." *Brookings Papers on Economic Activity* 2: 205–39.

Brewer, Elijah, III and Thomas H. Mondschean 1994. "An Empirical Test of the Incentive Effects of Deposit Insurance: The Case of Junk Bonds at Savings and Loan Associations." *Journal of Money, Credit, and Banking* 26 (February): 146–64.

Darity, William A., Jr. and Bobbie L. Horn 1988. *The Loan Pushers: The Role of Commercial Banks in the International Debt Crisis*. Cambridge, MA: Ballinger Publishing Company.

Eckstein, Otto and Allen Sinai 1986. "The Mechanisms of the Business Cycle in the Postwar Era." In Robert J. Gordon, ed., *The American Business Cycle: Continuity and Change*. National Bureau of Economic

Research Studies in Business Cycles, Chicago: Chicago University Press: 39–105.

The Economist 1993. "A Survey of Third World Finance." September 25.

Fergus, James T. and John L. Goodman, Jr. 1993. "The 1989–92 Credit Crunch for Real Estate." Federal Reserve Board Staff Study #164, July.

Friedman, Benjamin M. 1991. "Comment on 'Credit Crunch.' " *Brookings Papers on Economic Activity* 2: 240–44.

Green, Edward and Soo Nam Oh 1991. "Can a 'Credit Crunch' be Efficient?" *Federal Reserve Bank of Minneapolis Quarterly Review*, Fall: 3–17.

Kane, Edward J. 1989. *The S&L Insurance Mess*. Washington, D.C.: Urban Institute Press.

Keeton, William R. and Charles S. Morris 1987. "Why Do Banks' Loan Losses Differ?" *Federal Reserve Bank of Kansas City Economic Review*, May: 3–21.

Keynes, J. M. 1936. *The General Theory of Employment, Interest, and Money*. London: Macmillan.

Owens, Raymond E. and Stacey L. Schreft 1992. "Identifying Credit Crunches." Federal Reserve Bank of Richmond Working Paper 92–1, March.

Pecchenino, Rowena A. 1992. "Risk-based Deposit Insurance: An Incentive Compatible Plan."*Journal of Money, Credit and Banking* 24 (November): 499–510.

Scharfstein, David S. and Jeremy C. Stein 1990. "Herd Behavior and Investment." *American Economic Review* 80 (June): 465–79.

Sharpe, William F. 1970. *Portfolio Theory and Capital Markets*. New York: McGraw-Hill.

Wojnilower, Albert M. 1980. "The Central Role of Credit Crunches in Recent Financial History." *Brookings Papers on Economic Activity*, 2: 277–326.

______. 1985. "Private Credit Demand, Supply, and Crunches—How Different are the 1980s?" *American Economic Review* 75 (May): 351–6.

INDEX

Batch number: 10761599

Printed by Printforce, the Netherlands